Contents

Preface   v

1. Social Work and the Clinical Social Worker   1

2. The Helping Interview   41

3. Assessment   77

4. Planning Intervention   133

5. Implementing the Intervention Plan   184

6. Termination   224

7. Research on Social-Work Practice   245

   Epilogue: The Growth of the Social Worker and the Growth
             of Social Work   255

References   274

Index   291

CLINICAL SOCIAL WORK

Theory and Practice

HERBERT S. STREAN

THE FREE PRESS
A Division of Macmillan Publishing Co., Inc.
NEW YORK
Collier Macmillan Publishers
LONDON

a, Richard, and Billy

with love

The Free Press
A Division of Macmillan Publishing Co., Inc.
866 Third Avenue, New York, N. Y. 10022

Collier Macmillan Canada, Ltd.

Library of Congress Catalog Card Number: 77-90147

Printed in the United States of America

printing number

1 2 3 4 5 6 7 8 9 10

Library of Congress Cataloging in Publication Data

Strean, Herbert S
   Clinical social work.

   Bibliography: p.
   Includes index.
   1. Social case work.   I.   Title.   [DNLM: 1. Psycho-
therapy.   2.   Social work, Psychiatric.   WM30.5 S914c]
HV43.S862   361.3   77-90147
ISBN 0-02-932210-3

Preface

During my twenty-five years as a social-work practitioner, supervisor, administrator, researcher, and educator, many of my colleagues and students have expressed the need for a book that would serve as a guide through the labyrinth of clinical social work practice. This book has been written to provide such a guide.

The student or practitioner in social work is frequently confused by the vast array of techniques and approaches at his disposal. During the past decade particularly, such theoretical perspectives as system theory, role theory, communication theory, and organizational theory have appeared on the scene along with behavior therapy, rational therapy, gestalt therapy, and numerous other systems of intervention. One result of this knowledge explosion has been that many students and practitioners have been bewildered about what they are doing, why they are doing it, and where they are going.

My goal in this book has been to make the underlying rationale of clinical social-work practice as explicit as possible. By synthesizing concepts from system theory, role theory, psychoanalysis, and ego psychology, I have attempted to provide the basic skills necessary to work with individuals, dyads, families, groups, and communities. Regardless of the setting in which he is practicing or the unit of attention on which he focuses, the social worker always needs to make a comprehensive psychosocial assessment and an interventive plan, and to use himself dynamically and helpfully within the social worker-client encounter.

To enter meaningfully into the complex psychosocial gestalt of the complex person-in-his-situation, clearly defined interventive goals and disciplined use of a helpful professional relationship are more important than any technique or cluster of techniques. If students and practitioners can acquire a grasp of dynamic principles, they will be able to adapt their activities to the client and situation that confront them rather than slavishly follow some prescribed procedure.

The task of the social-work practitioner is an extremely trying and difficult one. More than any other helping professional, he or she works with the most oppressed in our population, who have been variously characterized as "hard to reach," "unmotivated," and "lonely and afraid." Frequently, these individuals are distrustful of anyone who wants to help them, have little faith in their own capacities, and are skeptical that agencies, organizations, and other bureaucracies exist to aid them. Rather, they often (and with some justification) regard helping professions and helping professionals as self-serving, insensitive, and patronizing. Consequently, the social worker who really wants to help people cope with their environments, must be flexible, creative, patient, and very knowledgeable. As one of my own teachers, Dr. Reuben Fine, has said, "Flexibility is the hallmark of the skilled practitioner, a flexibility that can only be learned on the basis of a thorough grounding in principles, rather than memorizing specific activities" (Fine, 1971).

The procedures and techniques described in this book are suitable for most clients in most agencies. They have been used over and over again with all kinds of people in all kinds of situations and with much success. This is not to deny that other roads may lead to Rome; for many of the clients who confront social workers, a variety of interventions are necessary before they can be involved in a helping process. What is extremely vital, as I have tried to demonstrate throughout the book, is that interventive procedures be adapted to the person-situation constellation and not the reverse. Individualization of the client-system is crucial to social-work practice at all times and in all its forms.

Unfortunately, social work at the present time is torn by dissension. Policy planners are at war with clinicians; behaviorists and dynamically oriented therapists find it difficult to cooperate with each other; and those who work with individuals and families are frequently at odds with those whose major efforts are devoted to larger units of attention.

In this book, I have tried to demonstrate that the material before social workers, people and their situations, should not and need not create rivalries and dissension among us. All social workers are faced daily with human beings beset by difficulties in living, and it is our joint task to help them cope more effectively with themselves and their environments. Contributions to social-work practice have come from many individuals and "schools," and the theoretical positions to which contributors claim allegiance have very little relevance.

Perhaps a unique contribution of this text is that every practice principle presented is illuminated by a live case example. The dozens of individuals described in these vignettes are very real people; certain identifying facts have been altered to respect confidentiality. The case examples are derived largely from my own work, but clients of students, supervisees, and colleagues also appear. I have used case illustrations very liberally because I believe that theory without practice is too abstract to be useful, and practice without theory is technique without meaning.

I should like to thank the many students, practitioners, clients, teachers, and colleagues who have contributed ideas and case examples to this text. I am especially grateful to Dr. Paul Lerman, Chairman of the Doctoral Program in Social Work at Rutgers University, for his encouragement and stimulation, to Dean Ralph Garber at Rutgers, who provided the time, space, and human kindness that were indispensable in making this book a reality, and to Mrs. Gladys Topkis, Senior Editor at Free Press, for her patience, encouragement, and constructive criticisms.

Rutgers University
August 1977

Chapter 1

Social Work and the Clinical Social Worker

Defining Social Work

In contrast to medicine, the law, the ministry, and most other professions, social work is difficult to define, even for its practitioners. Whereas most lawyers, doctors, and ministers probably share similar notions regarding their professional work, social workers demonstrate much variation in their responses when asked about the major tasks of their profession. Indeed, when the question was posed to a leading social-work scholar and educator, Professor Helen Perlman, she remarked, "To attempt

1

to define social work takes courage or foolhardiness or perhaps a bit of both . . ." (Perlman, 1957, p. 3). However, students and practitioners, in their search for a professional identity, continue to struggle to articulate with some precision and clarity just what social work is.

A single example demonstrates how difficult it can be to define social work. In 1949, Professor Swithun Bowers culled from the social-work literature for the period 1915–47 some thirty-four definitions of a single method in social work, social casework. When he presented his own definition of casework as an "art in which knowledge of the science of human relations are used to mobilize capacities in the individual and resources in the community" (Bowers, 1949 p. 127), he was severely criticized. Some social workers felt his definition was too general and others thought it limited the domain of social casework too much (Grinker, 1961)!

Social work has meant many different things to many people. It has meant alms to the poor and other forms of charity; it has meant marital counseling, child therapy, and family therapy; it has connoted income maintenance, adoption, work with the physically and mentally disabled, probation, parole, child care in institutions, and community planning. Many other fields of practice have fallen under the social-work rubric.

In addition, many different methods of working with people have been associated with the profession. Casework (working with individuals and families in counseling and psychotherapy) has been one of the most popular specializations in social work, and for many years it was the sole method. Group work (working with individuals and families in social, recreational, and therapeutic groups) and community organization (planning and executing change in sectors of the community) have been traditional methods in social work for over forty years. The methods keep proliferating; to the three long-established specializations have recently been added social-work administration, social policy, and social-work research.

Social work has been called an art by some and a science by

others. Some have perceived it as a semi-profession, and others are adamant in the view that it is a full-fledged profession. Some writers have argued that social work should regard itself as an essential component of modern society, serving the "normal" as well as the disadvantaged (Kahn, 1959), while others claim that social work should be concerned mainly or exclusively with those who are in distress (Witmer, 1942). While helping people to a better life is not inherently incompatible with working with sufferers from psychological or social pathology and disorganization, clinicians, or others involved in "direct service", are often thought to be in a different political camp from that of social planners and policy makers (Siporin, 1975).

To complicate the issue still further, a rich diversity of people with extremely varied types of formal education and training are called "social workers." A social worker who is a university professor or director of a federal bureaucracy like the U.S. Children's Bureau may have had many years of formal education and practice experience, with a doctorate in social work, and much research expertise; or the worker may hold a master's degree in social work and be a practitioner in a family agency, mental health center, or child guidance clinic; the social worker who is a parole officer connected with a prison may have a bachelor's degree from a university or college with a major in social work, English, philosophy, economics, or some other discipline. Finally, there are those who have had no formal academic training, such as workers in public assistance agencies, but who have also been categorized as "social workers."

The designation "social worker" has been applied to the unpaid volunteer who gives time to a children's institution, mental hospital, nursing home, or other social agency, and to those who hold high administrative posts in government and elsewhere. Social workers work in public agencies and private agencies, and a growing body in the past decade have become entrepreneurs, working with "clients", "patients," and "consumers" in private practice.

It has often been said that social work, with its multiple tasks, personnel, methods, and fields of practice, may have no unique function and therefore can have no unique operational definition. Like psychiatrists, psychoanalysts, and clinical psychologists, some social workers focus on the internal lives of individuals in an attempt to improve their psychological well-being. Like sociologists, some social workers concentrate on the situational forces in individuals' lives which cause stress, such as poor housing or deteriorated neighborhoods. Although the clientele of social workers ranges from communities to individuals, social workers are neither sociologists, psychoanalysts, psychiatrists, nor psychologists. Indeed, as Professor Alfred Kahn has averred (1959, p.7), "The unifying conceptual key to all of social work has not yet been identified and . . . the search for it may be comparable to the ancient alchemist's search for the philosopher's stone–valuable, the source of many innovations and discoveries, however unreal."

While it may be true that social work has no unique purpose, no unique conceptual key, no unique role for those who call themselves social workers, it has nonetheless made considerable progress toward defining itself over the years. Units of attention such as "the family" and "the poor", specific skills such as "dynamic interviewing," and knowledge of group, community, and individual psychosocial functioning have been integrated into casework, group work, and community organization. Concepts and values that all social workers share are also being carefully explicated as the entire profession in the 1970s accepts as its top priority an attack on civil injustice, poverty, and racism (Siporin, 1975).

The requirements of some fields of practice, such as family and child welfare, are being elaborated, and the utility of the social sciences for social work is being clarified. There is now an active and unified professional organization, the National Association of Social Workers, which stimulates scholarship, research, planning, social action, and legislation on local, state, and national levels. Finally, social work in the past decade or two has facilitated an enormous interchange of personnel and experience among the various fields of practice (such as work with the mentally ill, the criminal, and the addicted), and has demonstrated the ability to mobilize its resources to face new problems (Kahn, 1959).

Changing Goals of Social Work Practice

Social work's activities have become part of the very web of our society, and therefore some writers have referred to social work as a social institution (Bartlett, 1964). Others have referred to it as a human-service profession (Boehm, 1958), and many, as we have noted, have debated whether it is a science or an art form (Kidneigh, 1965). Social workers generally accept the notion that they are obliged to aid and represent their clients and that they are responsible to them, to the agency, and to the collective society (Siporin, 1975). Because social workers are concerned with individuals in their social situations, groups in their communities, and communities in societies, their focuses, functions, and roles cannot be divorced from the social context in which they work. Inasmuch as social work traditionally has carved out its tasks and assignments in response to society's concerns, its amorphous, ever-changing definitions and goals seem to be at least partially correlated with the concerns of society as they evolve through the decades. Consequently, in order to better appreciate the dimensions of social work today, it behooves us to review some of its history.

Until the seventeenth century, in England, the United States, and virtually everywhere else in the world, there was a fatalistic attitude toward misfortune and maladaptation; few attempts were made to override these problems other than providing the bare necessities to keep the victim alive. Social work, created initially to help the victims of poverty, emanates from a background in which the response to social, economic, and psychological problems was likely to be repression of the sufferer. Just as individuals afflicted with mental illness were incarcerated, chained, and sometimes brutally treated, those afflicted with poverty were frequently placed in almshouses for the poor. In fact, the mentally ill and the poverty-stricken were often placed indiscriminately in the same custodial institutions (and all-too-often treated sadistically) regardless of their social or psychological circumstances (Booth, 1904; Bosanquet, 1914; Fink, 1948; Webb & Webb, 1904).

Those societies that did help individuals paralyzed by poverty and other social and psychological misfortunes tended to rely on "mutual aid." Deriving from Judeo-Christian teachings, the most venerable component of our ideas about social work is charity (Leiby, 1971), and until the early seventeenth century most people who responded benignly to the disadvantaged did so in the context of the Biblical injunction to give alms and succor to the needy. The Christian was exhorted to love and care for his family, his neighbors, and even for strangers. "Inasmuch as ye have done it unto one of the least of these my brethren, ye have done it unto me" (Matt. 25:40). Even the most forlorn of humans, in this view, was in essence Christ Himself, appealing for and deserving of help (Leiby, 1971).

By the early part of the seventeenth century those in and out of government who had responsibilities in working with the poor began to recognize that people might be in trouble for a variety of reasons and that help given should be regulated according to the nature of the difficulty. The Elizabethan Poor Law, passed in 1601, provided an almshouse for the "impotent poor," and children whose parents could not support them were apprenticed (Queen, 1922).

Although governments and other social institutions in Europe and America have consistently sought legal and philanthropic measures to alleviate the lot of the needy, public relief has never been made an attractive alternative to gainful employment. England's Poor Law Revision of 1834 stated that "the conditions of paupers shall in no case be so eligible as the condition of persons of the lowest class subsisting on the fruits of their own industry" (Webb & Webb, 1904). Similarly, when Richard Nixon ran for

President of the United States in 1972 he averred, ''Those who receive the benefits of public welfare should never be as well off as those who don't'' (*New York Times,* Sept. 28, 1972).

While the poor have traditionally been considered second-class citizens by many societies, since the latter part of the nineteenth century there have been numerous changes in attitudes and in legislation toward the poor. Poverty has come to be viewed by many as a causative factor and/or a likely companion of mental and physical illness, retardation, child abuse, delinquency, crime, and many other social and psychological problems.

THE CHARITY ORGANIZATION MOVEMENT

Originating in England in the mid-nineteenth century with the Charity Organization Society, the idea of such an organization quickly spread across Europe and to the United States and Canada. The C.O.S. was, in effect, a private family agency that attempted to mobilize whatever resources existed in a community to help the needy person help himself become self-supporting. The forerunner of the modern social caseworker, the ''friendly visitor'' was the mainstay of ''The Society.'' He or she investigated the needs of the individual or family, but financial assistance was offered only when it was deemed necessary to accomplish some definite purpose. Special attention and encouragement were given to the ''worthy'' poor—i.e., those individuals who gave most promise of becoming self-supporting. The ''unworthy'' were forced to mend their ways in the almshouse and workhouse (Fink, 1948; Watson, 1922).

The ''friendly visitor'' attempted to understand the many forces impinging on the client's life that were inducing poverty. In addition to intervening in the client's environment, these early social caseworkers attempted to influence behavior by moral suasion and appeals to reason. One of the first textbooks on social work, *Social Diagnosis* (1917), by Mary Richmond, was a sociological attempt to locate the cause of the client's plight by examining the transactions between him and his reference groups. Much of the social worker's activity at that time was intended as intervention in the client's environment; attempts to directly influence him were largely limited to advice.

The C.O.S. movement fostered the development of family-service agencies, councils of social agencies, schools of social work, employment services, legal aid, and many other programs (Watson, 1922).

THE SOCIAL-SETTLEMENT MOVEMENT

Once social-work positions began to be established in Charity Organization Societies and in some public-welfare settings in the 1920s, the social settlements appeared as still another setting for the practice of social work. The Social-Settlement movement, like the C.O.S. movement, was launched in England by a few individuals who were concerned about the cultural and economic impoverishment of the working populations. These individuals began to live among the poor in slum areas, establishing "settle-ments," or neighborhood houses, there. The aim of the pioneers in the settlement movement was to develop a better understanding of the problems of people in the neighborhood and to bring them opportunities for education and wholesome group leisure-time activities (Kidneigh, 1965).

The settlement movement soon expanded its concern to pathological community conditions, and thus the rudiments of group work and community organization were established in United States in such places as Hull House in Chicago and Greenwich House in New York. The settlement houses became laboratories for studies of factory and sweatshop conditions (wages, the work of women and children, industrial diseases and accidents), the difficulties of immigrants, courts and correctional agencies, prostitution, and other important community problems and institutions (Kidneigh, 1965).

In the early 1920s there was also an effort to establish social policies and pass legislation that would provide more humane treatment for laborers, children, immigrants, and women. Through education, surveys, and legislation, efforts were made to bring change in economic and political areas. Women's suffrage, better health conditions in neighborhoods, and mental health programs were championed by settlement-house leaders, and the resultant changes enhanced in turn the conditions under which people lived.

ECONOMIC PROBLEMS AS PSYCHOLOGICAL CONFLICTS ("THE 1920s")

As caseworkers and other social workers in the early 1900s attempted to meet their clients' material needs and offered other forms of aid to individuals, groups, and communities, they found that their services did not always result in better psychological and social functioning in their clients; some responded positively to their interventions and some did not. Social workers began to recognize the existence of internal factors in clients' maladaptive behavior, and the personality of the client, his or her wishes, anxieties, and character traits began to assume importance. Social work made a rapprochement with Freudian psychoanalysis, and the client's feelings, thoughts, fantasies, and memories became important to the social worker in assessing and intervening in the client's life-space (Hamilton, 1958).

In the 1920s many writers in social work emphasized the salience of the client's *personality* in working with him. Thus in 1922 Richmond referred to social work as "those processes which develop personality through adjustments consciously effected, individual by individual, between men and their social environment" (Richmond, 1922, p. 98). Watson defined social work as "the art of untangling and reconstructing the twisted personality in such a manner that the individual can adjust himself to his environment" (Watson, 1922, p. 415), and Queen viewed social work as "the art of adjusting personal relationships'' (Queen, 1922, p. 18). A leading social-work educator and scholar, Porter Lee, defined social work as ''the art of changing human attitudes'' (Lee, 1939, p. 119).

From these definitions it can be seen that the primary focus of the social worker in the 1920s was responsive to the mood of the larger culture, which placed almost exclusive responsibility on the individual in coping with virtually any stressful social problem with which he was confronted. The 1920s in America were characterized by relative indifference to social reform; consequently, definitions of social work and social casework reflected a compatibility with psychoanalysis and psychology and an emphasis on the internal forces in the human personality (Kadushin, 1959).

Instead of saying ''case closed—client uncooperative,'' as many case records read in the early 1900s, social workers in the 1920s could now borrow from psychoanalysis the notion of ''resistance'' and understand how the idea of change might threaten the client and create anxiety for him. Social workers began to comprehend that some clients were poor because the acquisition of material goods might frighten them or activate guilt. Slowly, they began to perceive that not only could poverty lead to marital stress, poor parent-child relations, unmarried motherhood, and other psychosocial problems, but that these same problems could also lead to poverty (Strean, 1975).

In the late twenties and thereafter, social workers did not limit themselves to working with the poor alone but expanded their practices to include many other individuals with interpersonal and social problems. Psychoanalysis and dynamic psychiatry helped social workers recognize that personal, interpersonal, and social problems were interrelated.

The fundamental shift that occurred as a result of the growing popularity of psychoanalytic theory was that instead of exclusively treating the problem—e.g., alcoholism, desertion, poverty, or illegitimacy—the social worker began to consider the *person* with the problem. Social work by the end of the 1920s began to modify its essentially socio-economic orientation into an approach that could be termed "psychosocial" (Hamilton, 1958).

INTERDEPENDENCE OF MAN AND HIS SOCIAL ENVIRONMENT ("THE 1930s")

While an emphasis on the human personality, particularly on the conflicting forces within it, has always been characteristic of social work, the evolving tasks confronting the profession have caused it to alter its focus in different eras. During the 1930s the Depression brought into prominence the interdependence of man's personality and his social environment. Social workers noted that different personalities coped differently with social and economic problems activated by the Depression. They also began to realize that unemployment produced an array of tangible problems which caused stress for the individual, regardless of his coping-capacities. Consequently, definitions of social work in the 1930s emphasized the social as well as the emotional difficulties that produced maladjustment. Bertha Reynolds, who in the late 1920s defined social work as a process of counseling the client on a problem which was "essentially his own," by 1935 had come to view the task of social work as one of assisting "the individual while he struggles to relate himself to his family, his natural groups, and his community" (Reynolds, 1935). Rich, in 1936, defined social work as "the remedial and preventive treatment of social and emotional difficulties that produce maladjustment in the family" (Rich, 1936, p.3), and Lowry saw it as "a way of assisting people to meet their personal and social needs" (Lowry, 1937, p. 264).

By the 1930s American thought had moved toward acceptance of the notion that social and economic variables influenced man's behavior, and definitions of social work during this period seemed to express this theme. Just as the wider culture was tending to concede that people's functioning was dependent to some extent on external social and economic institutions, social work was attempting to assist the individual while he struggled "to relate himself to his family, his natural groups, and his community."

BRINGING THE "SOCIAL" BACK TO SOCIAL WORK

The experience of World War II once more altered social work's view of man and society, and definitions of social work were consequently further modified. As a result of working with military personnel and their families, social workers became even more sensitized to problems of marital and parent-child separations, the influence of group atmosphere on individual functioning, problems of leadership, the significance of communication patterns, and the effects of propaganda. The influence of the family, the social group, and the community on the individual's adaptive and maladaptive functioning became one of the major themes in social-work practice and in the social-work literature after World War II. Definitions of social work began to include the intricate network of socio-psychological forces operative in working with people (Kadushin, 1959). Group work appeared as a distinct method, and many social-work students became interested in participating in community organization. Family therapy, group therapy, and community mental health all came into prominence shortly after World War II. Social workers became interested in enhancing the "social functioning of people in life situations" (Boehm, 1958). They began to appreciate the utility of the social sciences; courses in sociological theory came to be required of every social-work student. By the end of the 1950s social work was described as "society's salvage and repair service," "concerned with the nurture of man," and being committed to build "a community of man" (Siporin, 1975).

The 1940s and '50s also witnessed the organization and conceptualization of social-work practice into three distinct methods, or fields of specialization: casework, group work, and community organization. Although elaborated and modified since the 1950s, in many ways these methods are practiced today as they were conceived then.

The Social Work Methods

CASEWORK

Casework is the oldest and most prevalent method in social work. Its aim is to restore, reinforce, or refashion the psychosocial functioning of individuals and families who are having trouble in their personal, interpersonal, or situational encounters (Hollis, 1964; Perlman, 1957). Through the provision of services and material resources, caseworkers attempt to modify the problems experienced by their clients; through counseling processes they try to alter clients' habitual modes of coping.

The problems brought to caseworkers are many and varied. Impairment of psychosocial functioning can occur in people of any age, among rich or poor, black and white; every member of society can be considered a potential recipient of casework help at some time of his or her life. The problems presented to a caseworker are frequently induced by some situational ''press''—unemployment, illness, death—with which the person has difficulty in coping. In addition, many individuals receive casework help because their personality disturbances get them into difficulty with others, as in marital, parent-child, and employer-employee conflicts. Whether the problem presented is externally or internally induced, the caseworker is always interested in how the client experiences and evaluates it in its interpersonal and social implications.

Social agencies that use casework as their major helping method are essentially concerned with problems of individual and family living; family and child-welfare agencies are the primary organizations using casework as their principal method, although schools, hospitals, courts, and many other institutions use it as well, either as the major method or as an adjunct to other services. For many years most caseworkers worked primarily with individuals. During the last two decades, however, the caseworker's units of attention have expanded to include dyads, families, small groups, and even whole communities. Furthermore, caseworker functions that were widely used in the early 1920s and were subsequently abandoned have lately been assumed once again; today many caseworkers serve as the client's advocate or "social broker." Techniques are also being developed to deal with involuntary and hard-to-reach clients.

Since the 1950s, several theoretical camps have emerged within casework, including the psychosocial approach, the problem-solving approach, the functional approach, and the behavior-modification approach.

The basic principles of the *Psychosocial Approach* were initially formulated by Gordon Hamilton (1951) and have since been elaborated and deepened by Florence Hollis (1964). Rooted in the Freudian theory of personality, this approach is concerned with both the inner realities of the human being and the social context in which he or she lives. Thus it concentrates not only on the situational components of the client's stress but also on his personality—including his history and his ego-functioning. The contributions of the client's family to his functioning is also held to be an important variable in diagnosis and treatment. The psychosocial viewpoint embraces both intervention in the client's behalf and direct work with individuals. It emphasizes the importance of diagnosis as part of the casework process, insisting on: (1) a dynamic diagnosis which involves study of the interaction of the client's environment with aspects of his psychic functioning—libidinal urges, ego functions, and superego admonitions; (2) an etiological diagnosis to determine how the client's past recapitulates itself in his present functioning; and (3) a clinical diagnosis to determine whether the client is neurotic, psychotic, or essentially normal. Intervention, as developed by Florence Hollis, consists of six identifiable procedures:

1. *sustaining* (supportive remarks)
2. *direct influence* (suggestion and advice)
3. *helping the client to ventilate* (catharsis)
4. *reflective consideration of the current person-situation configuration* (helping the client understand better his *present* functionings in his *current* relationships
5. *encouraging the client to think about the dynamics of his response patterns or tendencies* (helping the client to think about *why* he behaves the way he does)
6. *encouraging the client to think about the development of his response patterns or tendencies* (helping the client understand the contribution of his past on his current functioning)

The *Problem-Solving Approach* was introduced in the early 1950s by Professor Helen Perlman (1957). Buttressed by theories of ego psychology, learning theory, and role theory, this model makes the basic assumption that all human living is a problem-solving process and that inability to cope with a problem is due to lack of motivation, capacity, or opportunity to solve it. The chief aim of the problem-solving model is to help individuals or families to deal with whatever problems they are currently having difficulties with and to do so in ways that will make maximum use of their conscious efforts, choices, and competences. The problem-solving model does not consider diagnosis of the whole person as its relevant task. With its goal of helping the client to cope with some currently incapacitating situation, it focuses on those aspects of the personality involved in the problem (either as contributing causes or as powers for coping) and on the other persons and conditions in the client's role-network. In sum, the problem-solving process involves identifying the problem to be worked on, breaking it down into manageable parts, and establishing limited goals for and with the client.

Influenced by some of the teachings of psychoanalyst Otto Rank, the *functional approach* places major emphasis on the agency itself. Casework is not considered a form of psychosocial treatment but a method for administering some specific social service, and the caseworker's primary purpose is the accomplishment of the social purpose of the agency. All social casework of the functional school stresses the importance of time; the casework process is divided into beginnings, middles, and endings so that the potential of each time-phase for the client may be utilized. Although the functional approach was quite popular in the 1940s and early 1950s, it is a minority voice in casework today. However, some of its notions, like that of time and the agency's function, have been incorporated into many caseworkers' professional armamentarium (Smalley, 1967).

Based on the theories of B.F. Skinner and other behaviorists such as Wolpe, Pavlov, and Watson, the *behavior-modification approach* was introduced to casework by Professor Edwin Thomas (1968) of the University of Michigan School of Social Work and has since become very popular. Behavior modification focuses exclusively on the client's actions, utilizing such behavioral techniques as positive and negative reinforcement and operant conditioning. Many caseworkers are now attempting to help clients unlearn disabling behavioral patterns and learn new and adaptive ones by utilizing the behavior-modification approach.

GROUP WORK

Group work is a way of serving individuals within and through face-to-face groups in order to bring about desired changes in clients. Group-work practitioners serve in a wide range of settings: child guidance clinics, hospitals, courts, settlement houses, street gangs, and many others. The group is viewed as a small social system which is utilized to help the client develop abilities, modify negative features of self-image, resolve interpersonal conflicts, and find new and more constructive patterns of behavior. Group workers have always emphasized both the importance of small groups in maintaining a democratic society and the fact that an individual citizen's development can be facilitated by training in social skills. Furthermore, they have felt that social values can be inculcated through guided group experiences (Rosenthal, 1971).

As the group-work method has developed in social work, it has attempted to help clients not only by providing recreational and leisure-time activities, but also by fostering more mature and realistic identities through clinical work. Group work, then, aims to achieve social goals and foster therapeutic change in individuals through group achievement. A kind of "bifocal vision" is utilized by the group worker as he simultaneously relates to clients as individuals and guides the group as a small social system (Vinter, 1965).

The skills used in serving clients in groups include diagnosis, setting treatment goals, forming relationships (with a disciplined use of self), guiding processes toward treatment goals, and evaluating outcomes of intervention. A program is used according to the emotional and social needs of the members. The group worker is concerned with the social organization of the group and its pattern of roles and statuses; its activities, tasks, and decision-making practices; its culture norms, values, and shared purposes; and its relationship to the community (Vinter, 1965). As is true of casework, more than one model for group-work practice has evolved: namely, the developmental approach, the interactionist approach, and the preventive and rehabilitative approach.

Group work's *Developmental Approach*, initiated by Professor Emanuel Tropp (1974) of the University of Virginia's School of Social Work, is concerned with social functionality rather than with pathology. The underlying problems of clients are not emphasized; rather, clients are viewed as people facing life situations which involve stresses and challenges. The group worker using this approach is concerned mainly with the here and now. His focus is on *current* group and individual behavior rather than on personality dynamics, diagnosis, or motivation. As in behavior modification, the unconscious is not considered in the worker's planning; the realities of the group situation are the major guides to perceiving and evaluating what is happening.

The overriding consideration in the formation of such a group is that all prospective members share a significant common interest, concern, or life situation. The worker using the developmental approach sees himself as one human being interacting with others on a common human level, while realizing that worker and clients have different tasks to perform. This approach thus emphasizes a humanistic conception of the social worker's relationship to group members.

Introduced by Professor William Schwartz of the Columbia University School of Social Work (1961), the *interactionist approach* has developed a model in which clients with certain tasks to perform and a professional with a certain function to carry out engage each other as interdependent actors within an organic system. Attention is called to the ways in which each person in the system interacts and transacts with the others as all of them reflect on their respective reasons for being there; both sets of tasks—the clients' and the worker's—change from moment to moment. The interactionists emphasize experience and emotion, step-by-step processes, and situational rather than structural descriptions of people in difficulty. This approach puts the social worker in the path of the processes through which people reach out to each other in their mutual need for self-realization (W. Schwartz, 1962). The relationship between the individual and his group is described as "symbiotic"—each needs the other for its own life and growth, and each reaches out to the other with all possible strength at a given moment. Group workers who use the interactionist approach view the social worker's function as one of mediating the transactions between people and those systems through which they relate to society—the family, peer group, neighborhood, and others.

Introduced by Professor Robert Vinter (1967) and his colleagues at the University of Michigan's School of Social Work, the *preventive and rehabilitative approach* seeks to make changes that will alleviate specific handicaps in the functioning of individuals. In contrast to other approaches in group work, the preventive-rehabilitative approach focuses on the individual, and the worker attempts to attain specified group conditions only as they help to achieve specific goals for individuals (Vinter, 1965). Rehabilitation goals, according to this view, are more likely to be attained if expressed in precise operational terms. Goals are specified as the condition in which the social worker would like the client to be at the end of a successful treatment sequence. Here, the social worker stimulates and motivates the group so that individual goals and tasks can be accomplished. This approach has been used in schools, mental hospitals, and other settings that include emotionally and socially disturbed individuals.

COMMUNITY ORGANIZATION

Although the settlement movement of the 1920s, referred to earlier in this chapter, was concerned with the whole community as a client, it was not until the 1940s that community organization became a distinct and formally recognized method in social work. Community organizers have always been closely identified with the democratic process and with efforts to foster the evolution of the democratic community (Hart, 1920). Social workers involved in community organization view themselves as enablers in inter-group processes. They stimulate programs that involve interracial and interdenominational cooperation; secure, maintain, and co-ordinate the relationships among the agencies in a given community; and organize and administer "United Funds" and other welfare programs. Community organizers attempt to bring about a progressively more effective adjustment between social-welfare resources and needs. The method of community organization consists of activities which are usually concerned with fact-finding, raising standards, promoting teamwork, increasing public understanding, and enlisting public support and participation. In addition to its concern with the discovery and definition of needs and the elimination, prevention, and treatment of such social problems as racism, poverty, and civil injustice, community organizers are concerned with the readjustment of resources to meet changing needs; they have therefore been prominently active in community mental health and the war on poverty.

The community organizer, like all social workers, uses the

basic social-work skills—e.g., interviewing and dynamic assessment of individuals and their problems—so that he can sustain helping relationships with groups of people (Newstetter, 1947). The diverse activities of the community-organization worker can be classified in terms of function: health and welfare planning, community chest operations, social-service exchange administration, promotion of programs in specialized fields, research, public relations, legislative analysis, and teaching. The community-organization worker is an enabler because he is accountable and responsible to an aggregation of people, and is bound by the democratic mandate to enable the group to achieve its desires (M. Schwartz, 1965). Social workers in this method always stress that people in a community can cooperate effectively only through a social organization that provides a channel of democratic communication (Merle, 1971).

As the industrialized and urbanized society is producing problems from the womb to the tomb, community-organization workers reason that community services should be an institutionalized part of every community.

CURRENT CONCERNS AND CURRENT STATUS: TOWARD A GENERALIST APPROACH

The third "discovery" of poverty in the United States, in the 1960s, led social work to reexamine its functions as well as its definitions. The anti-poverty efforts, tied as they were to the determination to end racial discrimination and facilitate integration, brought education to the forefront. Social workers during these years became involved in the planning and development of new types of educational programs. Of particular interest to social workers were programs to help disadvantaged children overcome the effects of environmental and interpersonal deprivation so that they could enter into normal activities in school and at work. Such activities as tutoring (individual and group) and finding appropriate community resources for clients came into prominence (Kahn, 1965).

With poverty and discrimination attracting general concern, new roles and definitions were prescribed for the social worker. For the many clients with limited verbal and cognitive skills and who experienced much anxiety in relating to their environment, the social worker began to function as advocate and social broker. Like the larger society which had rediscovered poverty, social work began to rediscover some of its neglected roles and functions. As social work began to extend its traditional interests more and more into the lives of a total community, new functions have also been considered. Many social workers since the 1960s have been defining their task as intervening in a *crisis* (Parad, 1965), such as school entry, the death or illness of a loved one, or divorce. The social worker is now regarded by many as the "middleman" who negotiates disputes between welfare clients and their landlords and city officials. More recently, he or she has been considered by some as the "convenor" and "stimulator" who helps individuals in a community recognize that they have shared social problems and then organizes them to discuss and resolve some of them.

The 1960s and 1970s brought many new interventive modalities to the fore in social work, such as crisis intervention, short-term treatment, family therapy, and new forms of group therapy; also more and more social workers began to appreciate that personality change and social-system change require many of the same procedures—e.g., gathering information, establishing working relationships, assessing the transactions between people and their environments, and utilizing disciplined interviewing techniques. Recently many social workers have been conceiving of individualized direct services and social action as complementary helping activities; they do not see any inconsistency in holding both clinical and social-change orientations. The professional model of social-work practice being propounded more and more today recognizes that there is a common base of method (Meyer, 1970). Thus many social workers are using a combination of intervention techniques in their efforts to both help individuals and to modify social systems. New configurations of method, often referred to as a "generalist" kind of practice, are now emerging, and it is anticipated that such a practice will more effectively translate systemic work functions into helping procedures (Siporin, 1975).

The generalist approach has stimulated the profession to formulate the notion of "fields of practice". A field of social-work practice centers around some major human need or social problem. Social work itself is a part of the services organized to meet that need or problem, is clearly visible, and makes a distinctive contribution to the overall program and to the people being served. Social work in this so-called ecological sense embodies a full range of interventive measures and includes administration and research (Bartlett, 1971).

The following fields of practice have been identified by the National Association of Social Workers as areas in which social workers are employed. The worker may be in casework, group work, community organization, administration, planning, or research, but in most cases, he or she combines several of these methods.

Aging and the Aged
Alcoholism and Drug Addiction
Civil Rights and Civil Liberties
Crime and Juvenile Delinquency—Corrections
Economic Security
Family and Child Welfare
Health and Medical Care
Housing and Urban Development
Mental Health
Mental Retardation
Social Work in Schools

SOCIAL POLICY AND SOCIAL PLANNING

Until the late 1950s, social work education provided only limited instruction in policy making, and those most active in shaping social policy were frequently trained in other professions; if they were social workers, they acquired their social-policy training from on-the-job experience. In 1953, Charles Schottland (now Executive Director of the National Association of Social Workers) issued a challenge to social workers. He pointed out that social work could make itself felt, not by force of large numbers, but through its knowledge of the problems, programs, techniques, and solutions with which government must be concerned (Schottland, 1953). Since Schottland's call, social work, particularly social-work education, has shown increased interest in social policy. Social-work students at the master's degree level are increasingly being oriented to major social problems, governmental operations, participation in shaping policy, and systems for delivery of services. It is now widely recognized that every practice decision, whether it be in casework, group work, or community organization, has a policy implication.

It is not possible to ascertain how many social workers are employed in social-policy positions. It would appear that the number for whom this is a primary activity is small, but many administrators or researchers in social work are active in social policy.

The N.A.S.W. in 1968 published a document entitled *Goals of Public Social Policy,* which includes these objectives:

> ... to further the broad objective of improving conditions of life in our democratic society through utilization of the professional knowledge and skills of social work ... to provide opportunity for the social work profession to work in unity toward alleviating or preventing sources of deprivation, distress, and strain susceptible of being influenced by social work methods and social action.

The N.A.S.W. maintains an office in Washington, D.C. which attempts to keep members informed on matters of national social policy, to make representations at congressional hearings, and to influence policy development.

SOCIAL WORK ADMINISTRATION

A method introduced into social work fairly recently is that of administration, the process of defining and attaining the objectives of a social-work organization through a system of coordinated and cooperative efforts. Practitioners in social work, it is now recognized, need an understanding of administrative principles in order to make the most effective and efficient use of professional competence (Stein, 1965).

As social agencies are becoming large organizations with staff and clients demanding large inputs in decision-making, it has been deemed more and more necessary to have specialists in social-work administration who understand, relate to, and can help others with the intricacies and subleties of bureaucratic processes. The role of the social-work administrator is to stimulate new programs, be knowledgeable about and sensitize others to the restraints and constraints of bureaucracy, set requirements for specific job roles, and lead in fact-finding. The social-work administrator should be especially concerned with helping to establish agency policies which assist clients in getting faster and better service, also attempting to determine whether specific agency policies interfere with sound practice.

Practice theory and principles in social-work administration have been borrowed from public administration, hospital administration, and industrial management theory, as well as from social and behavioral science theory on organizational behavior. Social-work administration is considered a social-work method when it is concerned primarily with:

(1) Translation of societal mandates into operational policies and goals to guide organizational behavior: (2) design of organizational structures and processes through which the goals can be achieved; (3) securing of resources in the form of materials, staff, clients, and societal legislation necessary for goal attainment and organizational survival; (4) selection and engineering of the necessary technologies; (5) optimizing organizational behavior directed toward increased effectiveness and efficiency; and

(6) evaluation of organization performance to facilitate systematic and continuous problem solving (Sarri, 1971).

Training in administrative management is increasingly becoming part of the social-work executive's preparation. Most students in schools of social work today are required to take at least one course in administration to enhance their capacity to contribute to an agency and their understanding and acceptance of their responsibilities within such a system of cooperative effort.

SOCIAL WORK RESEARCH

In *The Assessment of Social Research: Guideposts for the Use of Research in Social Work and Social Sciences,* Tripodi (1969) and his colleagues define research as: "the application of systematic procedures for the purpose of developing, modifying, and expanding knowledge that can be communicated and verified by independent investigators." Ann Shyne, a leading social-work researcher, attributes the expansion and improvement of social-work research in the past two decades to the desire of the profession to verify and refine its theoretical base, the increased availability of social workers trained in research, new developments in research methodology, a rapprochement between social work and the social sciences, and the availability of new funds (Shyne, 1965).

Many agencies are now participating in research with full- and part-time social-work researchers on their staffs. Agencies are researching treatment modalities and comparing long- and short-term treatment, individual case work and work with groups, and the use of specific procedures in marital counseling. A host of other studies on casework, group work, and community-organization intervention have also been conducted. Many schools of social work during the past decade have established research centers in social work, now provide research facilities for faculty and students, and contribute to community research through consultation or contract research.

Among the major research projects in social work are studies on community needs, administrative questions (such as cost of service and utilization of personnel), client characteristics, and outcomes of service. As more doctoral programs are established in schools of social work and as the profession moves toward a closer liaison with the social sciences, it is expected that this research will continue to proliferate.

The Behavioral Sciences and Social Work

Although social work has its own unique processes, practice principles, and knowledge, it has always acknowledged its debt to the behavioral and social sciences. Social workers have long recognized that a comprehensive theory of social problems does not yet exist (Merton & Nisbet, 1966) and that social work must rely on the use of several behavioral and social science perspectives for its practice conceptualizations. The main behavioral-science orientations that have made and are making substantial contributions to social-work scholarship and social-work practice are as follows:

PSYCHOANALYTIC THEORY AND EGO PSYCHOLOGY

As noted in our historical review, when the friendly visitors of the 1920s were frustrated by the client who did not respond to help, they began to examine his personality in psychoanalytic terms, trying to determine whether there were complications and difficulties unrelated to outer circumstances, presented by the client's personality. The social diagnosis required a personality diagnosis, and the concept "psychosocial diagnosis" evolved. Psychoanalysis, with its notions of psychic determinism, the unconscious, psychosocial development, resistance, defense mechanisms, and transference, has been of inestimable value in helping practitioners to understand client behavior, assess client reactions to the social worker's verbal and non-verbal activities, and plan intervention. As is true of the other theoretical perspectives mentioned in this section, psychoanalysis and ego psychology have contributed greatly to the theoretical underpinning of basic social-work skills.

ROLE THEORY

As social workers began to focus on communication, interaction, and transactions among family members, they found a useful way of describing these phenomena in the concept of "social role." By this is meant behavior prescribed by the social situation, governed by the individual's motivation and his society's values. The stability of a transactional field such as a marriage, family, small group, or community depends upon a certain complementarity of roles. Hence, role theory has provided social work with a means of more precisely defining, assessing, and planning intervention for marital, family, group, and community interaction.

Psychosocial functioning can often be better appreciated by dissecting it into clusters of tasks accompanying certain roles, such as those of husband, wife, parent, or child. Each role implies a number of activities, some of which seem so essential for the role that impaired performance can be called psychosocial dysfunctioning.

SYSTEM THEORY

As the role concept became part of social-work thinking and activity, social workers began to assimilate facets of system theory, which embraces the role concept. Role interactions and transactions are considered part of a larger system of group behavior which strives for equilibrium. System theorists view the human personality as an open system in constant interplay with its surroundings, receiving stimuli from the environment, and modifying its internal mechanisms to maintain equilibrium while adjusting to changes from without.

Because social workers view the person, group, or community as constantly in interaction with other individuals, groups, communities, or organizations, they have been using the notion "client system" to designate the individuals and "subsystems" demanding diagnostic attention and interventive planning (such as the school, the extended family, and the welfare department).

COMMUNICATION THEORY

Much of what a social worker does involves understanding the communication of his clients and his own communication with his clients. Communication theory aids the social worker in conducting helpful interviews with client systems, deciphering hidden and latent meanings in clients' communications, and conducting himself or herself appropriately in the interventive situation.

Communication theory has also been helpful to the social worker in helping him understand how different socio-economic and ethnic groups have unique communication styles.

Because almost all of social work involves communication, communication theory is one of its most used and useful theories.

LEARNING THEORY

Problems in psychosocial functioning can be viewed as resulting from improper learning, and modifications in maladaptive behavior can take place through new learning, unlearning, or relearning. One of the better-conceptualized treatment models, which enjoys considerable popularity in social work, is behavior modification. Particularly in casework and group work, the concepts of conditioning, positive and negative reinforcement, reward and punishment are applied in considering how to account for and effect change in individuals, families, and small groups.

ORGANIZATION THEORY

The organizational model reflects a significant trend of social change—the increase in the number of large organizations whose members' significance is in their contribution to the organization's goals rather than in their personal qualities. Since most clients work in large-scale organizations, an appreciation by social workers of the impact of bureaucratic organizations on them is crucial to the study and assessment of their situations (Merle, 1971).

Almost all social work is performed in an organization—i.e., the social agency. The organization of the agency greatly affects the quality and quantity of services provided. Consequently, it behooves social workers to examine the organizations in which they work, the effects of organizational variables upon staff and client relations, the structural features of organizations in general, and the various issues and dilemmas pertaining to them.

With the recent knowledge-explosion of the 1960s and 1970s and more vigorous research in social work, more behavioral and social-science perspectives will come to form the theoretical underpinning of the social worker's practice wisdom and professional activities.

Social Work Values

Although social workers have always acknowledged the importance of values as a major dimension of professional practice, values have received increased attention during the past decade. Particularly as members of the profession have observed the utility of one common method, attempts have been made to identify values to which all social workers can subscribe. In order to justify an intervention or a practice decision, social workers have taken the position that it should derive from a value system that spells out ethical imperatives.

A value is an enduring belief that a specific mode of conduct or state of existence is preferable to the opposite (Rokeach, 1973). Some of social work's values are implied in the foregoing pages. Social work represents a social philosophy that expresses a moral vision of "the good life" and "the good society": mental health is valued, poverty is devalued; children should receive individualized love and attention and not be abused, etc.

The following values have been consistently identified with social work:

Belief in the dignity and worth of the human being regardless of his or her social, psychological, intellectual, or political orientation, sex, race, or age.

Although few social workers would disagree with the notion that all clients should be genuinely accepted and unconditionally helped, it frequently takes time to resolve one's negative feelings toward individuals who hate what we love, love what we hate, value what we devalue, and devalue what we value. The social worker, if he truly subscribes to a belief in the worth of every human being, must be able to empathize with the racial bigot or anti-Semite, listen attentively to the parent who abuses his or her child, offer hope to the mentally retarded and mentally ill, and see the world through the eyes of the slumlord, angry teacher, authoritarian policeman, etc. It is usually not difficult to accord dignity to clients whose beliefs are similar to our own, but it takes much self-examination and hard work to accept and identify with those individuals for whose attitudes we have customarily felt discomfort and hostility.

Belief in the human being's ability to grow and change toward social and personal ideals related to a liberal-humanistic concept of human betterment.

In working with individuals, families, groups, and communities the social worker is always attempting to diminish those forces which interfere with the human being's capacity to love, to participate in family and community life in an enjoyable and productive manner, to feel and act creatively and constructively, and to have an identity which is at the same time fulfilling and realistic. If intervention is successful, the human being becomes less hateful, enjoys bringing pleasure to others and himself, becomes more able to experience a wide range of feelings, and is actively engaged in mature love and work.

Client self-determination—i.e., the right of each person to live his or her life in a unique way, provided that it does not infringe upon the rights of others.

Thus, social workers do not impose their own goals or standards of behavior on the client but concede his right to make and pursue his own decisions and plans.

As the social worker in the 1970s is confronted more and more with clients whose life-styles may differ markedly from his own—e.g., members of "gay lib" and "women's lib," one-parent families, unmarried couples, "swingers," "switchers," etc.—it is all the more difficult not to prejudge clients' behavior. If the social worker cannot inwardly psychologically permit the client to function in a style that seems appropriate to the client, diagnostic assessments will be biased, intervention plans will be disrupted, and real therapeutic help will not be forthcoming. All too often mental health has been incorrectly assumed to be the enactment of behavior that is synonymous with the tenets of the Protestant ethic—introspection, restraint, hard work, limited sexual expression, etc. In order for the social worker to be an enabler and an enhancer of pleasureful and constructive living, he must be able to permit the client to find his own alternatives in living, even while finding these alternatives personally inimical to his own modus vivendi.

Acceptance of each client and client-system as unique.

One of the tasks of the social worker is to learn the distinctive features of each of his clients and client-systems. As the client (individual, family, or community) recognizes from contact with the social worker that he possesses skills, talents, values, and a history somewhat different from those of the rest of the world, self-esteem rises, optimism grows, and the client achieves more pleasure in living as he appreciates his own uniqueness.

Helping others to develop or recover the capacity for self-help.

The social worker in his work with clients always sets goals for and with them. One of these goals is to help the client achieve more autonomy, and learn how to master his own life with increased self-direction. Social workers assume that the more an individual can rely on his own resources and think through by himself how to master his own fate, the more his self-esteem, optimism, and self-confidence grow. Autonomy does not mean that the client becomes an island unto himself; it does mean that in the client's love and work relationships, he has a sense of who he is and who he is not, trusts his own capacities, relies on his own judgments, and learns what is realistically attainable from others.

Client participation—the human potential is always taken as a given by the social worker, and therefore he accepts the client as an interacting partner in a professional relationship that will psychosocially enhance him.

The social worker believes that all human beings, even those who are culturally or economically impoverished, intellectually retarded, or mentally ill, have a capacity for personal and social growth, a desire for "the better life," and therefore an interest and a right to participate in a professional relationship with a social worker intended to improve his personal and social potentials.

Practitioners sometimes face situations in which value implications are unclear or competing values require sensitive professional judgments. An example is the separation of social services from income maintenance which has come about as a result of recent amendments to the Social Security Act. Such separation reflects the viewpoint "that an individual may have a problem without being one and that economic dependency is not necessarily accompanied by personal inadequacy. On the negative side, money alone may offer dubious comfort to those who are too young or too old or too handicapped or uninformed to convert it on their own initiative into the goods and services they urgently need" (McCormick, 1975, p. 148). Professionals with a strong commitment to human dignity may stand on either side of such an issue. As the evolving profession relates to more and more complex issues in a complex society, many value dilemmas will continue to face the professional social worker.

Clinical Social Work

The term "clinical social work" has recently become popular in social-work parlance. Although since the early days of social work there have always been social workers interested primarily in direct practice with individuals, families, and groups, clinical social work as a distinct orientation to social work practice has evolved in the 1970s, for a number of reasons.

During the 1960s, when the profession turned its lens outward and became engaged in the war on poverty, racism, civil injustice, and other broad social problems, the status of the direct-service practitioner declined, and the positions of the social activist and social planner were elevated. Many educators, researchers, and administrators contended that the impact of social problems like poverty and mental illness could not be lessened appreciably by helping people through casework and group work, but that social action, social planning, and social legislation were required. Thus in the early 1970s one of the oldest and most prestigious casework agencies in North America, the Community Service Society of New York, drastically altered its policies to give priority to social action and social legislation, abolishing many of its traditional direct-service functions. Many social agencies emulated the C.S.S. and began to confine their direct therapeutic services to crisis intervention and short-term therapy.

The late 1960s and 1970s also witnessed another phenomenon

which lowered the status of the direct-service practitioner: Many agencies that traditionally employed graduates of master's degree programs as counsellors and therapists replaced these practitioners with personnel without graduate training in social work, i.e., B.S.W.'s. Schools of social work contributed to this trend by beginning to train and encourage graduate students to go into supervision and administration rather than direct service.

Research studies on direct-service practice carried out in the 1960s and 1970s led many individuals in and out of social work to question whether casework and group work could really improve clients' personal and social functioning (Siporin, 1975). In several studies it was demonstrated that individuals and families who did not receive the benefits of casework and group-work services functioned about the same as those in similar circumstances who had received several months to a year of social-work treatment (Mullen and Dumpson, 1972).

Many helping professionals outside of social work also moved away from their therapeutic roles toward an interest in modifying the social framework. Furthermore, not only were therapy and social change perceived by many professionals as two different realms of endeavor, each with its own separate technical requirements, but practitioners of each began to appear as feuding political enemies. As one writer concluded:

> Two major orientations are observable on the contemporary scene. One stresses dynamic inner psychological forces, psychotherapy, and individual change. The other emphasizes external forces and social manipulation and is antitherapeutic. The behaviorist, organic psychiatrist, and social worker-social manipulator are in one camp; the psychoanalyst, dynamic psychiatrist, and therapeutic caseworker are in the other (Fine, 1975, p. 447).

In response to these trends, direct-service practitioners in social work formed their own organizations and study groups, and started their own journals; they contended that those directing the national social-work organizations were overlooking their contributions and professional needs. Over and over again, direct-service personnel pointed out that they were not opposed to social change and planning but that a social worker's first obligation was to the individuals, families, and groups who were the victims of these broader social problems.

Thus the National Federation of Societies for Clinical Social Work was founded in 1971 to establish standards for direct-service practitioners and a peer-review system to serving the needs of providers and consumers of direct services. In this way its founders were also expressing publicly their conviction that the leaders of the social work profession were paying limited attention to their interests. The founding of the journal *Clinical Social Work* in 1972 can also be attributed to the feeling among many social workers in direct services that their professional interests were insufficiently addressed in the established social-work periodicals.

By the 1960s and 1970s, more and more social workers were entering private practice. These practitioners, like their colleagues in psychology and psychiatry, began to recognize that their expertise in marital counselling, family therapy, child therapy, group therapy, and individual counselling was something for which many clients were willing to pay substantial fees, and that these clients, most of them middle class, preferred to see the social worker in a private office rather than in an agency or clinic. There is no doubt that one of the reasons dozens of state societies for clinical social work were created in the 1970s was to help legitimize the role of the private practitioner.

As many social workers started chapters of clinical social-work societies throughout the United States, as some left social work and joined forces with psychiatrists and psychologists, the N.A.S.W. was forced to recognize clinical social work as a formal area of practice.

In 1976 the N.A.S.W. issued a *Register of Clinical Social Workers*, defining a clinical social worker as one who is:

> ... by education and experience, professionally qualified at the autonomous practice level to provide direct, diagnostic, preventive and treatment services to individuals, families and groups

where functioning is threatened or affected by social and psychological stress or health impairment (*Register of Clinical Social Workers,* 1976, p. xi).

Listing in the *Register* requires:

> A Master's or Doctoral degree in social work from a graduate school of social work accredited or recognized by the Council on Social Work Education; two years or 3,000 hours of post-Masters supervised clinical social work practice under the supervision of a Masters degree level social worker, or, if social work supervision could be shown to have been unavailable, supervision by another mental health professional with the added condition of giving evidence of continued participation and identification within the social work profession.... (*Register of Clinical Social Workers,* 1976, p. xi).

As a guide to the nature and scope of social-work settings, the *Register* offered the following: "Clinical social work is practiced within a private office or under the auspices of public, voluntary, or proprietary agencies and institutions addressing familial, economic, health, recreational, religious, penal, judicial, and educational concerns" (Ibid., p. xi). It set forth a model of clinical social-work practice: "Within the practice setting, the client's problem is identified, and a plan of intervention is designed and agreed upon with the client. The plan is supported by securing historical facts and clues to the latent forces within the individual's personality. Individual strengths in conjunction with community resources are activated and utilized to implement the treatment plan" (Ibid., p. xi).

Clinical social work as conceived in this text has a psychosocial orientation to the problems of individuals, dyads, families, groups, and communities. Personal, interpersonal, and social functioning are viewed as propelled by both inner forces (drives, defenses, and other unconscious stimuli) and outer ones (the influence of family, school, neighborhood, and community). The clinical social worker, regardless of the setting in which he works (school, family agency, mental institution) and regardless of his unit of diagnostic and therapeutic attention (individual, dyad, family, group, or community), needs to have certain basic clinical skills: skills in interviewing, making psychosocial assessments, planning intervention, implementing the intervention plan, and terminating treatment. Further, clinical social work as conceived in this text not only implies working directly with clients, individually or in groups, but also involves knowledge of and skill in working with the client's social environment—the police, landlords, teachers, lawyers, etc.

Clinical social work may be conceptualized as "psychotherapy plus." Psychotheraphy is a form of professional help which addresses itself exclusively to the internal life of the client and seeks to modify maladaptive defenses and increase ego strengths. Through a controlled professional relationship the therapist seeks to help the client discharge feelings and examine behavior and attitudes. But the clinical social worker never loses sight of the client's interactions and transactions with his social orbit, but rather seeks to modify those forces in the client's environment which hinder his personal and interpersonal functioning. He relates to and attempts to modify when he can "latent forces within organizations that determine the way people are served or not served" (Meyer, 1977).

Just as social workers were stereotyped in the past and often perceived as "do gooders" and "wild eyed liberals," the image of the clinical social worker is frequently distorted. Some picture him or her as a professional in a white coat working exclusively with middle class clients on their intrapsychic conflicts. Nothing could be further from the truth than this portrayal! The clinical social worker is one who is first and foremost a practitioner whose main concern is the psychosocial dysfunctioning of all individuals, families, groups, and communities. Like the policy maker, community organizer and social planner he is very much related to those dysfunctional forces in society which interfere with sound psychosocial functioning and he seeks to have them ameliorated, if not eradicated. However, he also recognizes that each individual experiences and shapes his life in his own unique

way, and therefore the clinical social worker, whether he be
helping a client through a "normal" crisis like death of a loved
one, illness, and so on, or trying to modify deleterious forces in
the client's social milieu, realizes that all individuals, rich and
poor, are propelled by unconscious wishes, anxieties, defenses,
ego strengths and weaknesses. The clinical social worker, though
first and foremost a practitioner and always involved with people
and their problems, works within a theoretical framework. Although there is variation among them, many subscribe to the
theoretical orientation used in this text—a synthesis of system
theory, role theory, psychoanalytic theory, and ego psychology.

When the clinical social worker *intervenes,* he is always working with the "person-in-his-situation." Like Sigmund Freud,
who advised that "one may reasonably expect the conscience of
the community will awake" and provide "material help" and
"help for the mind," (Freud, 1949), the clinical social worker
rarely sees himself exclusively behind a desk working solely on
dreams and fantasies of middle-class white clients.

Plan of This Book

Having examined social work's historical evolution, discussed
its methods and fields of practice, its knowledge-base and values,
and having reviewed the evolution of clinical social work as a
specialization, we can now turn to a discussion of the basic clinical skills required to help people cope better with themselves and
their situations. In Chapter 2, we examine the basic medium of
exchange between a social worker and his client, the *helping
interview.* The helping interview is utilized in all phases of the
social-work process—in gathering facts, assessing the client's
psychosocial functioning, and intervening in the client's life (by
helping him directly or attempting to modify his situational
presses).

Whether the client is an individual, a dyad, family, group, or community, the social worker must ascertain the meaning of the client's problems and behavior, how and why internal and external variables affect him, and how he affects them. Chapter 3 is devoted to the *assessment process*.

Chapters 4 and 5 consider *intervention,* the sum of all activities and services directed toward helping the client with his problems. On the basis of assessment, the social worker plans interventions for the client by using himself at various times as an authority, a troubleshooter, mediator, planner, guide, or parental figure, depending on the needs of the client and his situation. Chapter 4 deals with the planning of intervention. Chapter 5 discusses the specific procedures utilized by the social worker in intervention—e.g., supportive remarks and interpretations to the client, holding planned discussions with significant others, etc.

Chapter 6 discusses *termination* of the client–social-worker transaction, and in Chapter 7 we consider the methods and procedures involved in *evaluating the results* of social-work intervention.

The final section of the book, the Epilogue, is devoted to a consideration of steps the social worker can take to help the profession and himself grow and mature.

Summary

In contrast to most other professions, social work is difficult to define. It involves many different activities for many different types of people—marital counseling, work with the poor, adoption, etc. Individuals at several levels of education practice social work in a diversity of settings. The social worker sees as the focus of his professional activities intervention in the client's psychosocial malfunctioning; modification of the situational variables in the client's community, neighborhood, work situation or family insofar as they affect his welfare; and helping the client himself to alter his own personal and interpersonal functioning.

The social worker recognizes that people and their situations are interdependent; both must be assessed in trying to help individuals enhance their lives.

Synthesis Although it is still important for the student and practitioner to be aware of the traditional distinctions between casework, group work, community organization, administration, social policy and planning, and research, social work is moving toward a model of practice in which many "methods" intermingle. In this new generalist model, the programs and social services within which social workers practice take on new importance. For a field of social-work practice (such as work with the aged, the mentally ill, or the mentally retarded) to be considered as such, in addition to other criteria it must center around some major human need or social problem, and must make a distinctive contribution to the overall program and its clients.

All the methods and processes of social work are buttressed by common ethical imperatives and underlaid by a knowledge-base derived not only from accumulated practice wisdom but also from selected aspects of the social and behavioral sciences.

Clinical social work, as conceived in this text, has a psychosocial orientation to the problems of individuals, dyads, families, groups, and communities. It views personal and social functioning as propelled by both inner and outer forces. Regardless of the setting in which the clinical social worker works and regardless of his unit of diagnostic and therapeutic attention, he needs to have certain basic clinical skills: skills in interviewing, making psychosocial assessments, planning intervention, implementing the intervention plan, and terminating treatment.

Chapter 2

The Helping Interview

The basic medium of exchange between a social worker and his client is the helping-interview, whether the client is an individual, a dyad, family, small group, or community. Although each of these units of attention requires certain special knowledge and skills, all social workers need to master some generic principles and procedures of dynamic interviewing.

A great deal of social-work activity is conducted through interviewing. In the social-study phase of the process, it is through emphathic interviewing that the applicant is helped to become a client; an assessment of the client's psychosocial functioning then evolves largely through an examination of data from the interviews; and intervention with and for the client is provided largely by therapeutic and other forms of interviewing. Even when intervention is used to modify the client's environment, the social worker accomplishes this through interviews with teachers, policemen, lawyers, landlords, politicians, and others.

Because interviewing is basic to the social worker's transactions with clients and others (Kadushin, 1972; Edinburg, Zinberg, and Kelman, 1975), a single chapter cannot do full justice to the many facets of this essential process. Consequently, in this chapter we will have to be content with a review and examination of the major principles, concepts, and procedures involved in social-work interviewing.

What Is an Interview?

An interview is a purposive conversation, involving verbal and non-verbal communication between individuals during which ideas and feelings are exchanged. In any interview the participants reciprocally influence each other (Kadushin, 1972). In the social-work interview, however, the worker is considered the director of the process. The worker helps the client formulate his reasons for seeking help, helps him consider how he would like his person-situation–constellation to be modified, and focuses the interviews so as to help him talk about and reflect on salient issues.

The helping-interview in social work is designed to serve the interests of the client or client-system. The interviewer therefore conducts himself in a manner that encourages the interviewee to reveal a great deal about himself while the social worker reveals very little (Garrett, 1951; Kadushin, 1972). This affords the client the opportunity to feel, perhaps for the first time in his life, that another person is devoting exclusive attention to him—to his wants, needs, conflicts, and situational pressures.

The Social Worker and Client Meet: The Initial Interviews

Many factors determine what transpires in a social-work interview and how successful the outcome will be: the client's referral source, the problem he brings to the agency, the agency setting, the client's feelings about receiving help and the social worker's attitudes about helping, the personalities of the participants, their cultural backgrounds and verbal skills, and many other variables.

It should be recognized at the outset of any interview that the participants bring with them a history of living, working, and interacting with other people which heavily influences the communication between interviewer and interviewee. Every individual possesses what psychologist Alfred Adler (1927) termed a life-style, a modus vivendi, which consists in part of values, attitudes, and habitual defensive maneuvers designed to protect the person against anxiety; individual modes of expressing wishes; and ideas about "appropriate" and "inappropriate" ways in which interviews should be conducted and help given and received.

The social worker will constantly be engaged with individuals whose ways of conducting their lives are different from his own. If the prospective client believes that receiving help is his right while the social worker believes (and subtly conveys) that he is doing the client a favor, communication between the participants will not flow. Similarly, if the client disparages the idea of help, or demands it belligerently, or is not particularly verbal, and the social worker is not comfortable with this, the client will sense the worker's anxiety and will be reluctant to continue the transaction (Hamilton, 1951).

An old axiom of social work is that the client must feel free to be himself and behave in his customary ways of relating if the outcome of an interview is to be successful. The social worker's biases should not interfere with or in any way affect the manner in which the client conducts himself with the interviewer.

The following vigneete is an example of how a social worker may impose his own values on the client and thus alienate him:

> Mrs. Ayres, a thirty-two-year-old black mother of four, applied for income maintenance at a county welfare office. When she arrived for her initial interview, fifteen minutes late, the social worker, a white man of about twenty-five, told her to sit down and immediately asked, "Why are you late?" Mrs. Ayres responded, "I have four kids and a lot of things have to be done." The worker said, "If this was important to you, you would have been on time!" There was a long silence.
>
> The worker then asked, "Why do you want income maintenance?" "I can't work," Mrs. Ayres replied. "I've got to take care of my kids!" The worker gave Mrs. Ayres some forms to fill out, at which point she began to perspire profusely, got up from her chair, and was ready to walk out of the office. "Why don't you want to fill out the forms?" the worker asked. "None of your business!" Mrs. Ayres replied, and left.

The worker's imposition of his own standards clearly aroused in Mrs. Ayres feelings of anger, humiliation, fear, and scorn for him. Instead of asking whether Mrs. Ayres had had difficulty in finding the office, a strange and new place for her, the worker admonished her for coming late. He imposed his own value of ''promptness'' on his client, and this put her on the defensive immediately. The social worker did not recognize that his initial comment made Mrs. Ayres uncomfortable, so he could not have shared this observation with her even if he had wanted to. Consequently, Mrs. Ayres's discomfort did not abate. She therefore experienced the social worker's next question as an attack and again demonstrated, by her terse response, that she did not want to reveal too much to him. When the social worker told Mrs. Ayres to fill out the forms, an onerous task for many, Mrs. Ayres' anxiety was exacerbated. Because she could not share her doubts, confusion, and sense of vulnerability with the social worker, she abandoned him.

The client must be accepted as he or she is; otherwise, there is the danger of having no client, or at best a dissatisfied, disgruntled, and unhappy one. The following excerpt from the files of a child-welfare office demonstrates how the social worker can "tune in" to the clients' fears and wishes, helping them feel less anxiety so that they can better cope with their situation.

> Mr. and Mrs. Black, a couple in their forties, were visited by a social worker because they had been accused of child abuse. On her arrival, the social worker was told by Mr. Black, "We haven't done anything wrong. You social workers are out to get us. Sure, we hit our kid, but he's always starting up!" The worker responded, "I guess you don't much feel like talking to somebody who you think is going to accuse you of doing something wrong." "You're right!" said Mrs. Black. "That kid is a monster. He's horrible and deserves to be locked up." She continued to bring out many examples of how "horrible" her son was. When the social worker said, "Yes, Jack is giving you a hard time, he's so hard to cope with," Mrs. Black began to sob; Mr. Black then spoke of their feelings of helplessness and how they wanted help from the social worker "so we can deal with this better."

Note that the worker did not censure the Blacks for their behavior. Rather, she empathized with their plight and recognized their anger toward social workers as understandable and perhaps even legitimate. The Blacks therefore could be themselves and share their vulnerabilities with her. When a social worker imposes nothing, but instead respects the client's own ways of coping, the client feels accepted and therefore strengthened. He can *then* move on to examine himself and his situation with more ease.

ROLE EXPECTATIONS OF CLIENT AND SOCIAL WORKER

Related closely to social-worker and client values are the concepts "role" and "role expectations." "Role" refers to the socially prescribed behavior for the occupant of a particular social status (Biddle and Thomas, 1966), such as husband, policeman, and teacher. Each culture prescribes specific role-behavior for such a status occupant. Thus a mother is expected to nurture her children in certain prescribed ways; a policeman is obligated to preserve law and order through designated behavior (i.e., he wears a uniform, carries a gun, issues certain commands, etc.).

The notion of role always implies reciprocity; every status-occupant has a role partner. For every parent there is a child; for every student, a teacher; for every client, a social worker. Furthermore, if role partners are to interact and relate productively with each other, there must be some concurrence between them on their role-expectations. If husband and wife are to enjoy their life together, for example, there must be some agreement regarding the enactment of their separate roles.

Every prospective client has expectations for himself and for the social worker regarding how each should behave in the interviews. Furthermore, every social worker has his own notions on how a client and worker should interact. If an interview is to be productive and harmonious, there must be some mutual agreement regarding the role-behavior of the participants. If the client, for example, wishes to talk about his physical aches and pains while the worker wishes to have him explore the antecedents of his maladaptive behavior, there will be role-strain and the client may leave the social-work encounter.

One of the variables that accounts for failure in social-work practice is that the client's and social worker's role-behavior has been incongruent. If a client is action-oriented and not particularly interested in verbalizing, the social worker should focus the interview in terms of what can be *done*. Similarly, if a client expects to be asked questions and the worker sits back passively, tension develops, and the interview can deteriorate. The sensitive social worker finds out in the early stages of an interview what the client expects. Frequently, these expectations can be gratified to some extent. If they cannot, the interviewer must relate to the client's dissatisfaction and hear him out on why he needs a social worker to behave in a certain way (Aronson and Overall, 1966).

In the following excerpt from a group interview, the social work interviewer puts these notions into practice:

A group of six youngsters aged twelve and thirteen years were referred to the school social worker because they were "behavior problems" in class. When the social worker entered the room, one boy, Tom, immediately remarked, "You're going to tell the teachers and principal that we're crazy, huh?" The social worker responded, "Is that what you expect?" Turning to the other children, she asked, "Do the rest of you feel that way?" Two other youngsters bellowed, "Yes!" and another, Sally, continued, "A social worker is a snooper and everybody knows that!" John then remarked, "Sure, you're a tattler and just want us to straighten out!"

Further remarks from the children related to the theme of "the social worker can't be trusted." The social worker, sensitive to what the children expected of her, said, "You all feel I'm against you and that I'm for the people that you're angry at. I guess you don't want to have too much to do with me if I'm going to hurt you rather than help you!" The children's tone shifted dramatically. They shared their anger and hurt with each other and with the social worker about being labelled "bad kids" and moved rapidly toward making up an agenda with the social worker on how future meetings could be made productive.

The social worker must recognize his clients' attempts to cast her or him in a variety of roles in their interviews. Frequently the client's expectations can be gratified, as when he expects the social worker to listen, ask questions, and offer understanding and empathy. However, sometimes the client may expect the social worker to be a persecutor (as in the vignette above), manipulator, or lover, or to enact some other role the worker feels he cannot or should not enact. If an interview is to be sustained and move productively, the client's expectations, even if they are destructive or unrealistic, must be recognized by the social worker and fed back empathically to the client; otherwise, the client's anxiety level becomes too high, making him unable to relate to the issues at hand.

BEGINNING WHERE THE CLIENT IS

It has already been implied that the interviewer should recognize the futility of passing judgment on other people's values, standards of behavior, or expectations. To tell an angry client to be calm or an inarticulate one to verbalize only creates barriers in communication. The interviewer, to be successful and helpful, must be genuinely concerned about the client and respectful of his biases, coping mechanisms, and ideas on problem solving. Real acceptance of a client involves acceptance of the many dimensions of his personality and the contradictory forces in his modes of relating.

Although most clients are in some conflict and pain to begin with, there are rarely quick solutions to their plights. Every social worker learns that regardless of how miserable a client is in his situation, the idea of changing his attitudes or altering his situation usually evokes a great deal of anxiety. The status quo, however unpleasant and dysfunctional, is often the best he can manage (Hamilton, 1951).

The social worker must permit the client the opportunity to "talk out" the many facets of his problems and examine alternatives; only later should a course of action be considered. Social-work students and neophyte practitioners, in their genuine zeal to ameliorate the clients' distress, too often rush to solutions without first obtaining a sound understanding of the individuals and their situations. Such a procedure can be destructive; it is hardly ever helpful. To advise a marital couple to stay together or to divorce without first making a comprehensive assessment of their personalities, interactions, values, expectations, and loves and hates can only exacerbate their distress. Similarly, to advise a student to drop out or stay in school without first obtaining knowledge of his interests, abilities, anxieties, resentments, and relationships will in no way help him. All clients have conflicting wishes, loves and hates, wishes to approach and avoid; they usually feel ambivalent about themselves, significant others, and their situations. Consequently, to prescribe a course of action prematurely, before letting the client talk about the many sides of his problem and of himself is to silence parts of him. This can only lead to resentment and depression in the client and may induce him to drop out of the social-work transaction.

The following vignette demonstrates the necessity of *beginning where the client is:*

Mrs. Cantor called a family agency and asked for help with "my deteriorating marriage, . . . my poor relationship with my children, . . . my many arguments with everybody." After the social worker, over the phone, had elicited the names and ages of the other family members, he scheduled a family-therapy session for the Cantors at the agency. The time given, Mrs. Cantor said on the phone, was "quite convenient."

Yet the family did not appear for the scheduled appointment and failed to come for three others made by telephone. When the social worker reflected on his initial telephone conversation with Mrs. Cantor, he recalled that Mrs. Cantor spoke of "*my* marriage, . . . *my* children," etc., and later recognized that perhaps she wanted to be seen alone in the agency rather than with her family. Because he had not met her "where she was," she sabotaged the worker's plan.

When the social worker called Mrs. Cantor and said that perhaps he had foisted the idea of family therapy on her when she wasn't really interested in it, Mrs. Cantor heaved a sigh of relief and said, "You mean, you'll see me for myself?" She quickly arranged an appointment for herself, which she kept.

It is inevitable that every social worker will have his own biases and predilections among the many modalities of social-work intervention available. Beginning ''where a client is'' means listening carefully to the client's requests, his wishes, and his ideas for help. Only *after* listening to the client can the social worker *suggest* a possible type of intervention, such as family therapy, group treatment, or a community clinic.

DIFFERENTIATING REQUESTS FROM NEEDS

When prospective clients seek out a social worker or are referred to one, they usually have some requests to make of him or her. Sometimes they want advice; on other occasions they may want a tangible service such as financial aid, legal aid, adoption, or placement; still other clients may want recreational resources, advocacy, or brokerage. The requests clients make are as varied as the person-situation–constellations of the clients themselves. Because of their distress they often ask the social worker for permission to behave in a certain way—or for a warning, a limit, protection, or a combination of these things. Every client's request, no matter how far-fetched, needs to be heard in all its details and explored further. One cannot merely tell a group of delinquent youngsters that their wish to make the agency into a kind of fort to be used to protect them from their enemies is antisocial and against the policy of the agency. Instead the group may need several interviews with the social worker on how and why they want the agency to be a fortress, why they fight in street gangs in the first place, how they feel about social workers, etc. When the client's requests are explored carefully by the social worker, he frequently finds new alternatives—and different needs, often more constructive, can assert themselves.

Most people who seek help from a social worker are very much troubled by their problems. In a society that generally views the idea of receiving help as a sign of lack of strength or maturity, the fact that an individual requests aid usually connotes that his anxieties have risen to such a pitch that he can no longer cope by himself. The anxiety the client feels may make it very difficult for him to see his problem clearly or state it lucidly. Frequently, a client's simple request is a disguised cry for help in dealing with more complex needs and conflicts. For example, a man who comes to an agency requesting a job may in fact need medical attention. A husband and wife who request guidance for their child may need help with their marriage. Parents who ask the worker to place a child in an institution may need help in examining some of their feelings toward their children. Thus one of the essential tasks of the social worker is to help the client look beyond manifest purposes to more basic latent ones that may be present (Garrett, 1951; Hamilton, 1951).

THE ART OF LISTENING

A good interviewer is a good listener. This may appear at first blush to be a simple statement. However, it sometimes takes many years of experience for a social worker to truly comprehend that when an individual is given the opportunity to have a concerned listener attend to his thoughts, feelings, ideas, and memories, his tensions are reduced and energy previously used to suppress disturbing feelings and thoughts becomes available for more productive functioning.

Most people who become clients of social workers do so because there is no one in their immediate environment to hear them out. Most listeners, when hearing someone else describe a conflict, voice indecision, or discuss feelings of helplessness and hopelessness, feel obliged to give advice, offer notions and experiences of their own, or in some other way be "helpful." They fail to realize that one of the most effective means of being helpful is to permit the interviewee plenty of latitude to voice what is on his mind (Barbara, 1958).

In most societies it is a unique experience to talk with someone who, instead of advising, criticizing, or bringing attention to himself, listens attentively and does not judge. When the client is given the opportunity of being with a person who does not ask anything for himself but focuses his interest solely on him and listens, wonderful things can happen to and for him. He begins to feel that he is a person of value, and this feeling of self-worth induced by an accepting interviewer often frees and strengthens the client to use his coping mechanisms more effectively. The client begins to see that his problem—unemployment, marital distress, poor housing, or whatever—does not mean he is totally helpless and doomed to defeat.

Psychologist Carl Rogers described effective, non-judgmental listening as offering the client "unconditional positive regard" (Rogers, 1951). When the client feels that he is regarded positively by the interviewer, which is usually transmitted by non-intrusive listening, he begins to regard *himself* more positively. The interviewee full of self-hatred often reacts with suspicion to compliments and other supportive remarks. He may feel that he is being patronized and demeaned if the interviewer uses these well-intentioned procedures. However, the client can begin to learn to value himself much more when the interviewer values what he says by carefully listening (Benjamin, 1974).

Good listening, of course, means following what is implied as well as what is being said. It requires being expectantly attentive and receptive, with a relaxed alertness in which the interviewer extends himself fully to appreciate what the interviewee is saying (Kadushin, 1972). Most interviewees sense when the interviewer is somewhere else; silent listening without being attentive to the clients' spoken and unspoken messages rarely achieves very much.

The value of attentive listening may be seen from the following interview between a ten-year-old girl and the social worker at a therapeutic camp for disturbed youngsters.

Peggy's counselor brought her to the social worker because, after two days of camp, Peggy refused to eat or to have anything to do with other youngsters or adults. She sulked most of the time and appeared very depressed, keeping her thumb constantly in her mouth.

When the social worker and Peggy sat down, there was an initial silence. The social worker then said: "You seem very unhappy in this camp. Would you like to talk about it?" Peggy was at first a little reluctant to talk, then said that she didn't like the food, the kids, the counselors, the bunk, or the activities. She felt that being at home was much better; at home, she knew everybody and they really cared about her. She could tell her mother and father what was going on in her life and they would listen. "Nobody at this camp wants to listen to me," Peggy said tearfully. After another short silence, Peggy said, "You see, my social worker in the city thought I would like camp since I could meet kids and do things, and because she always listens to me, I thought I'd do her a favor and come here. But I hate being alone!" Peggy then looked at her interviewer and asked, "Will you be at the hot-dog roast tonight?" When the social worker asked, "Would you like me to be there?" Peggy said, "Maybe you'll sit next to me and we can talk some more. I think I'll go swimming now!"

Like so many clients, Peggy needed somebody to listen to her. When she was given the opportunity to ventilate anger, criticize the camp, and voice her longing for what was comfortable, she felt accepted and valued. Feeling accepted and valued, her depression lifted for a while and she could begin to enjoy the here and now of the camp. It will be noted that the social worker in this vignette, did not say a single word after her opening remark, but instead listened attentively. As a result, Peggy endowed the social worker with the positive characteristics that she was searching for in another person; she could then use the worker effectively as a transitional object so that she could make the break from home and use camp to her advantage.

Whether the problem of the client is homesickness, unemployment, marital conflict, or any other form of distress, effective listening by the interviewer inevitably reduces anxiety and unleashes energy for more constructive problem-solving.

The Social Worker Speaks

Our discussion up to now has been concerned with initial interviews and the importance of good listening has been stressed. Although good listening is a sine qua non in good interviewing, no interviewee wants a completely passive and silent listener. Particularly as the course of the interviews progresses, if the social worker does not respond but exclusively listens the client may conclude that the worker is not interested.

An attentive listener must demonstrate that he has grasped the essential points of his client's story. The client usually feels that he is being heard if the interviewer, through his questions and comments, illuminates and clarifies significant features of the interviewee's own account. If the interviewer demonstrates that he is attending to the major details of the client's story, this conveys the stimulating feeling that the listener not only wants to but does understand what the client is trying to say.

One of the central procedures in good interviewing is posing good questions. Questions can be asked to elicit pertinent data in order to arrive at a psychosocial assessment of the client and his situation; they can also be asked to help the client himself explore and reflect upon his own and others' role in his interactions, and to direct his conversation to fruitful channels. A question that truly engages the client will be one that clarifies ambiguities, completes a picture of the client's situation, draws out more detail on his thinking, and elicits emotional responses (Kadushin, 1972).

In order for a question to be considered helpful by the interviewee, he has to experience it as one that, if answered in full, will enhance him in some way. Questions that can be answered with "No" or "Yes" or "I don't know" do not really help the client discharge distress, explore his situation more fully, or increase his understanding. For example, asking a client, "Are you happily married?" gives him little opportunity, because of the way the question is phrased, to reflect on his marriage, discharge his complaints, or examine his role in it. However, if the social worker says, "Could you tell me about your marriage?" or "How do you and your wife (husband) get along?" more data will be elicited and a fuller exploration of the client's marriage may ensue.

Questions have to be phrased so that they can be understood. They should be unambiguous and simple enough so that the client can remember what is being asked. In asking a question, the social worker should have a clear purpose for doing so.

Perhaps more important than the precise formulation of a question is the attitude with which it is presented. The client must feel that the question evolves from the interviewer's empathy and identification with him. This helps the client want to talk freely, communicate more in depth with the interviewer, and really tell his story.

Empathic questions can supplement good listening and contribute to the interview's success. The following brief vignettes illustrate this.

> After a group of Army trainees spent about twenty minutes with the social worker in the mental-health center of the army post criticizing every feature of the Army—the food, the personnel, the living arrangements, the early rising, K.P., etc.—the social worker asked, "How do you men feel about being away from home?" After a moment's silence, Jerry spoke about how he missed home-cooked meals, his warm bed, his girlfriend, and his job. This induced Bob and Vic to speak about how much they missed their usual activities, particularly the fact that "no one ordered us around at home!" Soon all the men were sharing their homesick feelings, and Joe expressed the group's new-found insight: "The Army is very tough but when we can get it out of our system how much we really miss home, we'll be able to deal with the Army better!"

The social worker was sensitive to the fact that the group's ventilation of their complaints was not only an expression of dissatisfaction with their current reality but was also an indication that the men missed home. One question, properly timed, helped the men to release their tension, go on to support each other, and gain some insight.

> When Mr. and Mrs. Erikson came to the family agency to see if they could place their mentally retarded daughter in an institution, they described her in intellectual terms, focusing on her limitations, vulnerabilities, and pathology. After listening to these affectless descriptions for about fifteen minutes, the social worker asked, "How is it for you people when you have to live with a youngster who does so little for herself?" Within seconds, both Mr. and Mrs. Erikson began to talk about how the child was "draining, . . . very hard to take, . . . and gets us angry all the time.
>
> They voiced their anger, their despair, and their hurt for the next fifteen minutes. Then Mrs. Erikson with her husband concurring, said to the social worker, "You know, before we place Edith, we'd better talk some more about how we feel. I'd hate to place Edith if it was just out of our anger. Let's see if she really needs an institution, or if we just want to get rid of her. Can we see you again?"

In addition to listening attentively and asking well-timed questions to help clients discharge anxiety, and explore and reflect on the situation, the social-work interviewer also comments at appropriate times. Such comments, like questions, should be made with a purpose. Often they are used to encourage the client to talk more fully and freely, as when the interviewer says to a silent, inarticulate client, "It seems difficult for you to talk to me" or "There seems to be something about me which makes you feel uncomfortable." These are leading-remarks designed to encourage the client to reflect on his behavior.

Comments are also made to help the client feel accepted and to strengthen his self-esteem, such as "You certainly have been giving a lot of yourself to your family!" or "You've managed very well on little income." When the social worker has enough data and the themes of the client's life situation are very clear, comments can be made to clarify, suggest, or interpret them to him.

Students and inexperienced practitioners are usually too eager to clarify, advise, or interpret in order to defend themselves against the inevitable anxiety regarding their own competence. As we have reiterated, the good interviewer is a good listener and one who asks well-timed questions. When he comments he is taking a stand. Consequently, the social worker should be very sure that the observation is correct and that the client is ready to accept it. Often a worker may be correct in discerning his client's "underlying hostility", "ambivalence," or "dependence"—but if the client is not ready to hear his appraisal, he will fight the help offered.

Two useful rules in deciding whether or not to comment are: (1) when in doubt, don't! and (2) comment—i.e., clarify, suggest, or interpret—when the client is almost ready to make the statement himself. Continued listening with occasional questioning is rarely destructive to clients, but premature interpretations or other such comments can activate anxiety and increase defensiveness. It requires tact, empathy, patience, and restraint to wait for the appropriate time to interpret something to a client of which he is only partially aware.

After five interviews in which unemployed Mr. Ferguson had constantly talked of his shyness, indecision, and withdrawal and had given many instances of it, the social worker said: "You know, Mr. Ferguson, you seem to be afraid of asserting yourself. What do you suppose the danger is?" Mr. Ferguson smiled and said, "You know, that's what I told my wife about myself last night! I'm afraid I'll offend people with my temper, and that's why I keep it very much under control. If I didn't keep a lid on myself, all hell would break loose. You see, I have a lot of hateful thoughts toward a lot of people!" When Mr. Ferguson discussed his hateful thoughts in several more interviews, it turned out that they were generally confined to figures of authority. The social worker recognized this and said, "People in authority seem to get you sore. Perhaps you have some unsettled business with your parents?" Mr. Ferguson corroborated the suggestion and a few interviews later concluded, "I am still battling with my father. No wonder I get fired from jobs!"

Not only must the social worker time his comments according to the client's pace, but the comments should be brief and clear (Fine, 1971). Furthermore, the worker's use of language should take into consideration the client's social, economic, and cultural circumstances. Terms like "hostility", "coordinated and integrated", and "composed" may be more meaningful to a middle-class literate adult client than they would be to an ill-educated, lower-income teenager. The sensitive interviewer recognizes language differences among different ethnic, socio-economic, and age groups and flexibly adjusts his own choice of words and phrases so that the client can feel that he is in his particular life-space.

THE CONTRACT

During the early interviews, after the client has elaborated on his problems, discussed his requests, determined some of his needs, and given some clues to his expectations, the interviewer and client should come to a working agreement on what each plans to accomplish in the transaction. The working agreement includes not only such practical arrangements as the frequency, length, and site of interviews, and fees (where indicated), but non-administrative matters as well. The client's responsibilities as well as the social worker's need to be comprehensively discussed and consented to. For example, when a client is unemployed, the contract may be that the client agrees to discuss his feelings about work, his conflicts with peers and authorities, his work habits, etc. The social worker in turn might agree to listen, ask questions, and comment on what the client might be doing that interferes with keeping a job. There may be further agreement between client and worker as to which of them (if not both) will seek out job openings; and then as to discussing the pros and cons of a particular job with each other.

A contract is reviewed frequently. A client's needs may change as his requests are explored, and social worker and client may then agree to renegotiate their contract. Although the term "contract" has a legalistic connotation, in social-work it evolves from the dynamic interaction in interviews where the client is helped to talk and the social worker tries to understand and help. Rarely, do client and social worker put the contract in writing, because it is their feeling towards each other that will influence how it is carried out—not the written words.

When a client is given the opportunity to discuss his notions about what his role and responsibilities should be as well as his ideas of what the social worker's should be, he begins to feel that he is an individual who has rights. This usually creates in him a feeling of importance. Furthermore, taking on responsibilities in the interviews can induce in the client the willingness to consider other responsibilities in his day-to-day life and to ponder whether he is not responsible enough or perhaps is too much so.

When a contract is negotiated and renegotiated, it helps bring a focus to the interviews; client and worker are less likely to get sidetracked by extraneous issues, and the interviews' productivity can be sustained.

> When the Green family came for a group interview it became obvious to the social worker, and eventually to the Green family members, that every individual in the family was all for himself. They all talked in terms of their individual dissatisfactions, but nobody in the family considered the other family-members' needs, conflicts, and miseries. After the theme had been noted several times by the social worker, she suggested that a contract be made: in the interviews she would help the family members see how they avoided each other, neglected each other, and were insensitive to each other. But the Greens would have a responsibility, too. When some member felt slighted, he would be singled out to ex-

press his hurt and anger, with everybody listening and thinking about how to help the injured person. The Greens agreed to follow this procedure at home as well.

Much progress occurred as a result of this agreed-upon contract. Each member of the family became more sensitive to the others, and as a result each family member felt more valued, with self-esteem enhanced. Although increased family harmony was observed at home and in the agency interviews, another conflict later emerged. The Greens seemed to be setting up teams, with the son, Jack, and Mr. Green listening more to each other than to anyone else; Sandra, the daughter, was in collusion with her mother "against the guys". When this phenomenon was remarked on several times by the social worker and then later noted by the Greens themselves, a new contract was formulated. Whenever this collusion was detected in the interviews or at home, the dyads (Mr. Green and Jack—Sandra and Mrs. Green) were to discuss what they could do to overcome it. Although this new contract was more difficult to carry out, with the social worker's help the Greens were eventually able to become a group of more sensitive, more humanly related, and happier individuals.

THE FOCUS

Closely related to and evolving from the dynamics of the contract is the issue of *interview-focus*. Once a contract is formulated and all the participants in the transaction agree to it, each succeeding interview should have a specific purpose or focus. The focus might be specific marital conflicts, parent-child stresses, unemployment, group restlessness, community tension, etc. When the social worker observes that the individual, family, or group is deviating from its purpose or focus, it is his responsibility to help the client recognize this, so that those forces interfering with the maintenance of the interview-focus can be explored and aired. If the social worker does not keep the focus in mind, interviews can deteriorate into idle chitchat and the client will not feel (and probably is not being) helped.

For any interview to be productive and helpful, the social worker must always keep in the forefront these questions: What are our goals for this interview? Are we in the process of meeting them? Is the focus the correct one? Am I or is my client deviating from our focus? If so, why, and what can I do to bring us back?

> After Mrs. Hynes agreed to a contract in which she would discuss some of her feelings and anxieties regarding sex, she spent a lot of time in the interviews criticizing her husband for his general shortcomings. When the social worker recognized this movement away from the focus, she told Mrs. Hynes, "Sexual feelings and sexual anxieties seem to be kind of dangerous to talk about with me. What's the danger?" Mrs. Hynes was able to talk about how "weak, vulnerable, inferior, and empty" she felt as a woman. A discussion of sex seemed to activate these feelings of low self-worth, and "I guess that's why I avoid them." Able to discuss her distress, with the worker showing empathy without criticism, Mrs. Hynes moved back to the focus of the interviews.

Obstacles in Interviewing

Asking for help is rarely easy to do. Most individuals who feel a need for professional help postpone making the initial interview, and sometimes weeks, months, and even years go by as the potential client tries to defend himself against the idea of being helped. Because most of us like to think of ourselves as autonomous and independent, participating as a client in social-work interviews can stir up feelings of resentment, vulnerability, weakness, and ambivalence. This phenomenon was noted in part in the above episode with Mrs. Hynes and could be observed in some of the other interviews presented.

No social worker can be effective unless he or she realizes

emotionally and intellectually that every client, no matter how much he consciously desires to participate constructively in the interviews, is also frightened of what will be discovered. As the one who is being helped, he frequently feels inferior to the interviewer and often feels he has to fight the interviewer covertly or overtly. Feeling trapped in a situation where he is expected to reveal things that most of the time are kept guarded, he consciously and unconsciously erects obstacles to block communication.

It is never easy for a client to focus on unrealistic romantic ideals which may be contributing to his marital disharmony; it is often anxiety-provoking to look at hidden and forbidden sexual, aggressive, or dependent feelings; and it is of enormous concern, what the social worker thinks of him when he reveals material that he experiences as shameful, evil, or embarrassing. Often the client anticipates receiving blame, criticism, or punishment from the social worker.

Compounding the reluctance and resistance to receiving help from a social worker is the fact that many such individuals have had negative experiences in the past when they were the recipients of help. Because they may have experienced the counsel of parents, teachers, guidance counselors, or a previous social worker or psychiatrist as arbitrary and judgmental, they understandably raise barriers to the communication process in the social-work interview.

Recognizing that every client has some resistance to the idea and process of being helped should alert the social-work interviewer to the fact that not every part of every interview can flow smoothly. Most clients at one time or another will find participation difficult or may even refuse to talk at all; others will habitually come late and some may be quite negative toward the agency, the social-work profession, and the social worker. From time to time many clients will tell the interviewer that they are not being helped or that their situation, problems, and anxieties have worsened. As a result, they may cancel interviews or fail to appear at all.

While every social worker, usually quite early in his career, will experience failure and not be able to engage a client in further interviews, some of the obstacles to successful interviews can frequently be resolved. One of the forces that sometimes blocks resolution of a client's resistance to help is that the social worker experiences the client's criticism, lateness, or absence much too personally. It is important to remember that when a client poses such obstacles he is feeling vulnerable and anxious, even though he may be behaving defiantly and negatively. When the social worker relates to the fear, anxiety, or anticipated criticism that is usually at the root of the resistant behavior and communicates it to the client, the resistant behavior is often overcome. Such resistant behavior usually connotes anxiety—the client feels that there is danger in the interview and he must defend against it either by keeping it short, not coming, or criticizing the social worker.

HABITUAL LATENESS

Persistent lateness is not uncommon, and frequently the client is quite unaware of the reasons for it. Usually the phenomenon indicates some anger and fear. As one client put it, "I resent being put into the position of underdog and I will not let you control me." By being habitually late, the client postpones being put on the "hot seat" and reduces the significance and importance of the interviewer's position. Sometimes lateness is the client's characteristic defense in coping with anxiety. For this reason, habitual lateness should never be overlooked by the interviewer but should be tactfully explored (Fine, 1971). In discussing the client's lateness with him, it is important not to appear as an accuser. The interviewer should bear in mind that the client is already feeling desperate, vulnerable, and weak. He might ask questions like: "Is it difficult to get here?" "Am I doing something that makes coming here unpleasant?" or "I've noticed that you've been coming late to our interviews. How have you been feeling about them?"

The interviewer should not explore the phenomenon of client

lateness until it becomes habitual. Many factors may interfere with appointments; consequently, lateness should not be questioned until it has become a clearly defined pattern (Fine, 1971). Furthermore, it is hardly ever helpful to tell the client one's interpretation of the meaning of his lateness. The interviewer should tactfully question the phenomenon and then sit back and listen to what the client has to say.

> When the social worker observed that the chief of police, who had agreed to meet with him to discuss the community delinquency problem, was habitually late for the scheduled appointments, he decided to confront the issue in the fourth interview. "You know, Chief Jones," the social worker said, "I get the feeling that I'm a bit of a pain and that maybe I'm imposing on you." "Oh no," the police chief replied. "What makes you say that?" "Well," said the social worker, "unless I've misunderstood our schedule, I believe you are always late!" "Well, you see," said Chief Jones, "I'm a busy guy, much busier than you social workers. I'm not a bleeding heart. I'm for law and order. I'm feeling that you look at delinquents differently than I do and perhaps we can't work together so well."
>
> The social worker thanked Chief Jones for his sincerity and asked if "we could spend more time so I can learn more about your point of view? I think it will help me be a better social worker." With less reluctance, Chief Jones went on to explain his point of view on delinquents, agreed to more appointments with the social worker, and began keeping them, arriving on time.

When the social worker recognizes that the client's lateness expresses a sense of being threatened and calmly questions him without blaming or censuring, the client feels less defensive and more valued, and can frequently resolve his anxiety and start coming on time. In the example above, the social worker, without being submissive and conciliatory, was willing to take some responsibility for his client's lateness. Chief Jones then became more cooperative because he felt less threatened.

CANCELLATION OF APPOINTMENTS

What has been said about lateness pertains in many ways to cancellations. The client frequently is resentful of his client status, fears what will be revealed, feels a loss of power, and may therefore want to spite the social worker.

The same procedures discussed above also apply in trying to resolve the anxiety of the client who cancels appointments. It should be reiterated that the client is most helped here when the social worker does *not* suggest or interpret the reasons for the cancellations but instead tactfully explores the situation through good questions. Sometimes the answers are surprising, as the following vignette demonstrates:

> After Mr. Isaacs had cancelled two interviews the social worker called him and asked, "What's the trouble?" "It's about time you called me!" Mr. Isaacs angrily bellowed over the phone. "I thought you didn't give a damn about me and that's what I almost proved. Do you really want to see me?" "Of course!" the social worker reassured him, and Mr. Isaacs came for his next interview and succeeding ones on time.

A client who has experienced real or fantasied rejection in the past may test out the social worker. He really wants acceptance and recognition but doubts that it will be forthcoming, so he tries various ploys in order to secure what he so deeply craves. It is important, therefore, when a client cancels an appointment to get in touch with him as soon as possible and make another appointment.

SILENCE

Silence in the interview usually upsets the novice interviewer. He feels self-conscious because communication has stopped; he begins to question his abilities. In his attempts to resolve his own discomfort the interviewer may ask irrelevant questions, change the subject that induced the silence, or barrage the client with interpretations. But silence almost always means that the client has thoughts, questions, ideas, or memories which he feels are irrelevant, embarrassing, shameful, or in some other way unacceptable. Like other resistant behavior, the silence of the client is a message that what he is feeling or thinking is too dangerous to articulate.

Frequently the interviewee's silence denotes that he has feelings or thoughts about the interviewer which he cannot express. These thoughts may be quite positive—admiration, sexual fantasies, the wish to love or be loved—or they may be thoughts of condemnation and resentment, or aggressive fantasies. Because the interview is an interpersonal process, it is inevitable that the client will have thoughts about and feelings toward the interviewer. These thoughts and feelings are never completely based on reality but usually emanate from the client's past and are transferred to the social worker. Their subjective and sometimes irrational nature does not mean that these thoughts and feelings should be overlooked; on the contrary, they should be explored. (We shall have more to say about transference and countertransference in chapter 5, "Implementing the Intervention Plan.")

It can even be argued that every form of resistance—lateness, cancellation, prolonged silence, and others—is to some extent an expression of feeling, positive or negative, toward the social worker. Silence in particular is usually a defense against anxiety due to unacceptable thoughts or feelings about the social worker.

In dealing with silence, it is important first to accept it and let the client remain silent for a minute or two. Often he will break the silence himself and tell the interviewer what is on his mind. If he does not, questions like, "What are you thinking now?" "What comes to your mind?" or "What are you feeling now?" usually help the client to move on. If the interviewer has good reason to believe that it is related to feelings the client may be harboring toward him, he may ask tentatively, "How are you feeling about our interview? What are your feelings toward me right now?"

Sometimes the client enjoys a silence, and the social worker may ask if he would like the worker to help sustain the silence or break it. This question often elicits much dynamic material. Clients frequently welcome being consulted on how the interview should be conducted, and from time to time their prescriptions are quite sound (Strean, 1970d).

> In a family-therapy session with the King family, there was a three-minute silence. The social worker said, "You folks are having some difficulty talking." More silence. Then the interviewer said, "I think you're having feelings toward each other and me that you are finding hard to express." Mrs. King said she felt uncomfortable talking about sexual matters. When the social worker said she was glad Mrs. King had mentioned this and that perhaps the other family members were also uncomfortable about discussing sex, the family agreed and said they felt this was "none of the social worker's business."
>
> The social worker told the Kings they didn't have to talk about sex if they didn't wish to do so; she wouldn't press them. However, she commented that it seemed to be one of the areas that made the Kings uncomfortable with her and each other. Feeling accepted and understood by the social worker, the family embarked on a productive discussion of how sinful and anxiety-provoking sex seemed for all of them.

Silence, as in this example, can occur after an anxiety-laden subject has been broached. Mrs. King in effect helped the social worker recognize that references to sex earlier in the interview had induced the silence. When silence is prolonged the worker should consider what content in the interview preceded it, and then may say to the client, "We were talking about X and you became silent. What were you feeling as we talked about X?"

IINTERVIEWING THE INTERVIEWER

We have noted that the social-worker–client interaction is usually a unique and intimate one in which the client shares a great deal of himself, it is inevitable that the client will have feelings and thoughts about the social worker. Frequently these feelings and thoughts are difficult to express directly; they therefore take the form of questions. The client is interested in knowing whether the social worker is married or not, has children, why he chose social work as a career, whether he himself has experienced psychosocial problems, etc.

Inexperienced social workers frequently become anxious when questions are asked of them. They feel exposed, frightened, and defenseless. Fearing that if they frustrate the client and get him angry they "will lose the case", many workers feel an obligation to answer these personal questions. Another way of reacting to the anxiety aroused by personal questions is to answer every question mechanically with a cold, "Why do you ask?" Hardly ever do these defensive responses truly engage the client and help him communicate what he feels and thinks.

Inasmuch as personal questions almost always reflect hidden wishes and anxieties, the social-work interviewer should attempt to ascertain the latent meaning of the client's questions and help the client appreciate their significance. When a client asks if the worker is married, for example, the question may reflect the wish to use the social worker as a role-model for his own marriage; he may wish to expose immaturity on the worker's part, thereby indicating his resentment and fears of the helping situation; he may be having loving and sexual fantasies about the social worker; or he may be competing with the social worker and attempting to put him in the position of interviewee. Because these and other possible motives may lie behind the questions, it is rarely helpful to answer them directly.

To eventually assist the client to cope with his situation, it is important to relate such questioning to the ongoing interview sessions. For example, when an adolescent boy had been talking about "hating all adults over thirty" and then asked the social worker how old she was, the interviewer directed the client's attention to this sequence of events and asked, "Are you wondering whether to hate me or not?"

The social worker interested in helping the client gain increased autonomy and higher self-regard will use questions asked to promote the goals of the interviews and not worry so much about frustrating the client. No social worker need fear saying to a client, "We want to understand you better. Let's see if we can figure out why you asked me." or "I don't mind telling you if I have children of my own, but let's see what your real concern is."

When the client sees that the social worker uses everything he says as grist for the interviewing mill, he begins to explore the thoughts and feelings that propel his questions.

> Mr. Lewis, aged 40, a father in a child-guidance clinic, asked the social worker if he was an athlete. When the social worker replied, "I know athletics interest you, Mr. Lewis. Would you like me to be an athlete?" Mr. Lewis responded, "Well, if you aren't you must be some kind of fairy! Are you?" "You have some question about how much of a man I am", the social worker responded. Mr. Lewis eventually went on to discuss his own fears relating to masculinity and his consequent discomfort with his sons.

Personal questions, if explored fully, will tell us something more about the interviewee. Whatever information a social worker reveals about himself usually has limited effect on the outcome of interviews. Therefore questions such as these should be answered only under very rare circumstances.

Whether the client's questions are about the worker's life or not, the same principle holds: Find out why the client is concerned with the issue at hand.

GROUP INTERVIEWING

It is now a normal occurrence in many agencies and clinics to conduct interviews with a group—a family, a group of parents, a group of spouses, or a group of patients in a mental-health center or mental hospital, to cite just a few examples. Clients are interviewed in groups for different reasons. Perhaps they share certain common problems (e.g., physical or emotional handicaps), similar situations (welfare clients, war veterans), or mutual interests (parent groups, teachers' groups); or they wish to improve their interpersonal skills by interacting with peers in a group.

Whether the client is an individual or a group, all the principles that we have been discussing in this chapter apply in conducting interviews. In the early interviews with a family or a therapy group, when the social worker wants to help the group move from applicant status to that of client, the purpose of the interviews, as of those with an individual, is to understand the problems, the situation, and the personalities of the clients who have come for help. However, the processes of negotiating a contract and determining a focus in group interviewing are much more complex than they are in one-to-one interviews. The members of a family or therapeutic group have different expectations about the help they will receive and different investments in the helping-process. Because their perceptions of the social worker and their motivations for help differ, it takes longer for group members than for individuals to achieve consensus with the social worker on the purpose of the interviews and the roles of the participants.

Although obstacles increase and resistance becomes compounded in group interviewing, there are many situations when it is more desirable than the one-to-one interview. The school social worker who wishes to effect changes in the school's environment, for example, will probably achieve more by conducting group interviews with the teachers in which resentments, fears, and concerns are ventilated and clarified than by interviewing them one by one. Group interviews are also the likely modality of choice in consultative work with policemen, physicians, nurses, paraprofessionals, and other occupational groups in the client's environment.

In group interviewing many interactions and transactions take place that the social worker needs to understand. Who is in competition with whom? Who are the more cooperative members? Which members keep the group contract and focus in mind, and which do not? What are the forces in the group that retard progress? What are the members' different perceptions of the leader? How does the leader feel toward the members? Does he favor some over others? Does he resent some of them, and if so, why?

When the social worker speaks in the group, he must always remember that he has a responsibility to the whole group, not just to a few individuals. Consequently, he formulates his questions and comments with the entire group in mind. He might ask, for example, "What is the *group* doing to keep Mary so quiet?", "Why does *this family* like Mother to dominate it?" "Why does *the group* seem to become silent when John voices his anger?" or "What's happening *among us* that keeps Sally from coming to sessions on time?"

Group interviewing, like interviewing with individuals, must begin where the clients are. It requires listening carefully to the members' wishes and expectations for help, differentiating between their requests and needs, asking pertinent questions, and eventually helping them to resolve the problems that brought them to the social worker. (We will discuss the indications and contraindications of group interviewing in more detail in Chapter 4, "Planning Intervention.")

FEES

As the professional esteem of social workers has risen, along with recognition of the value of their services, more agencies and clinics have arranged fee schedules for their clients comparable to those established by private practitioners. Usually a fee is set after a contract has been formulated by client and worker and is determined by the client's ability to pay—his income as against his financial obligations.

Most social workers have difficulty in setting fees. Unable to value their own competence, they tend to ask for too little. Many of them find it difficult to charge a client for a missed appointment because they fear the client's hostility and because they recognize that frequently such an absence is a communication about his feelings toward the worker.

Both client and social worker reveal many of their own feelings about the helping process as they negotiate the fee. The client who feels that he deserves help and that the social worker can help him will probably not resent paying. However, clients who devalue themselves and/or the social worker will often argue about the unfairness of the fee. Other clients who have fantasies of being indulged or treated in a very protective way will voice surprise when a fee is charged for services, particularly when the worker charges for a missed appointment.

If the social worker wishes not to indulge his client but to help him, he will probably have little difficulty in asking for a fee or in listening to the client's feelings about it. However, if the worker questions his own competence or has a need to be a rescuer or to be omnipotent, he will find it difficult to set appropriate fees and will probably react defensively when clients question or complain about fees.

The social worker, like the landlord whose tenant goes away on vacation or the college official when a student is absent from class, should charge his usual fee when the client is absent from interviews. This procedure helps the client in many ways: He is not treated like an overprotected child, and this lack of indulgence helps him to cope better with other frustrations in his day-to-day life; he begins to view the social worker as a human being who has needs of his own rather than as an omnipotent parent with unlimited resources; his feelings toward the social worker and the helping process are more likely to be discussed when he is charged a fee for a missed appointment; and finally, he is simply more likely to come for appointments if he is charged for missed ones.

After Mr. Mann mentioned to the social worker that he could not be present at his next interview because he would be out of town attending a convention for teachers there was a minute's silence. When the worker asked Mr. Mann what was on his mind, Mr. Mann said that he had a question. "The question I have is whether you charge for absences or not. What *is* your policy?" Mr. Mann queried with some beligerence in his voice. "I charge," answered the worker.

Mr. Mann angrily decried the social worker's fee policy, claiming that the social worker was "money-hungry," "undemocratic," and did not appreciate that there was nothing Mr. Mann could do about the forthcoming absence. "Should I change my job on account of you? Do you also charge me if *you* go out of town? I have to pay a penalty even if my job requires me to be elsewhere!" Mr. Mann exclaimed in a vitriolic manner.

When Mr. Mann saw that the social worker did not respond defensively but waited for Mr. Mann to continue to discuss his feelings about the fee policy, the client began to look at his relationship with the worker and his feelings about being helped. "I guess I feel in a secondary role with you and that you are an arbitrary boss. It is the same feeling I had with my father. I resented his unfair rules and regulations. You always appear so authoritarian to me! The only thing that is different between you and my father is that I can tell you how I feel. But wait a minute, if I see you as a big boss all the time, then of course I want to fight with you! Do you think I want you to be unfair so I can battle it out with you?" Mr. Mann asked with some insight.

When the social worker asked him what he thought about his wish to battle, Mr. Mann laughed and said, "You know, if I didn't get paid when they closed the school where I teach, I'd think that was unfair. I'm putting you in a funny position, eh?"

Mr. Mann unconsciously viewed the worker as an arbitrary, omnipotent parental figure who did not really need money as most people do. Because he put the worker in an elevated position, he resented him and had to challenge him on many issues. When the social worker refused to argue with him, Mr. Mann was able to look at his relationship with the worker and see how he was maintaining a father-son relationship with him and then hating him for it. Mr. Mann further realized that it was really he who was imposing unfair rules on the relationship with the social worker—he, Mr. Mann, should be paid when his school was closed, but the worker should not be paid when in a similar situation.

Sometimes the client is ready to quit treatment if the worker insists on charging for a missed appointment. Unable to relinquish the psychological position of a child who should be cared for by a parent with few needs of his or her own, the client feels humiliated, imposed upon, and derogated if he has to pay for something he did not receive. Rather than argue with the client, which is hardly ever productive, it is frequently helpful if the social worker tells the client that he does not have to pay for the time being and that it's more important to understand why he feels the way he does. This stance usually helps most clients who resent paying for broken appointments because they soon realize that the worker is interested in more than money; he also cares about the client's feelings and thoughts.

RECORDING AND NOTE-TAKING

Because the social worker is accountable to the client and to his agency, he keeps records on what transpires during interviews. Beginning workers often take notes during the interview. This is usually contraindicated, for it may give the client the feeling that the record is more important than what he says.

If the worker records the main theme of the interview a few minutes after the interview is terminated, he will usually be able to fill in the details later so that he can have a lucid summary of the interaction.

Summary

The basic medium of exchange between a social worker and his client is the helping-interview. An interview is a conversation with a definite purpose. Although both parties reciprocally influence each other, the social worker is considered the director of the process, and the interview is designed to help the client cope better with himself and with others.

An interview is colored by the expectations of the participants; it therefore behooves the social worker to be sensitive to the client's values and in control of his own biases and needs. The social worker must begin where the client is and not rush prematurely to judgment or action. Good interviewing requires patient listening and enormous respect for the client's defenses. However, the client's wishes and demands must be carefully distinguished from what he truly needs.

Social-work interviews are governed by a contract, a working agreement on what the participants plan to do in their transactions with each other and in the client's social orbit. The contract, usually expressed overtly but sometimes only implied, may be renegotiated as new needs appear during the client's further interactions with the social worker.

While interviews always involve some resistance, by beginning where the client is, respecting his view of the world, listening carefully, and making appropriate interventions, the social worker can help the client learn to like himself more and to function more constructively.

The principles and procedures of group interviewing are similar to those used in one-to-one interactions. However, the work is more complex in that the social worker has to relate to multiple transference-reactions and different expectations of help.

If the worker feels secure about his own competence, he should also feel comfortable about setting a fee, charging for broken appointments, and listening to and evaluating the latent meaning of the client's reactions to his fee policy.

Because the social worker is accountable to the client and to his agency, he keeps records of all interviews, generally making notes a few minutes after the interview has terminated.

Chapter 3

Assessment

Essentially, diagnosis is the worker's professional opinion as to the nature of the need or the problem which the client presents. It is not a "secret labeling of the client," it is not an uncontrolled adventure into the mysteries of life; it is a realistic, thoughtful, frank and "scientific" attempt to understand the client's present need, which is always a person-in-situation formulation, including interpersonal relationships.

Gordon Hamilton
Theory and Practice of Social Casework (1951)

What Is Diagnostic Assessment?

If the social worker is to be of help, he must obviously understand what is troubling the client and what seems to be contributing to his problems. The assessment is always "psychosocial" because the social worker recognizes that people and their situations are in dynamic interaction and that both contribute to adaptation and maladaptation.

In social-work assessment, the client and the worker, although having different roles and responsibilities, are collaborators. As the client is helped to tell his story, the worker and the client together arrive at an understanding of what the problem is, later deciding together what needs to be done about it. With the client's help, the social worker seeks to arrive at a sound professional judgment of what is causing the distress.

> Mrs. Andrew's social worker amassed considerable evidence before coming to the conclusion that her depression, lack of energy, and sexual unresponsiveness derived from feelings of self-hatred and self-punishment. He was able to pinpoint many instances in and out of the social-work interviews in which Mrs. Andrew had deprived herself of pleasure and derided herself. In addition, the social worker had learned that Mrs. Andrew had many hostile feelings and fantasies toward her husband and children.
>
> In the interviews, she expressed feelings of guilt and self-debasement after her hostile remarks about her family. "Even when they are nice to me, I get upset," Mrs. Andrew lamented. As these patterns recurred, the social worker hypothesized that for Mrs. Andrew, anger had to be punished, and consequently she could not permit herself to enjoy life. The notion became more than a hypothesis when the worker began to notice how Mrs. Andrew frequently rejected his statements of support and encouragement by saying or implying, "I don't deserve such kindness."

Professional judgments must be supported by evidence and reason; they have to be checked and rechecked. They take into consideration the client's current behavior in and out of the social-work interviews, his or her personality, situation, and modes of relating to the social worker. The social worker does not rush to any conclusion but makes sure that the diagnostic assessment meets logical and professional criteria—that is, that the assessment derives from facts that would be clearly apparent to any other professional observer.

Many authors refer to the social worker's assessment as a "social study." Siporin (1975), for example, sees the social study as the identification, examination, and individualized understanding of the psychosocial problems of a client or "target human unit." On the other hand, Hamilton (1951), Hollis (1972), and Pincus and Minahan (1973) view the social study as a *preliminary* process, undertaken prior to making an assessment.

Despite this apparent disagreement, it is clear that the worker must gather facts and make pertinent observations of the client and his situation in order to understand the client-system well enough to guide intervention wisely. As Hollis has pointed out, "It is extremely important to separate observation and classification of facts, on one hand, and diagnosis, on the other. A diagnostic assessment represents the *thinking* of the worker about the facts. It is a professional opinion that is influenced by the frame of reference that he uses to guide him in understanding the meaning of the facts. If observation and diagnosis are not kept separate in the worker's mind, he is in great danger of skewing the facts to fit his theoretical biases" (Hollis, 1964, p. 251).

A diagnostic assessment is no better than the facts it rests on. This was recognized very early in social-work practice when Mary Richmond (1917), quoting a physician who worked closely with social workers, said: "In social study you open your eyes and look; in diagnosis you close them and think."

DEFINING THE PROBLEM

In making an assessment, the social worker is always interested in the client's *statement of the problem,* although he may wish to reformulate it when he gathers further data. As we noted in Chapter 2, any client's statement, whether a request or perception of a problem, needs to be explored before it can be confidently accepted by the social worker.

> When Mrs. Andrew was referred to the family agency by her priest for family counseling, she claimed that her sole reason for coming to the agency was to locate a recreational facility for her son, John. While the social worker did not dispute John's need for recreation, further exploration convinced him that Mrs. Andrew in addition was feeling so guilty about her hostility toward the boy that she wanted to protect him from her temper tantrums by keeping him away from her as much as possible. As the interviews continued, it became clear that the problem had to be restated: Mrs. Andrew's anger and guilt were inducing problems in her interpersonal relationships, and she needed to understand this much better before she or the worker could take responsible action on her behalf.

How a problem is viewed and stated are functions of the definer, reflecting many variables—societal imperatives, religious and other institutionalized belief-systems, clients' values and hopes, agency practices, the practice theories currently in vogue, the worker's values and training, and many others (Strean, 1976). Thus Mrs. Andrew's priest saw her problem as one of family conflict and her need as one of help for her son; the social worker viewed the problem as Mrs. Andrew's difficulty with interpersonal relationships. Furthermore, one's conceptualization of the client-system as an individual, a family, or an organization may affect one's definition of the problem (Siporin, 1975).

THE CLIENT'S PERSONALITY

In any form of social-work activity, the worker must get attuned to and genuinely understand the individual's coping-capacities, role functioning and dysfunctioning, and relationships with significant others. Whether the client is an individual, a family, a group, or an organization, the competencies and incompetencies, defenses, drives, and self-images of the people involved must be understood by the social worker.

One means of assessing the client's personality is by examining his use of various *ego-functions,* those capacities of the individual which determine how well or poorly he can adapt and function in his day-to-day living—e.g., his perception, judgment, impulse control, frustration tolerance, capacity to feel guilt, and ability to identify and empathize with others. Some social workers incorrectly assume that to explore the strength or weakness of the client's ego-functions implies a weakness in the client's personality and a belief that the personality is the only variable contributing to his plight. However, when we conceive of the client in his or her situation as a system, we see that every factor in the system affects every other factor, and that both people and their situations contribute to the problem and its resolution (Hollis, 1972; Parsons, 1951).

In assessing the personality of a client, recognition must be given to his strengths as well as his limitations. Noting these strengths will influence plans for intervention, help in formulating a prognosis, and alert the worker to how much can be expected from the client.

> After only two interviews with Mrs. Andrew it became quite clear that she ran the Andrew home with enormous skill and responsibility and had many other strengths as well. She had been an excellent high-school teacher, interacting very well with students and colleagues, and was well-liked by most of the people with whom she had contact. Furthermore, she had always been very popular among her friends, and played a prominent role in her church and community.

This information greatly enriched the social worker's diagnostic assessment. He began to understand that the conflicts besetting Mrs. Andrew tended to be found in her roles as mother and wife and that in many other areas she was conflict-free.

In formulating a personality assessment, it is also important to understand the client's history. Functioning in the present is formed not only by current situational and personal variables; there are always sources from the past that contribute to difficulties and strengths as well.

As Mrs. Andrew, with the social worker, reflected on her difficulties, she mentioned that her mother had died when she was eight years old. Mrs. Andrew subsequently formed a very close, mutually seductive relationship with her father and in many ways enjoyed her role as wife-and-mother–substitute. Mrs. Andrew was not consciously aware that this situation represented fulfillment of the universal childish wish that some day she would get rid of her mother and take her place with Father. Her mother's death gave Mrs. Andrew the feeling that she was a very powerful human being who could control life and death.

It could now be seen that the assumption of maternal and wifely roles made Mrs. Andrew feel unconsciously like a murderer. Hence she was full of guilt in these roles, could not like herself in them, and felt deserving of punishment, not kindness, for being a mother and wife.

Part of her history, therefore, could explain some of her difficulties in her current familial relationships.

THE CLIENT'S SITUATION

We have noted that the client's interactions and transactions with family, friends, extended family, job, neighborhood, and community are fundamental aspects of his functioning and therefore must be assessed. "Significant others" may enhance the client's functioning, hurt it, or keep it in relative equilibrium (Bertalanffy, 1968). In social-work parlance, the *client's situation* refers to his relationships with these "significant others."

The client's "situation" defines his role, status, identity, and responsibilities in various social contexts. Sometimes the role in one situation is in conflict with that in another, as with, for example, the wife who is expected and expects herself to be waiting at home for her husband with a smile at the end of his working day, but also expects herself to finish her harried P.T.A. job or some other communal or work effort (Meyer, 1959).

Many clients present several role-conflicts to the social worker. Because of the complexity of our "future shock" society, people have to cope with an array of role responsibilities that conflict with one another. Most men and women wish to be successful in their work, with their families, and in their communities; consequently, an individual may be tortured by the need to decide on a given evening whether he or she should do some leftover work from the office, play with the children, or attend the church meeting. Furthermore, differing role responsibilities often present value dilemmas—e.g., the teacher or social worker who has strong political or social values but feels some pressure to violate those values in work with students or clients.

When the social worker assesses the situational components in the client's constellation, he frequently comes to appreciate how the client's significant others are contributing to his personality problems. Consider, for example, a client on public welfare:

> The modal welfare client is an individual trapped in a vicious cycle of grinding poverty. . . . He is frequently living in a rundown neighborhood and exploited by landlords. Schools and other services in his locale are usually inferior; when physicians or attorneys are needed, his usual experience is to wait on long lines and often he receives superficial help. The bulk of welfare clients are blind, disabled, or mothers of young children who must cope without a husband who has been shunned by the job market. . . . All too often the individual who ends up on welfare does so involuntarily, and this parallels the fact that he was frequently an involuntary victim of a broken home. Most frequently he has experienced limited emotional, physical, or economic satisfaction during his life (Strean, 1971a).

Although clients also affect their social milieus, negative feedback from their environment can have a profoundly depressing effect on their faltering self-images. This is true not only of impoverished clients. Mrs. Andrew's difficulties, for example, were compounded and reinforced by significant others:

> When she had been involved with the social worker for about two months, it emerged in the interviews that Mrs. Andrew was the scapegoat of her family. Although she lent herself to this problem, Mr. Andrew and the children consistently poked fun at the way she prepared meals, dressed, talked, sat down and stood up. The family's disparaging remarks reinforced Mrs. Andrew's negative self-image, and she found herself concluding that their apparent attitude was just punishment for "all my meannesses."

To recapitulate: on the basis of an understanding of the problems presented, of the people involved and the situational forces confronting them, the social worker will make decisions as to which aspects of the client's situation he will deal with and how he will deal with them, in order to eventually formulate with the client goals and means for person-situation alteration (Compton and Galaway, 1975; Pincus and Minahan, 1973).

Changing Orientations Toward Assessment

As will be recalled from the historical review of social work in Chapter 1, the "friendly visitor" in his assessment of the client's problems emphasized the contributions of the client's social orbit, his reference groups, family, school, neighborhood, etc. The first text in social casework, *Social Diagnosis* (Richmond, 1917), was a notable effort to translate good neighborliness into a methodology (Meyer, 1970). Because the social orbit contributed to the client's problems, the social worker of Richmond's day tried to influence the client's family, school, and other reference groups to respond differently to him, reasoning that if the client were supported by a more benign environment, he would function better.

Although Richmond implied a person-in-situation orientation in *Social Diagnosis,* most of her case illustrations placed the focus of the assessment almost exclusively on social contributions to the client's plight; very little emphasis was given to personality factors. If a child, for example, resisted attending school, the social worker prior to the 1920s would assess the contribution of parents, teachers, school, neighborhood, etc. The child's feelings and conflicts received little attention in this diagnosis. His developmental needs, history, major defenses, and ongoing, reverberating interactions and transactions with others were, for the most part, neglected. Furthermore, a critical and comtemptuous tone often appeared in the worker's assessment.

From the mid-1920s until the 1950s social-work practice drew its major theoretical sustenance from Freudian psychology (Hellenbrand, 1972). Those who championed Freud felt that recognition of basic unconscious needs in behavior as opposed to rational factors offered a valid view of the human being as he struggled with inner and outer forces, a more realistic one than that typified by the moralistic and self-righteous attitudes which previously underlay many diagnostic assessments.

Gordon Hamilton has pointed out that what Freudian psychology did for social work was to modify the social diagnosis so that it became a psychosocial diagnosis (Hamilton, 1958). An understanding of the effect of significant others on the client was meshed with an understanding of his primitive desires (*id*) as well as of the reasoning, integrating self (*ego*) and the conscience (*superego* and *ego ideal*). Freudian theory also recognized the importance of the past in determining behavior and the special importance of childhood experiences in the formation of personality.

On the basis of a Freudian orientation, a child with a school phobia had to be assessed not only in terms of the impact of significant others but also in terms of his own sexual and aggressive fantasies. What defenses was he using? How were his ego-functions working? What about the quality of his superego? What about developmental fixations and traumatic experiences of the past? These and other questions became part of the psychosocial diagnosis of the psychoanalytically oriented social worker. However, just as Richmond's social orientation had its limitations, there are limitations in an exclusive use of Freudian psychology in making a diagnostic assessment.

LIMITATIONS OF A FREUDIAN DIAGNOSTIC ASSESSMENT

The major orientation of Freudian theory is toward the inner life of the client. Freud himself felt that family members were natural enemies of psychoanalytic treatment (Freud, 1933); consequently, many social workers have concluded that Freudian theory is of limited use in an attempt to appreciate the family as a system with interacting and transacting parts. Adherents of this view would probably also conclude that there is little in Freudian theory to help the social worker assess the effects on an individual, family, or group of the deplorable housing conditions in a ghetto area of a decrepit city (Meyer, 1970). Because the social worker's unit of attention is usually, if not always, more than the inner life of a single client, extending to dyads, families, groups, communities, and complex social institutions, Freudian psychoanalysis, with its crucial preoccupation with the individual, is limited in the help it can give the social worker in making a comprehensive assessment. Its range is too narrow.

Although many Freudian analysts contend otherwise, the Freudian orientation to assessment appears to many social workers as a medical model, and medicine is not the practice of social workers. One of the reasons social workers prefer the term "assessment" to "diagnosis" is that the latter term has medical connotations. Furthermore, when one anchors a "diagnosis" to a medical definition, one becomes interested in the symptoms of an individual. Social work, as we have indicated, includes a myriad of other factors in its assessment of functioning and malfunctioning—interpersonal relationships, self-esteem, group affiliations, ego-functioning—and not merely individual symptoms and pathology (Compton & Galaway, 1975; Hamilton, 1951; Hollis, 1972; Meyer, 1970; Pincus & Minahan, 1974).

A Psychosocial Model

Social-work theory and practice dealing with assessment have swung back and forth over the decades, emphasizing first "the situation" and then "the person." As we discussed in Chapter 1, Richmond's "social diagnosis," while still useful, has been augmented by concepts from the social sciences: role theory, systems theory, communication theory, group dynamics, and organizational theory. Concepts from the social sciences have been extremely useful in clarifying aspects of the person-situation gestalt so central to the psychosocial approach of social work.

Just as the "social" part of the "psychosocial diagnosis" has been enriched by contributions of the social sciences, so the "psychological" part has been enlarged by contributions from personality theorists, whether Freudian or non-Freudian (Strean, 1975). Ego psychologists Anna Freud (1937), Heinz Hartmann (1951), Erik Erikson (1950) and others have focused on such notions as the saliency of a nurturing environment and its contribution to mature functioning, the fact that the ego has some functions which are "conflict-free", and the "normative crises" through which all individuals pass—school entry, adolescence, the loss of a loved one, etc.

Many social workers feel that a merging of certain social-science concepts falling largely under the rubric of social-systems theory and role theory with certain psychoanalytic concepts from Freudian psychology and ego psychology can serve social workers well in assessments (Siporin, 1975; Hollis, 1972; Meyer, 1970). Although social-systems theory, with its emphasis on interpersonal interactions and transactions in a system such as a family or small group, will probably be more useful in certain instances than psychoanalysis and ego psychology, with their focus on individual behavior, it would appear that certain concepts from social-systems theory, role theory, psychoanalysis, and ego psychology are all pertinent, if not indispensable, to assessment in social work.

A CAUTION

Some social-work theorists contend that social-systems theory alone, with its focus on the gestalt of the person-situation–constellation, can organize all the data the social worker needs for diagnostic assessment (Compton and Galaway, 1975; Hearn, 1969; Pincus & Minahan, 1973). This seems to be rather short-sighted. It is important to recognize that sociology and psychology focus on different aspects of human functioning. Social-systems theory can help us understand the dynamics of group interactions and transactions but tells us little, if anything, about individual motives and individual dynamics. Similarly, psychoanalysis can explain a great deal about the meaning of unconscious behavior and ego psychology can help us assess the client's coping-capacities, but neither psychoanalysis nor ego psychology offers very much help in understanding familial, small group, or community transactions. Consequently, both orientations, social and psychological, seem necessary in assessing the person-in-his-situation. The state of knowledge in the human sciences is such that to use psychology or sociology alone would be to either psychologize society or sociologize personality (Meyer, 1970).

Virtually all social-systems analysts and role theorists emphasize that the mechanisms of personality as a system are not the same as the mechanisms of a social system like a family or small group. Although the study of psychology and psychodynamics does offer insight into motivational processes and is therefore applicable to the study of family, small group, and organizational systems, it has a limited contribution to make to the analysis of the social processes of role interaction and transaction. As Parsons (1951) has pointed out: "Social systems do not 'repress' or 'project,' nor are they 'dominant' or 'submissive'; these are mechanisms of the personality."

It is therefore incumbent on the social worker to recognize that in assessing social systems like the family, small group, or organization, concepts from systems theory and role theory such as reciprocity and complimentarity are more appropriate and pertinent than such psychodynamic concepts as projection or repression. A family does not project, but family members may.

As the social worker comprehensively assesses an individual, family, or group, he will of course go back and forth in his thinking as he concerns himself with the psychodynamics of individuals and the social processes of dyads and groups. However, to help the reader gain more mastery in adapting social-science theory and psychological theory to assessment, we shall, for purposes of explication, keep the two orientations separate in the next two sections of this chapter.

UTILIZING SOCIAL SYSTEMS THEORY AND ROLE THEORY IN ASSESSMENT

A social system is a group of individual actors in a transaction who have interrelated tasks and the capacity for certain kinds of performance (Bertalanffy, 1968; Buckley, 1967; Compton & Galaway, 1975). Each actor in a social system influences the others. Therefore, one may consider a marital dyad, a family, a small group, or an organization as social systems in that each consists of transacting actors with interrelated tasks and interdependent functions.

There is general agreement on three principles of social-systems theory. According to the principle of *stability*, social-systems theory emphasizes input and output, and the equilibrating processes that keep the system in a state of stability, or homeostasis. Stability means that a change in one part of the system is followed by a change in other parts. Therefore, if a mother starts going to work, or a child leaves for camp, or a father's change of job necessitates a move, the behavior of the other members of the family will be modified in order to adapt to the change (Grinker, 1967; Bertalanaffy, 1968).

The principle of stability is a crucial one in social-work assessment for it recognizes that regardless of how much difficulty marital, family, group, and organizational members might have with each other, how much they complain about one another, or how miserable they feel when together, the fighting, arguing, and conflict serve some purpose for the role partners and keep the system in a steady state.

> When Mr. Bergen first met the social worker he talked about his deteriorating marriage. Referring to his wife, he said, "She's always putting me down, criticizing me, demeaning me. How can I possibly feel good or be nice to her?" However, at a subsequent interview at which both Mr. and Mrs. Bergen were present, it became very clear to the social worker that whenever Mrs. Bergen appeared to be understanding and compassionate Mr. Bergen found fault with her. The same was true when Mr. Bergen tried to be empathic with Mrs. Bergen. Neither party ever thought of separation, but they seemed to maintain the *stability* of their marital union by engaging in constant "one-upmanship" fracases. This emotional seesaw seemed to be in constant motion, with both Mr. and Mrs. Bergen preserving the equilibrium through their respective "outputs."
>
> Whenever either of them attempted to modify the power struggle through understanding, the other was sure to cooperate with the mandate that "bickering is here to stay."

In a study conducted several years ago, I attempted to enlarge the diagnostic assessment of Freud's six-year-old patient, Little Hans, who suffered from a phobia of horses (Strean, 1970b). I was able to demonstrate that not only was Hans's phobia a symptom expressing his unconscious sexual fantasies toward his mother and hostile competitive feelings toward his father but that marital, parent-child, and parent-parent subsystems all had to be assessed carefully in order to comprehend the full meaning of Hans's plight. In reexamining the data, it became quite evident that Hans's phobia also expressed his ambivalent feelings concerning his parents' tempestuous marriage. Because the boy's malady was one of the few concerns that Hans's parents shared, when Hans was cured of the phobia, the parents divorced.

The principle of stability is frequently witnessed in small groups (Rosenthal, 1971) and organizations (Merle, 1971), and is a useful concept in assessing the interactions and transactions of the members.

In a fathers' group of six men, Mr. Cohen was consistently scapegoated by the other members. They were critical of his impulsive behavior toward his children, his demeaning remarks toward his wife, and his arrogant behavior toward the group members and leader.

At one meeting from which Mr. Cohen was absent, the group members fell silent. When the leader attempted to explore the meaning of their silence, one of the members, after some resistance, voiced the group's sentiments: "I guess we enjoy picking on Mr. Cohen. He's nice to have around to beat up. If he's not here to beat up, we're all dead. We better find another guy to fight with."

One of the important implications of the principle of stability for social-work assessment, particularly of larger units, is that whenever one member of the system modifies his behavior, other members inevitably follow with alterations in their behavior to restore equilibrium. When Mr. Cohen was absent from the group meetings, the members fell silent and looked for a new scapegoat. When Mrs. Bergen was cordial to Mr. Bergen instead of debasing him, he provoked a fight to preserve the marital stability. When one uses a social-systems approach and considers the implications of the principle of stability, notions like "sado-masochistic marriage" and "scapegoating" take on an added dimension. We learn that "deviant" or "aberrant" behavior can serve a function in a system for which all members have some responsibility.

A social worker in community organization and social planning was consulted about an organization that was having personnel problems. The staff was up in arms because of the "tremendous authoritarianism" of the executive. The staff members said that they could not get their work done, felt humiliated by the executive, and claimed that "everything was going to pot." However, when the consultant suggested that the executive be replaced by a subordinate, most of the staff members protested, claiming that the replacement "would be too liberal" and "would not run a tight enough ship."

A second principle of systems theory states that a system is transactional. That is, a reciprocal relationship exists between all parts of the system, not merely an interaction which is an effect of one unit upon another. When an organism is "in process" with the environment, knowledge of the organism or environment alone is inadequate. The full system must be observed (Grinker, 1967). Transactions occur between whatever people under discussion are involved with each other.

By infusing diagnostic assessments with transactional processes, we can appreciate not only how one member affects another, but also how their conjoint behavior is forever influencing each of them. For example, not only are the partners in a marital subsystem constantly influencing each other, but the marital subsystem (husband and wife), parent-child subsystems, parent-parent subsystem (husband and wife in their roles as parents), and sibling subsystems are all influencing and affecting each other (Stein, 1971).

To recognize the profound implications and impact of transactional processes, let us look at a case situation in which a child was ill with rheumatic fever:

> When Sally Davis became ill, her mother panicked and became quite depressed. Mr. Davis resented his wife's withdrawal and became quite critical of her. As a result, Mrs. Davis could not fully concentrate on helping Sally recover, and the doctor admonished both Mr. and Mrs. Davis for not attending to Sally properly.
>
> Then, Mr. Davis's mother became infuriated with him for not visiting her weekly. He felt upset by his mother's criticisms and this induced him to blame Sally for his mother's resentment toward him; therefore he withdrew from Sally. Because he developed insomnia, he was late for work on several occasions and forfeited some of his salary; as a result he could not pay the doctor on time. When the doctor threatened to abandon the case if he did not receive his fee, Mrs. Davis became even more depressed.

From this example, we see that when two systems are in transaction because they have a common member, occurrences in one system will affect the other system. In systems theory this is referred to as *input* from one system to another. Mr. Davis's input at work caused tensions between him and his boss. When Mr. Davis's mother became irritated with him, this fed back into several subsystems of the Davis family. *Feedback* from other systems intensified the tension in the Davis family and induced all family members to modify their behavior in the subsystems of which they were a part.

Hollis (1972) has pointed out, in referring to such transactional processes, that the possible chain of events is endless, and the individual being influenced by the many forces at the same time has to arrive at some resolution within himself that ultimately determines how he will act. If the transactional processes involving just one individual's illness and its impact on several subsystems are complex, as they certainly were in the Davis case, transactional processes in small groups, communities, and organizations are, of course, even more so.

An important feature of a social system is the _communication of information_. Communication is an essential feature of the transaction between two or more people. What information is communicated, what is withheld, and the manner in which it is delivered influence the reciprocity or lack of reciprocity between members. If feelings and thoughts are directly communicated without fear of reprisal, the system is stable; on the other hand, if communication is indirect or squelched, resentment arises between members and the system can deteriorate or break down (Ruesch, 1961; Spiegel, 1960).

Communication can be verbal or non-verbal. The presenter may convey a latent message in his overt statement, as in a _double-bind_ message (e.g., the mother who admonishes her child, "Be careful as you go downstairs that you don't fall, smash your teeth, break your arms, and bleed to death!") In the double-bind message the speaker overtly manifests one set of intentions which only superficially mask other intentions, usually hostile or destructive ones.

Communication occurs, of course, at all levels of interaction and transaction, directly and indirectly, covertly and overtly, and symbolically. Social agencies, through their policies, staff hierarchy, physical plant, and services, communicate messages to their clients regarding the system's priorities and values. Because the agency is a social system, its communication patterns, particularly as reflected through agency policies, must be evaluated as part of the diagnostic assessment.

In a study conducted a few years ago (Strean, 1974a), it was clear that an agency's communication patterns with welfare clients were producing poor social work. The welfare clients were offered short-term service by inexperienced social workers while middle-class clients were seen by more experienced workers in long-term treatment. Frequently, such modalities of treatment as family therapy, group therapy, and sensitivity groups were withheld from the more impoverished clients; in addition, these clients were frequently labelled at intake "hard to reach," "poorly motivated," and the like.

An agency communicates its biases, prejudices, and value-priorities through its informal and formal arrangements. In the example cited above, the agency was communicating its contempt for impoverished clients and its keen interest in middle-class clients.

Another important dimension of social-systems theory is the *hierarchical factor* in social systems, with its implications and consequences for communication patterns and relationships among system-members. A social structure that emphasizes status-differences often creates barriers in communication and undue formality in interpersonal relations (Stanton & Schwartz, 1954). Not only the nature and sources of the system-strains but how these strains are mediated, balanced, or resolved is important.

> In assessing the ego functioning of several patients in a mental hospital, the social worker was able to demonstrate that when the patients were no longer obliged to wear uniforms, were addressed by name rather than number, and were offered statuses in the "Citizens Council" of the mental hospital—in short, when the hospital system, in effect, ascribed a different status to the patients and began to view them as active participants in the hospital system—their behavior changed remarkably. Their self-esteem, impulse control, and other ego-functions improved dramatically.

The social context in which behavior is enacted always affects the social worker's assessment. If mental patients are treated as third-class citizens, they will, of course, be assessed that way; if impoverished clients are given statuses of ''hard to reach'' and "poorly motivated," they will be assessed accordingly. The assignment of a status to individuals, groups, or organizations is to some extent a self-fulfilling prophecy; in the end, the way people will act, react, interact, and transact is influenced in many ways by the statuses assigned to them.

It is assumed in social-systems theory that systems are *closed* or *open.* A *closed system* is self-contained and not dependent upon other systems for survival (Buckley, 1967). Certain families, small groups, and organizations tend to isolate themselves and become like an island unto themselves; this is characteristic of some communes, orthodox religious groups, delinquent and criminal organizations, and other subcultures.

In an *open system* there is an exchange of energy with other systems (Buckley, 1967). A social-work department in a hospital that exchanges information with physicians, nurses, patients, and other sub-systems is an example of an open system. An essential factor in a system's continuity and change is its engagement in interchanges with the environment.

The *open* system receives input from and gives output to its environment. The environment and the transactions with it are basic to the existence of the system. It is because of this quality of openness that human systems can grow and mature. *Closed* systems, on the other hand, are systems that do not interact with other systems, neither accepting input from them nor producing output for them. Such systems have the quality of *entropy;* this means that, over time, they tend to become disorganized and to degenerate (Compton and Galaway, 1975).

Social-system theory is not in itself a science or a body of knowledge; nor does it contain prescriptions for intervention. It is an orientation, a way of thinking, of viewing and organizing data. Its major contribution to social-work practice and theory is its emphasis on interaction, transactions, reciprocal roles (hierarchy), and communication. It provides a perspective for the range of elements that bear on psychosocial functioning, including what units are involved, their interrelationships, and how change in one part of a system affects others.

ROLE THEORY

Inherent in any study involving social-systems theory as a frame of reference is the concept of role. The structure of a social system, including its formal and informal aspects, is defined as a network of roles. Role theory views human behavior and its organization as social acts; it provides a means of studying the interactions and transactions of a system's members. Roles, mentioned in Chapter 2, are linked to positions or statuses in a system, and the norms governing the statuses provide guides for the expected, permitted, and prohibited attitudes and behavior for them (Biddle & Thomas, 1966).

Stability, equilibrium, and integration of a social system are achieved through the *complementarity* of roles. Complementarity exists when a role partner carries out the reciprocal role automatically, without difficulty, and in the expected way.

Particularly in the assessment of family, marital and parent-child relationships, the notion of complimentarity is useful in determing the contribution of all the partners to interpersonal conflicts.

> When the social worker interviewed Mrs. English to try to understand some of the etiological factors of her alcoholism, his initial assessment was based exclusively on Mrs. English's psychodynamics and personal history. Later interviews with Mr. English enlarged his diagnostic understanding and eventually altered his treatment plan. It became quite clear that although Mr. English overtly repudiated his wife's drinking, he was vicariously enjoying it; this was evidenced by his going for walks with her to bars and giving her bottles of whiskey as Christmas and birthday presents. As a willing accomplice to his wife's drinking, Mr. English could be regarded as her complementary role partner in alcoholism.

The concept of complementarity helps the social workers maintain a neutral stance in assessing relationship-difficulties. There is much less of a tendency to identify with one partner against the other when the worker realizes that a husband's sadism is usually complemented by a wife's masochism, one spouse's dominance is inevitably complemented by the other's submissiveness, and a child's provocative behavior is frequently aided and abetted by his parents.

Role conflict, as we have noted, occurs when the status of a member is defined differently by two reference groups (Rosenblatt, 1961). Although it may not be apparent at first, many clients' difficulties turn out to be role-conflict problems.

Fred, an 18-year-old high-school student, had received poor grades in school, was suffering from a deep depression, and bickered with his parents virtually every day. After several interviews with the boy, the social worker could account for many of Fred's difficulties in terms of his role-conflicts. In order to feel accepted by his peers on the football team, Fred felt an obligation to shun girls. However, he felt quite attached to one particular girl but, to avoid censure from his male friends, saw his girlfriend secretly. The girl resented the arrangements Fred made, and her anger upset him. Fred's conflicts with his parents, peers and girlfriend interfered with concentration on his studies; consequently he received low grades. Fred's parents were extremely upset about his grades and tried to curb his time with both his girlfriend and football team. This, of course, exacerbated Fred's anger toward his parents.

Role incongruency (Spiegel, 1960) is a stress situation in which the perception of one's own role is different from the expectations of significant others in the role-system. For example, in a group of boys who had been adjudged "delinquent" and who met with the social worker weekly, much role incongruency occurred. The boys thought the social worker and agency would help them attack their "enemies"; the social worker conceived of his role as helping the boys curb their delinquent impulses. Had the social worker more comprehensively assessed how the boys perceived their own roles and the roles of agency personnel, he would have moved more cautiously in his interventive plan, thus avoiding much strain between the boys and himself.

The notion of role usually involves some form of *prescription* (Biddle and Thomas, 1966); some behaviors "should" be performed. If the roles prescribed by and for each member of a marriage, a family, or any group are at variance, strain occurs. Utilizing a systems and role-theory perspective, the social worker recognizes that for a system to sustain itself in relative equilibrium, what the prescribed role expectations actually are is less important than whether they are complementary.

Research related to prescriptions of marital roles (Jacobson, 1952) indicated that divorced couples exhibited greater disparities in these prescriptions than did married couples. Jacobson concluded that for a marriage to sustain itself with limited strain, the complementarity of partners' role prescriptions regarding sex, work, recreation, religious practices, and so on, is more important than what they actually are. Similarly, if the prescriptions regarding child-rearing practices within a family are in reality what all the members feel they ought to be, this fact is more important for the family's stability than the specific child-rearing practices.

The notion of role prescription is particularly important during the early phases of the social-worker–client encounter, when information is gathered, problems are assessed, and the contract is formed. The phenomenon of early client dropout is one that several writers in social work have explored (Perlman, 1960; Stark, 1959; Overall and Aronson, 1963). One of the underlying factors that has been proposed to explain why some clients leave the agency after only one or two interviews is that the client's understanding and expectations of the agency and social worker were not clear to the worker, and vice versa. In other words, the barriers between client and worker in the early phases of the assessment process may fruitfully be viewed from a role-theory perspective—the role partners have uncomplementary and incongruent expectations regarding their respective roles.

When a welfare-rights group sought out the social agency
for help, strain soon developed between the group and the social worker. The group was interested in using the social
worker's influence to petition politicians, administrators, and
civic officials for higher welfare-allotments, while the worker
expected to help the group discuss their familial, marital, and
economic conflicts. Because the role partners prescribed
behaviors for each other that were incongruent with their
self-expectations, strain developed and the group withdrew
from the agency.

In work with lower socio-economic groups the matter of role
prescriptions is particularly salient. Many individuals in these
groups do not regard verbalization of feelings, thoughts, and
memories as a legitimate or prescribed part of any role-set. Consequently, to the more action-oriented client, the social worker's
reluctance to provide for him materially and tangibly is baffling
and may be interpreted as disinterest or rejection.

Applying the notion of role prescription to the assessment process, particularly during its initial phase, it would appear that a
fundamental task of the social worker is to clarify the respective
role prescriptions of clients and worker so that they may attain
some agreement regarding them. As Perlman (1960) has
suggested, certain understandings must evolve before the applicant can undertake the role of client. What an applicant will do in
the initial phase of the assessment process is, of course, conditioned by his perception of what the worker expects of him and,
in turn, what he may expect from the worker and the agency
(Perlman, 1957). If the applicant wants to discuss his aches and
pains or his wishes for the worker to be his "social broker" or
"advocate," while the worker prefers to discuss the client's
psychological dynamics, dropout will probably occur. Unless the
social worker and the applicant come to some tentative agreement
about their present and future transactions, the worker will not
have a client to assess and eventually help.

ROLE-SET

Another construct from role theory which has applicability to the assessment process is the notion of *role-set* (Merton, 1957). A "role-set" signifies an array of associated roles related to a specific status. The status of social-work students, for example, has a complement of associated role reciprocators, including field-work instructor, agency executive, client, agency social workers, fellow-students, and others. The compatibility and fit of expectations within this array of complimentary roles affect the student's performance in any one of his roles (Strean, 1971c).

When the applicant adds the status of client to his existing role-set, a host of conflicts may be generated (Rosenblatt, 1961). He may feel that the role of client is incompatible with his role-set of, say, father and wage-earner, and that the reference groups which support and sanction his usual role-set (e.g., family, colleagues at work) may not support his being a client as well. This is why it is crucial, as an applicant moves to the client role, to ascertain how his reference groups react to his becoming a client and how he, in turn, feels about their reactions.

Boehm (1959) has utilized the notion of role-set for purposes of diagnostic classification in social-work practice. If role performances are classified and all clients are viewed as enacting various roles, assessment can be more comprehensive and may point more clearly to the direction of intervention. Boehm classified role performance in four levels:

Level I.—Role performance violates minimal societal standards and may cause stress to individuals and groups in the client's role-network. Clients who have been engaged in criminal activity would be an example; they have violated societal standards and have caused stress to many individuals and groups in their community.

Level II.—Role performance meets minimal societal standards but causes stress to individuals and groups with whom the client is in constant interaction. In this category would be clients whose behavior is disruptive to members of their own work-group, school, or other important reference group. They could be children who antagonize or alienate their peers and/or teachers, or workers whose role-behavior causes stress to their fellow-employees and/or employer.

Level III.—Role performance meets minimal societal standards for members of the reference groups (e.g. family, work) but is not commensurate with role-performance potential. In this level are clients whose overt behavior does not induce stress in anyone in day-to-day interactions, but who feel dissatisfied with their performances—e.g., the student who is receiving passing grades but feels he could do better; the worker who is gainfully employed but could produce more; the client who is functioning reasonably well but has a shaky self-image.

Level IV.—Role performance meets minimal societal standards and is commensurate with role-performance potential. At this level the client is conforming to what is expected of him by society and significant others and is creatively and constructively using his capacities in the roles he is enacting.

Clients classified at Level I are generally referred to social workers by courts and penal institutions and might be served in prisons or similar institutions. At Level II the impetus would come chiefly from families, work or recreational groups of which the client is a member, or from the client himself. The clients would be seen in mental-health centers and family agencies. Public health and community mental-health measures would seem to be required for individuals and groups at Level III, who are frequently self-referred or referred by their families. The usual social utilities would be the services needed for people at Level IV; these individuals are not usually seen by any social worker.

The scheme's usefulness is that it provides a clear picture of the role of society in the provision of social services, clarifies the social-control aspects of social work, and, finally, suggests that certain tasks of the client should be taken into consideration by the social worker as he assesses role-set performance. Because role performance is viewed against certain norms, Boehm's scheme tends to locate areas of potential dysfunction. Because the client is seen almost exclusively as a role carrier, these classifications suggest the appropriate diagnostic direction by helping the social worker assess what aspects of the role-set the client accepts or rejects.

A study by Dinitz et al. (1962) of the relationship between role-expectations of family members and the performance of female mental patients following their discharge from a mental hospital found that the higher the expectations held for the patient's role performance, the higher the level of her actual performance.

While role theory embodies some psychological and biological considerations, its major emphasis is a social one. Its chief value for assessment in social work is that it focuses on the task-oriented aspects of social functioning, points to conflicts that the client may have in his role relationships and role-set, and suggests areas of misunderstanding that may arise between the social worker and client in the early phase of the assessment process.

APPLYING PSYCHOANALYTIC THEORY AND EGO PSYCHOLOGY TO ASSESSMENT

As was suggested in Chapter 1, the psychoanalytic model met the need in social work for a personality theory that could enlarge upon the sociological model already in existence; it also replaced the moralistic orientation toward personal reform of the individual client that characterized many of the early charity workers and "friendly visitors" (Meyer, 1970).

In contrast to many other theories of personality, which explained only fragments of the human being, Freud postulated the principle of *psychic determinism,* which holds that in mental functioning nothing happens by chance. Everything a person does, feels, thinks, fantasies, and dreams has a psychological motive. Whom the client chooses marry, what he does or does not do in the marriage, where he works and how he conducts himself on the job, who his friends are, and so on, are all motivated by *unconscious* inner forces (Freud, 1939).

Although situational factors are always impinging on the client, the notions of "psychic determinism" and "the unconscious" help the social worker to recognize that the behavior of individuals, dyads, groups, and organizations is not only a reaction to such external variables as family, friends, and neighborhood, but is also shaped by the client's idiosyncratic wishes, hopes, fears, and ethical imperatives.

> When Mrs. Gordon discussed in her Mothers' Group at the agency her conflicts in her three marriages, all to alcoholic men, the social worker and the other group members had to take note of the repetitiveness of this behavior. As her history unfolded and her coping patterns became clearer, she was slowly able to recognize "how much I like protecting weak guys and even get a kick out of seeing them impotent."

Freud saw the human personality from five distinct but intermeshing points of view: the dynamic, the genetic, the topographic, the structural, and the economic (Freud, 1938; Freud, 1939).

The Dynamic Approach   Freud's instinct theory is concerned with the libidinal and aggressive drives. The drives or instincts represent the "nature" factor in the development of behavior (Rapaport, 1951). An instinct has four characteristics: a source, an aim, an object, and an impetus. The source is a bodily condition or need—e.g., hunger, sex, aggression. The aim of an instinct is gratification or pleasure, and the object includes not only the object upon which the need is focused (e.g. food), but all the activities necessary to secure it—walking to the refrigerator, eating, and so on. The impetus of an instinct is its strength, which is determined by the force or intensity of the underlying need; that is, hunger, sexual need, or aggression may vary in impetus among different individuals or in the same individual at different times.

In making an assessment, the social worker will want to ascertain whether and how the client's instincts are being gratified. Is he getting enough food and enjoying it? Is he able to have consistent sexual gratification? Is the client capable of mature love, friendship, and trust, or is he handicapped by an unusual degree of narcissism? Is he capable of asserting himself appropriately, or is his aggression characterized by too much destructiveness? The answers to these questions, which the *dynamic* point of view suggests, help the social worker to pinpoint conflict, plan intervention, and gauge the client's motivation and capacity for a working relationship with the social worker.

The Genetic Approach   Each individual's past participates in and shapes his present. During the first five or six years of life the child experiences a series of differentiated dynamic stages which are of extreme importance in the formation of personality. In the oral stage, the mouth is the principal focus of dynamic activity; in the anal phase the child turns his interests to elimination functions; in the phallic stage he forms the rudiments of a sexual identity; in latency, there is a quiescence of erotic and libidinal interest; and at puberty, there is a recrudescence of biological drives (particularly of the Oedipal interests that emerged during the phallic phase) and ambivalence toward parents and other authority figures (Freud, 1939).

Ego psychologist Erik Erikson (1950) greatly expanded Freud's theory of *genetic* stages of instinctual development by placing development in a social and cultural matrix and emphasizing the tasks of ego mastery presented by each stage of maturation. He has identified eight nuclear conflicts or developmental crises in the life-span—trust vs. mistrust, autonomy vs. shame and doubt, initiative vs. guilt, industry vs. inferiority, identity vs. role diffusion, intimacy vs. isolation, generativity vs. stagnation, and integrity vs. despair—which correspond to Freud's stages of orality, anality, genitality, latency, puberty, etc.

According to Erikson, not only does the human being unfold

according to predetermined biological phases, but human maturation cannot be viewed apart from the social context in which it transpires. For example, the infant's functioning during the oral phase cannot be assessed without taking into consideration his transactions with his mother. If the infant and mother mutually gratify each other in many basic ways—e.g., during feeding, playing, etc.—the child will learn to "trust" rather than "distrust" his environment. Similarly, if the child is helped to forego certain pleasures and take on some frustration during toilet training (anal phase) he will develop a sense of "autonomy" rather than one of "shame and doubt." If parents help the child to feel comfortable with sexual interests and impulses, the child will be more likely to participate creatively and constructively in interpersonal relationships and be "industrious" rather than feel "inferior."

Frequently individuals who become clients of social workers have been placed under stress by some environmental factor. In response, they may regress to earlier, more immature modes of psychosocial functioning. The depressed woman who cannot relate to her children and friends because her husband is ill and she feels angry and lost due to his lack of support can be described as having regressed to a level of functioning more appropriate to a child struggling to be autonomous but plagued by much shame and doubt. Diagnostic questions that this genetic orientation would prompt us to ask are: "What triggered the client's regression?" "At what level of psychosocial functioning is the client now operating?" "What is occurring in the present that is reminiscent of the past?"

When Mr. Howe, a 35-year-old man, appeared at the social agency, he was full of anger and was quite depressed. He had recently learned that his fiancée was having a sexual affair with another man. He found himself obsessed with the affair, could not get it off his mind, and was thinking of suicide. In addition he was not eating or sleeping. He did not want to talk to anyone, resented his lawyer for referring him to the agency, and felt "social workers never even give you the time of day."

Further interviews helped both client and worker to realize that Mr. Howe had never felt very secure as a man, had spent a great deal of his time trying "to take women from men I know," and usually lost the battle with himself. This was reminiscent of his Oedipal competition with his father and older brother during his teens. His reponse to his girlfriend's affair was a regression to the trust–mistrust phase of development. He wanted understanding and to be symbolically fed (oral phase) but was too angry to ask for help. Therefore, he had much difficulty in trusting the social worker or anybody else.

Many individuals who are referred to social workers have never in their lives matured beyond a certain point of psychosocial development. The term "fixation" is used to describe them because they are "fixated" at a certain level of development and are unable to mature further. As part of his assessment the social worker will have to determine where such a client is fixated. Has he ever learned to trust? Has he established sufficient ego autonomy? Has he ever mastered the maturational task of learning how to relate intimately with another human being? (Wood, 1970).

The Topographic Approach   The *topographic* model examines the personality in terms of conscious, preconscious, and unconscious states of mind. The conscious mind is that part of our mental activities that we are fully aware of at any time; the preconscious refers to thoughts and feelings that can be brought into consciousness fairly easily; and the unconscious refers to thoughts, feelings, desires, and memories of which we are not aware but which powerfully influence all of our behavior. The unconscious not only consists of drives, defenses, and admonitions but also contains memories of events and attitudes that have been repressed (Freud, 1938, 1939).

The social worker in his assessment of a client-system needs to know the ways in which the unconscious influences the individual, for the unconscious is always operative in all behavior, adaptive and maladaptive.

> Ten-year-old Joseph went from one tutor to another trying to overcome his "reading block." In addition to faithfully keeping his appointments with his tutors, he overtly complied with all of their instructions and did the homework they required of him. Despite all his conscious efforts, Joseph continued to fail.
>
> When a social worker was consulted by one of the tutors, the worker was able to determine, from Joseph's history as well as from his other relationships, that *unconsciously* Joseph needed to spite every authority with whom he had dealings. While consciously Joseph wanted to please, his reading block expressed his unconscious wish to defeat parental figures.

When the social worker becomes attuned to the unconscious meaning of behavior, he is in a much better position to plan intervention. He realizes that the sexual impotence of a man or the frigidity of a woman serves an unconscious purpose; the constant bickering of a marital couple, the lack of intimacy in a family, the divisiveness in a group, and the dissension in a community all have unconscious meaning which he must understand to help resolve the manifest difficulties of the particular client-system.

The Structural Approach   The *structural* approach refers to the psychic structure of id, ego, and superego. The id, the most primitive part of the mind and totally unconscious, is the repository of the drives and is concerned with their gratification. The ego, which develops out of experience and reason, is the executive of the personality and mediates between the inner world of id drives, superego commands, and the demands of the external world. Some of the functions of the ego are judgment, reality testing, frustration tolerance, and relating to others. The ego also erects defenses against anxiety. By assessing the client's ego strengths and weaknesses we can determine how well he is adapting; the more severe the client's disturbances, the less operative are his ego-functions and vice versa (Erikson, 1950).

The superego is the judge or censor of the mind and is essentially the product of interpersonal experiences. It is the storehouse of "do's and don'ts," values, imperatives, etc.

It remained for the ego psychologists to conceptualize the ego as something more than Freud's "mediator." They see it as a structure with autonomy and power of its own. The ego's power arises primarily from the development of the secondary process—those aspects of the ego that are rational, adapted to reality and derive from interpersonal processes and experiences: locomotion, cognition, memory, perception, and rational thought and action. Heinz Hartmann (1951) saw these ego capabilities as "conflict free" even though they are intimately connected with id drives and superego commands.

Ego psychologists encouraged social workers to assess their clients' _strengths_, those functions that give their clients pleasure, the parts of the personality that can be supported rather than modified.

> Everyday behavior is a complex psychosocial phenomenon. We must analyze it in various ways—as a social role and as family interaction, as an expression of ideals and values, as physical processes, as an expression of psychological processes such as instinctual drives and defensive operations.... [Social-work] practice requires that we use all these frames of reference and ego psychology constructs offer such a unifying theory for the diagnosis and understanding of all these frames of reference, a way of "pulling together" and extracting meaning and perspective from the worker's various discrete sub-diagnoses [Stamm, 1959, p. 86].

By applying aspects of ego psychology the social worker can assess the level of development of the client's perceptive, executive, and integrative functions: "Have the ego's defenses been overdeveloped?" "Is the client's social situation such that his defenses are vitally necessary adaptations to it, as in the environment of a decrepit ghetto?"

One of the important ego-functions to which all social workers must give attention is that of the client's defenses—those ego structures which protect the client from anxiety. The defenses include *projection* (ascribing to others one's own unacceptable feelings, thoughts, or behaviors); *denial* (stating that something that is anxiety-provoking, such as an illness, possible job-loss, etc., just does not exit) and *isolation* (separating parts of an experience so that matters that are actually interrelated appear not to affect one another). Other defenses used by the ego are *turning against the self, regression, undoing, repression,* and *reaction formation*.

When the individual experiences certain emotions toward another individual but finds them unacceptable, he can *turn against the self.* For example, rather than feel anger towards a valued person, the individual can attack himself instead.

As has already been suggested, if reality presents a danger, the individual can *regress* by returning to a more immature form of functioning. This is often seen in children when a sibling is born; they soil or urinate in bed, even though they have been toilet-trained for sometime.

Undoing is an action which has the purpose of disproving the harm which the individual imagines may be caused by his aggressive or sexual wishes. For example, a child whose angry feelings toward a younger sibling cause him anxiety may defend against his anxiety by being a rescuer and trying to nurse sick and injured animals back to health. He *undoes* the harm he thinks he can inflict on his siblings.

The defense mechanism which Freud recognized early in his career is *repression*. This defense bars from consciousness id impulses that cause anxiety. It is important to note that when the individual represses—or utilizes any defense mechanism—this is an unconscious process. One is never aware that he is repressing, undoing, regressing, and so on.

Reaction formation is a mechanism whereby one of a pair of ambivalent attitudes is rendered unconscious by an overemphasis of the other. For example, an individual may find himself feeling uncomfortable with certain hateful feelings; therefore, he over-emphasizes his love.

In the use of all defense mechanisms, there is always an attempt to repudiate an impulse (A. Freud, 1937). To the id's "yes," the ego defends by saying "no" to avoid the danger of a forbidden impulse becoming conscious. More often than not, there are complex interactions between many drives and many anxieties. A defensive struggle is rarely brought to a successful conclusion by one particular defensive activity. Defenses may be more or less successful; they may work under certain circumstances, or be insufficient under others.

Seemingly irrational, provocative behavior that appears to be disruptive to the social-work encounter can often be understood and related to with empathy if the social worker is aware that all human beings defend themselves from ideas, thoughts, and feelings that arouse anxiety.

When the community social worker was attempting to persuade an elementary-school principal to permit the childdren to have milk and cookies during the school-day, she met with enormous resistance. "Children should not be fed, they should be taught," he bellowed. "You spoil them by indulging them and give them no reason to work hard," he continued. All his remarks demeaned children and he was particularly adamant about children not being "fed," "given to," etc.

As the social worker listened to the principal and took note of his own obesity, his inability to give, his anger at children being given to, she began to realize that the principal was projecting his own "hearty appetite" onto the children as well as his own wish to be given to, both of which were unacceptable to him. Recognizing that the principal was really talking about himself as he damned the children, the social worker could explore with him why food, milk, and fatness were so taboo. As she maintained a non-critical attitude toward the things that the principal unconsciously craved but consciously condemned (oral supplies), the principal could get

more in touch with his real wishes. At one of the interviews
he concluded, "Just because I don't like myself as a fat slob, I
shouldn't be so tough on the kids."

Sometimes a social worker generalizes about ego strength and
weakness without specifying what functions are being referred to.
Is it that the ego has insufficient energy to control instincts and
selectively discharge tension? Is the reference to an ego domi-
nated by aggressive impulses or by a punitive superego? Or is it
that the ego makes a poor choice of defense mechanisms to cope
with a problem (Stamm, 1959)?

Determining the level and quality of superego functioning is
also part of every good psychosocial assessment. If the client is
very strict with himself and others, an understanding of superego
development and functioning will sensitize us to his self-image,
interpersonal relationships, and other modes of coping. Similarly, when clients are destructive, manipulative, and damaging
to others, an understanding of the development and functioning
of their superegos will guide us in assessment and intervention.

The Economic Approach   The *economic* dimension of
Freud's theory of personality holds that all behavior is regulated
by the need to dispose of psychological energy. Psychological
energies cannot be expressed in mathematical formulae, yet they
are referents of phenomena that seem to abide by the laws of
energy-exchanges—laws of conservation, entropy, and least action (Rapaport, 1951).

Assessment of the economic weightings and equilibria involved in the client's intrapsychic functioning, interpersonal
transactions, and interactions with the social environment help us
to answer such questions as: "What is the relative force and
weighting of libidinal and sexual needs?" "What is the state of
equilibrium in a particular marriage or family?" "Is the problem
of this child in the family not only an expression of family dysfunction, but perhaps also a way for other members, through their
scapegoating of him, to maintain a family homeostasis?" "What

will happen to the rest of the family if one member changes and disturbs the equilibrium?'' ''Does this welfare mother, burdened and harassed by a destructive reality situation, have sufficient inner resources to improve her functioning if the social worker provides some relief from external pressures?'' (Wood, 1971).

Neurotic Symptom Formation When the individual's impulses—sexual or aggressive—are unacceptable to the ego, the ego utilizes defenses to protect the person against conscious awareness of the impulses, ideas, thoughts, or memories which are unbearable. Anxiety, according to Freud (1923) is a warning to the person that some unacceptable thought or action will reach consciousness. If the drive is too strong or the defense too weak, anxiety erupts and the person forms a *neurotic symptom*—e.g., a phobia, obsession, or compulsion. The sympton expresses simultaneously the individual's impulse and his dread of the impulse. In a phobia, for example, two variables are at work: the very situation that the individual fears, also excites him—an aggressive situation, a sexually stimulating scene, etc. Neuroses, then, are ''arranged'' by the person to effect a compromise between the id and those parts of the personality which repudiate an expression of sexual or aggressive impulses.

When Gloria, a seventeen-year-old client, reported that she could not go to high-school dances because she would vomit there, get hives, become speechless, and sweat profusely, the social worker saw a neurotic phobia at work. As she herself realized, Gloria had strong sexual fantasies which were seeking discharge and which caused unbearable anxiety for her. Puberty induced erotic feelings which Gloria felt had to be condemned. Her defenses of denial, repression, and avoidance were not strong enough to keep her libidinal desires away from consciousness. Anxiety erupted, and she began to suffer from a painful phobia.

Just as we concluded that systems theory and role theory did not provide a complete arsenal for the social worker's assessment of his clients, so too must we consider psychoanalysis and ego psychology of only partial use. Although Freudian psychoanalysis and ego psychology are comprehensive theories, they have some limitations for assessing the social interactions and transactions of dyads, families, groups, and organizations.

It would appear that where systems theory and role theory are strongest—in helping us assess the social interactions and transactions of two or more people—psychoanalysis and ego psychology are weakest. Where the latter are strong—in helping us assess the human being in terms of his internal life and unique coping patterns—systems theory and role theory appear to be deficient. This is why social workers need to consider both orientations as they dynamically assess individuals and groups in their situations.

The Clinical Diagnosis

One of the most controversial issues in clinical social work (and in psychotherapy and psychoanalysis) is the clinical diagnosis. When the social worker makes a clinical diagnosis he categorizes the client as "neurotic," "psychotic," having a "character disorder," or uses some other diagnostic label.

There are several reasons why categorizing a client has been a debatable issue. Firstly, such labels as "neurotic" or "psychotic" fail to individualize the person-situation–constellation under discussion. A diagnosis of "anxiety-hysteria," for example, does not tell us much about the intensity, pervasiveness, or disruptive effects the client's neurosis has on him or on his interpersonal relationships. It tells us little about the strength of the client's drives and ego-functions, and nothing about the flexibility of his superego. The label contains little information about the client's unique conflicts, the etiology of his stresses, or the environmental contributions to his coping or inability to cope.

A clinical label often stereotypes an individual, influencing how he responds to himself and how others will view him. If a client is labelled "schizophrenic," he and others may think of him as "crazy," and he will often be shunned by relatives, friends, and associates. It has been found that if a person is given the title or label "patient in a mental hospital," one form of behavior will be elicited, but if the same individual in the same hospital is given the title "President of Citizen Government," another form of behavior will manifest itself, and usually it will be more adaptive and mature (Goffman, 1961).

Recently the American Psychiatric Association recognized that individuals labelled "homosexual" were stereotyped in many sectors of society and often had many of their civil rights curbed. The A.P.A. therefore dropped the clinical label from their diagnostic nomenclature. While many therapists in and out of social work contend that homosexuality, bisexuality, and other non-mainstream forms of sexual behavior may be indicative of maturational lags and emotional conflict, they also realize that there is no correlation between such unconventional sexual behavior and job performance, empathy for others, impulse control, and other dimensions of personality functioning.

Because such clinical diagnoses as "psychopath" or "character disorder" do not fully describe an individual but tend to stigmatize him, many clinical social workers have rejected this form of assessment altogether. And there is no doubt that one can assess and help an individual without clinically labelling him. However, clinical diagnoses frequently appear in the literature, are utilized in case discussions and supervisory conferences, and sometimes can serve as a useful short-cut in discussion. Florence Hollis (1964) has pointed out that when social workers use, for example, the label "obsessive-compulsive neurotic" most of them are referring to an individual with a tyrannical superego, with strong sadistic impulses that he must defend against, and who is very ambivalent, orderly, parsimonious, and overly intellectual. Yet, most social workers would also agree that there are many differences among obsessive-compulsive individuals. Among other things, their social, family, and marital situations differ, offering to some of them much protection and to others, stimulating danger. Furthermore, they differ in the rigidity of their defenses, the strength of their ego-functions, and their drive endowments.

It has been determined that social workers, more than any other professional group, diagnose and treat the most disturbed of our population. They work with more "psychopaths," "schizophrenics," people with "character disorders," and "neurotics" than do psychiatrists and psychologists (Strean, 1974b). As a result, social workers are often called upon to function in the roles of consultant, supervisor, or teacher in helping psychiatrists and other professionals make differential diagnoses and work on interventive plans. This is another reason why the social worker should be familiar with clinical categories: psychiatrists and psychologists tend to use them a great deal in discussions.

In the review of the major clinical categories which follows we will be discussing them as they have been conceptualized by Freudian psychoanalysts and ego psychologists. Consequently, for each label under discussion—e.g., schizophrenia, obsessive-compulsive neurosis—we will examine the relationship between certain childhood experiences and maturational deficiencies, on the one hand, and certain adult manifestations of adult pathology, on the other. It must be stressed again that there are a vast array of variables that contribute toward psychosocial dysfunction in addition to the client's history, maturational development, and parent-child relationships. Only some of these significant variables can receive major consideration in our discussion.

SCHIZOPHRENIA

When a client is referred to as "schizophrenic," the diagnostician may be implying that he is suffering from hallucinations and delusions, distorts reality severely, and/or is plagued by powerful murderous fantasies (usually projecting his murderous wishes onto others as well). Because the schizophrenic believes that the world is an evil, torturous place, he frequently withdraws from reality and remains seclusive, often talking to himself. He may become obsessed with a non-human issue or activity such as physics or mechanics and devote all of his energy to this non-human environment.

There is continuing debate about the etiology of schizophrenia. On one side are those who contend that it is strictly a constitutional, biological phenomenon that should be treated by drugs and other pharmaceutical agents to deal with the toxins in the client's system. On the other side of the controversy are those who view the schizophrenic as an individual who has been poorly nurtured during the early phases of psychosocial development and is therefore distrustful, suspicious, and paranoid because he has never been responded to appropriately by a trusting person; he suffers from disorders in thought (hallucinations and delusions) because his ego, like that of a very young child, has not had the opportunity to develop and mature in a favorable climate. While not negating the notion that every organism is a bio-psychosocial amalgam, most social workers subscribe to the second point of view.

Like the infant who is primarily narcissistic in that the systems of his mental apparatus are not yet differentiated from each other, the schizophrenic client is also highly narcissistic. Just as the infant has not yet developed to the point where he can relate to people on a thoughtful, considerate basis, so, too, the schizophrenic client has no emotionally significant contact with people. Furthermore, just as we do not expect the infant to have well-developed ego-functions such as judgment, reality testing, impulse control, and perception, the schizophrenic client has parted with reality and most of his ego-functions have broken down. Like early infancy, which has no "reality," the schizophrenic client is one who has "lost reality." His ego has turned to its original undifferentiated state and has dissolved almost entirely into the id, which has no real knowledge of people and reality (Fenichel, 1945).

The schizophrenic client may be considered not only a psychological infant, but an infant who has been poorly fed, poorly loved, and poorly comforted. Psychologically he is an extremely angry infant with powerful feelings of murderous rage which he is helpless to discharge because he needs his parents, the primary object of these feelings. Therefore he bottles up his rage, for were he to discharge it he might, in his mind at least, kill his parents. Instead, he feels like an extremely unworthy child, and this murderous rage pervades his entire psyche and prevents him from maturing, much as powerful infectious toxins can retard physical development (Josselyn, 1948).

Because the schizophrenic client has withdrawn his *libido* (energy) from people to himself, he not only is very narcissistic, with feelings of estrangement and depersonalization, but, again like a baby, is preoccupied with body sensations. Regression to or fixation at the infantile narcissistic state accounts for his megalomania, in which he fantasies that he is somebody very special, such as an emperor.

Erikson (1950) describes the schizophrenic individual as one who has either lost or never gained a basic sense of trust and therefore resorts to a narcissistic, paranoid orientation to the world. His thinking falls back from the logical to the prelogical level, and he is consumed by archaic wishes which give rise to hallucinatory and delusional thinking (Fenichel, 1945).

Just as the baby wishes to have a relationship with a mother figure, so the schizophrenic adult does not completely abandon his wish for contact with people (except for the catatonic schizophrenic, who has given up the search and lies mute for hours or days, often having to be fed intravenously). The schizophrenic often demonstrates his wish to have a relationship by his infantile thought-processes and often manifests it in a megalomaniacal form, holding to the conviction that, "Everyone is looking at me!"

MANIC-DEPRESSIVE PSYCHOSES

The manic-depressive psychotic also is a very infantile person. His mood alternates from deep depression, like that of a baby who has lost his mother (therefore, the world has stopped), to an oceanic feeling that he has been reunited with Mother and that life is now perfectly blissful. Although there is some evidence of the operation of biological factors in manic-depressive psychoses, the alternating states of acute depression and intense joy seem to mirror a situation in which the baby is alternately abandoned and then loved intensely, only to be abandoned again. Differing from the schizophrenic client who seems to have suffered from consistent estrangement, the manic-depressive client appears to be the product of a very tempestuous, unpredictable environment that offered much pain but also sporadic pleasure. However, as Glover (1949) has pointed out, the exaggerated self-love of the client during the manic phase is also indicative of pathology in that it is often accompanied by intense feelings and impulsive actions. It is as if the client is holding desperately onto a joyful state, knowing that at any moment it will disappear (Mother will go away).

In the depressive phase of the manic-depressive psychosis, one can usually see that the client has suffered decisive narcissistic injuries which must have taken the form of severe disappointments in the parents at a time when the child's self-esteem was being regulated by them (Fenichel, 1945).

The ego-functions and narcissistic state of the manic-depressive–psychotic client are quite similar in nature to the infantile state of the schizophrenic client. However, the manic-depressive seems to be continually alternating between hunger and satiety, and seems to expect this pattern. Thus he anticipates pleasure after every pain and pain after every pleasure. As Fenichel (1945) has pointed out, the primitive idea is set up that any suffering bestows the privilege of some later compensating joy, and vice versa.

Manic-depressive psychoses and schizophrenia are two clinical entities that fall under the overall category of psychosis. Clients diagnosed as psychotic have few if any ego-functions working for them. They have lost their hold on reality, have defective judgment, relate to others on a very infantile basis, and have extremely poor impulse control and frustration tolerance. They tend to harbor strong murderous fantasies and are very distrustful of others. As with schizophrenic clients, their prognosis for complete recovery is usually guarded.

BORDERLINE AND SCHIZOID STATES

Individuals who do not manifest a true psychosis but function at a trust-mistrust or oral level of development have been variously referred to as borderline, schizoid, ambulatory schizophrenic, and pseudo-neurotic schizophrenic. These clients, although frequently suffering from the extreme narcissism, feelings of omnipotence, lack of true object-relatedness, departures from reality, and poor judgment associated with psychoses, usually have some ego-functions that are operative, at least at certain times. Sometimes they can use good judgment on a job but do not relate well in a marriage (or vice versa). They may be extremely preoccupied with their bodies but manage to operate for periods of time in a symptom-free manner. As is also true of the schizophrenic and manic-depressive, huge quantities of aggression pervade their psyches. Such persons are potential psychotics: they have not broken with reality, yet under unfavorable circumstances they may become psychotic (Fenichel, 1945; Glover, 1949).

The borderline person may be psychopathic in that he functions with a limited superego or conscience and does not concern himself with the needs of others. At times he deceives others by his pseudo-independence, but in reality he is a little child handling narcissistic hurts by denial and with a protective increase in his narcissism. He tends to react to frustrations by losing object-relatedness, although the loss is partial and temporary. Occasionally the client appears "normal" because he has succeeded in substituting "pseudo-contacts" for real relationships (Erikson, 1950). Like other clients who have been improperly nurtured, borderline or schizoid clients are frequently paranoid (distrustful of others).

ADDICTIONS

The drug addict, food addict, heavy smoker, or heavy eater are all trying to satisfy a strong hunger, either because they have not been appropriately given to or because higher levels of development have created so much anxiety they cannot master them. Once the hunger is satisfied, the client feels a temporary sense of security and self-esteem. Addicts are frequently distrustful people and have hardly ever held others in high esteem; that is why they resort to self-pleasure. Through drugs, food, or tobacco, they are literally feeding themselves because the desired object is not available. The drug or food is experienced as equivalent to warmth and comfort from the mother and her body.

Addicts bear a resemblance to the manic-depressive client in that they frequently live in a state of alternating elation and depression, corresponding to the alternation of hunger and satiation in the very young infant. The depression is particularly observable in the addict's "morning after" syndrome (English and Pearson, 1945). While the "morning after" syndrome is painful, the alcohol or drug, like gambling and other addictions, initially has removed inhibitions from consciousness so that frustrations appear smaller and wishes nearer. Yet, most addicts usually suffer from acute depression and frequently feel quite persecuted.

PSYCHOSOMATIC DISEASE

Because the growing organism is a system comprising biological, psychological, and social subsystems, alteration in any one part will affect others. It is well known that undischarged quantities of anger can lead to a migraine headache or insomnia, unfulfilled dependency-wishes unacceptable to the person can lead to an ulcer, and undischarged aggression and frustrated libidinal longings can induce heart conditions. Note terms in common parlance like, "That was a heartbreaker"; "He gives me a headache"; "I couldn't stomach that!"

Some authors contend that psychosomatic illnesses are merely expressions of damned-up excitation and tension and do not express a unique set of psychodynamic conflicts (Glover, 1949). Others have concluded that the particular body-zone selected reflects a unique psychological conflict. According to Fenichel (1945), for example, bronchial asthma reflects a passive-receptive longing for the mother expressed in pathological changes of the breathing function. The asthmatic seizure may be interpreted as a cry for help directed toward the mother whom the client tries to introject by respiration in order to be permanently protected. Similarly, dermatitis can be viewed as crying out through the skin, and colitis may express the wish to withhold because of defiant feelings.

The clinician working with clients who have psychosomatic diseases cannot fail to note the disease's diminution when the client is given the opportunity in treatment to verbalize what his "grinding stomach" or "heavy heart" is saying. Somatic distress is a reflection of psychic tension that attaches itself to a weak constitutional zone. When the heart or stomach is given a chance to "speak" about a psychological conflict, the pains tend to lessen (Fenichel, 1945).

Just as the infant expresses his tensions by calling attention to his body, so, too, does the frustrated adult resort to this infantile form of expression. Hypochondriasis may be viewed as an attempt on the part of the client to have the therapist or others view his shaky body, comfort it, and hold it. In hypochondriasis, feelings the client has toward parents and significant others but cannot discharge because of the fear of retaliation or abandonment are often somaticized and "kept inside" the body.

Many somatic disorders may be viewed as expressions of inhibition on the part of the client. Stuttering and stammering may occur if the verbal expression of feelings is experienced as potentially aggressive. Eye tics may occur if the patient feels that seeing something is forbidden. Just as a bodily part may be inhibited to restrain an impulse, so impulses that cannot be discharged through normal channels are expressed inappropriately. Just as a frustrated infant who cannot verbalize his affects thrashes, kicks, and screams, the adult equivalent may be noted in such psychomotor discharges as petit mal epilepsy. Clinical experience would seem to indicate that epileptic personalities are generally very narcissistically oriented and manifest features of a primitive ego. They also have very intense murderous drives that can be discharged in a seizure (Glover, 1949).

Psychosomatic disease then, is a phenomenon that clearly shows the interdependence of psyche and soma—one subsystem expressing the tension of the other.

SEXUAL DISORDERS

Homosexuality A clinical category that has stirred enormous controversy during the past decade is that of "sexual disorders." Because so many non-mainstream life-styles have gained acceptance, such as those of "gays", lesbians, and "swinging," "swapping" couples, some social workers are not ready to regard unconventional forms of sexual behavior such as homosexuality and bisexuality as indicative of psychopathology. As we have already noted, the American Psychiatric Association has struck "homosexuality" from its diagnostic nomenclature. The issue for the social worker is not the client's overt behavior but how he experiences himself and his partner. What fantasies are operative while engaging in sex? What defenses are at work? What is the client's capacity for empathy and object-relatedness as he or she expresses himself or herself sexually?

In the process of growing up, everyone develops a certain amount of sexual feeling toward members of the same sex. In certain situations where there are no members of the opposite sex, as in prisons, individuals who have been heterosexual may turn toward homosexual relationships. This is what Fenichel (1945) has referred to as "accidental homosexuality", citing as proof that every individual is latently capable of a homosexual object-choice.

In any discussion of homosexuality it is important to remind ourselves that what is termed "masculine" or "feminine" depends more on social and cultural factors than on biological ones. Gender role is based on a host of factors—economic arrangements, ethnic values, traditional mores, etc. Yet there is no doubt that biological factors such as hormonal balance do contribute toward a particular predisposition. However, we still have to answer the question, "When members of both sexes are available to the client, why does he or she choose members of his or her own sex for sexual gratification?"

In Freudian theory, the prime etiological factor in male homosexuality appears to be castration-anxiety. The male, usually because of strong Oedipal fantasies, would rather submit to Father and be his lover than oppose him and compete with him. To the homosexual man, the idea of losing his penis is so terrifying that he avoids it by rejecting any sexual relationship with a woman. According to Freud (1939) the homosexual man cannot feel comfortable unless his sexual partner possesses a penis. Recognition of the fact that human beings may be without a penis leads to the threatening conclusion that he might also become such a being.

Frequently male homosexuals have an exaggerated love for their mothers, and homosexuality can express itself not only as submitting to Father but also as mothering oneself. The homosexual man gives to his partner in the manner in which he wishes his mother would give to him. He chooses as love-objects young men or boys who are similar to himself, whom he can love and treat with the tenderness he has desired from his mother (Fenichel, 1945).

Another etiological factor in homosexuality is identification. Children tend to identify themselves with the parent from whom they have experienced the more impressive frustrations. This explains Freud's finding (1939) that men who are more inclined to become homosexuals had a weak father or no father at all and were frustrated in crucial areas by their mother. However, it is also important to note that boys who have had no mother are also inclined to become homosexual, because the enjoyment of passive pleasures at the hands of a man creates a disposition toward homosexuality (Glover, 1949).

In female homosexuality, the etiological factors usually emanate from Oedipal conflicts (sometimes referred to as the "Electra Complex") and penis envy. Many women clients respond to the disappointment of their Oedipal wishes by identification with their father. In their anger toward Father for not loving them the way they would like, they incorporate him in fantasy and become him, thus assuming an active masculine relation to women. This "inverted Oedipal situation", identifying with the parent of the opposite sex, wards off Mother's disapproval and possible abandonment. Usually the female homosexual client regresses to the early mother-daughter relationship; the activities of such homosexual women consist mainly in the mutual playing of mother and child roles (Fenichel, 1945). Frequently, the sight of a penis creates in the homosexual woman a fear of impending violation, but more often it mobilizes thoughts and emotions about the difference in appearance between the male and female. The female homosexual, in effect, is saying to the man, "I hate you for what you have and for the pleasures you can have with your penis. I will have nothing to do with it. I will relate to women sexually and do a better job than you can."

Impotence and Anorgasmia   It should come as no surprise that those who cannot trust are not able to tolerate the intimacy inherent in a sexual relationship. The tenderness, movements, and closeness in sex recapitulate the experiences of the early oral period. Lovers frequently refer to each other in oral terms—"honey," "cookie," "sweetie pie"—and, of course, as "baby." Frequently, the individual who has difficulties in a sexual encounter fears that his impulses will overwhelm him or his partner. In effect, in sex he becomes a psychological infant, ascribing omnipotence either to his partner, who will devour him, or to himself, who will devour the partner (Cameron, 1963).

Frequently, such clients experience sex as if they were submitting to an arbitrary parent. They see it not as a source of mutual pleasure but as "putting out" and being exploited by a tyrannical parent. In the same manner as the child who refuses to defecate or urinate for his parent because he sees no pleasure in it for himself, the client sees "nothing in sex for me." In addition, just as the child can view assertiveness and the spontaneous expression of "animal" impulses as bad, so the adult client can experience sexual expression as something "bad" which his introjected parental voice or superego prohibits. Sex, if it is to be culminated successfully, requires the individual to discharge his sexual tensions and enjoy an orgasm. Some clients equate the sexual discharge with anal or urinary discharge, feeling that sex, like urine or feces, is something "dirty." It is as if they are either urinating or defecating on or in their partner, or vice versa.

Common forms of sexual dysfunction are *impotence* and *anorgasmia*. The impotent man unconsciously equates his sexual partner with his mother, is aggressively competing with his father, and becomes impotent to punish himself for his aggressive fantasies. Often impotence in a man reflects an unconscious wish to be a woman, and the inability to have an erection expresses the man's reluctance to own a penis and his wish to have a vagina instead.

Anorgasmia, like impotence, may have at its root an unconscious comparison of the sexual partner with the parent of the opposite sex; hence the client fears possible injury or loss of love if she allows herself orgastic pleasure. As in impotence, the degree of severity may vary; some women can be aroused but never achieve climax, and others can't be aroused at all. Finally, there are cases of total frigidity where the genital erogeneity is entirely blocked. In these situations there is probably also a strong competitive feeling toward the man—i.e., penis envy. Feeling hostile to the man, the woman cannot enjoy him because her unconscious wish is to castrate him (English, 1945).

OBSESSIVE-COMPULSIVE NEUROSIS

The obsessive-compulsive neurotic is plagued by unwanted thoughts, and/or he feels compelled to perform certain actions over which he has little or no conscious control. He is in a constant struggle between his sadistic wishes, which stimulate him toward being destructive, and his overly strict superego, which tells him that he is a bad child for hating and wanting to hurt and torment. The compulsion or obsession is a compromise between two opposing forces—the id's wish to destroy and the superego's wish for punishment. The ego compromises by forming the obsessive or compulsive symptom.

Several forms of obsessions and compulsions are well known. In the handwashing compulsion, the client must continually clean away his dirty thoughts; the housewife who must constantly check the gas-jets is attempting to cope with her wishes to burn down the house; the obsessive thought, "God, strike me dead!" is the response to the death wishes that the client has toward important persons in his or her life.

The unconscious conflicts in obsessive-compulsive neurosis deal with problems of love and hate, right and wrong, cleanliness and dirt, orderliness and disorder. Plagued by a demanding superego, the client suffers from much guilt. One of the paramount features of the obsessive-compulsive client is his sense of omnipotence of thought, or magical thinking. The client, like the child, really believes his thoughts can kill (Cameron, 1963).

The obsessive-compulsive neurotic is typically afraid of his feelings because, in his mind, they will do damage. He lacks spontaneity and is frequently sexually impotent or frigid. He must organize life for fear that he will "step on a crack and break Mother's back." Angry and revengeful, he must obey his strict superego, thus placating his introjected tyrannical parents.

ANXIETY HYSTERIA

Two major forms of neurotic illness derive from faulty resolution of the Oedipal (initiative-vs.-guilt) conflict. One is anxiety hysteria and the other is conversion hysteria.

Characteristic symptoms of anxiety hysteria are pervasive anxiety and/or anxiety attached to special objects or situations, as manifested in phobias of the dark, animals, airplanes, etc. The phobic situation activates wishes and fears; in a phobia of darkness, for example, the darkness has stimulated sexual wishes and because these are unacceptable to the client, anxiety erupts. The hysterical patient, like the Oedipal child guilty about incestuous and aggressive wishes, fears abandonment, death, and mutilation.

The hysterical client also shows dramatic qualities associated with the excitement and exhibitionistic features of the neurosis. Fearful of losing love, this client is eager to please others. He often simulates more adequacy than he feels in order to conceal his neurosis (Fenichel, 1945; English and Pearson, 1945).

The hysterical client has been totally or almost totally unacknowledged in his sexual development. He or she attempts as an adult to gratify Oedipal desires, but guilt and inhibition usually result. Frequently the client has been conditioned by incestuously seductive experiences which he keeps secret because of guilt over the excitement they engendered (Austin, 1958).

Freud (1948) originally thought that the patient suffering from anxiety hysteria was always a victim of a sexual seduction. He later learned that the memory reported was often a fantasy of seduction which was a defense against the memory of sexual activities such as masturbation.

Austin (1958) has pointed out that the presenting problems of the client with anxiety hysteria may take the form of difficulties in family relationships, in the job situation, or in personal adjustments. The external event which stimulates the anxiety signifies a psychosexual danger.

The emotional deprivation that the anxiety hysteric has experienced is of a particular kind (Perry, 1958). It is not that the client has not been loved, but that his parents could not accept his sexual wishes. The client, when a child, repressed his or her desire to be wholly masculine or feminine, and the difficulties manifested are usually in the sexual sphere—frigidity, impotence, diffuse anxiety when sexually stimulated, and phobias designed to lessen exposure to sexual relationships. His job problem, for example, emanates from the anxiety that evolves from his unconscious competitive wishes toward parental figures of the same sex. Job satisfaction in the client's mind is equated with an oedipal victory.

CONVERSION HYSTERIA

In conversion hysteria, the client's psychodynamics are quite similar to those of an anxiety hysteric, except that symptomatic changes in physical functions occur which, unconsciously and in a distorted form, give expression to instinctual impulses that previously had been repressed. The organ of the body that is chosen is expressing the client's specific conflict. In Freud's famous case of Anna O. (1938) the patient suffered a paralysis of the arm whenever she was unconsciously reminded of her sexual and aggressive feelings toward her father. At the time when her father died, Anna had been sitting at his bedside with her arm pressed against the chair and her paralysis expressed her feelings toward her father at that time.

The somatic compliance in conversion hysteria is determined in part by unconscious sexual fantasies and a corresponding erogeneity of the afflicted body part—i.e., non-genital zones are "genitalized." Spasms, rhythmical muscular contractions, and sensory disturbances often prove to be simultaneous defenses against and substitutes for masturbatory activities.

In sum, the client suffering from conversion hysteria is blocking the expression of sexual impulses. His sexuality, dammed up inside him, is manifested in unsuitable places and at inconvenient times.

CHARACTER DISORDERS

In contrast to clients with symptomatic neuroses (obsessive-compulsive neurosis, anxiety and conversion hysteria) the client with a character disorder does not suffer symptoms but expresses his psychological conflicts in such character traits as stinginess, demandingness, and Don Juan behavior. In contrast to the client with a neurosis from which he suffers *ego alien* symptoms, the person with a character disorder induces suffering in others. He sees his character traits as an appropriate way of coping with life and will defend them as the "right way." His character traits, in contrast to those of a symptomatic neurosis, are *ego-syntonic*.

The client with an *oral* character is one who seeks mergers with practically everyone he encounters. Although consistently fed and nurtured as a child, he was never successfully weaned. Consequently, if he cannot control a relationship and get what he wants at once, he will persist for long periods of time. This very narcissistic individual knows little autonomy but, like a baby, must symbiotically attach himself to a person in order to feel some sense of identity. Often the product of a mother who has never permitted her child to separate from her, this client feels empty and depressed when alone. He has to hold onto and psychologically devour a person in order to feel alive. The oral character devours knowledge, particularly other people's business, and feels a compulsion to take in everything he can.

Freud (1933) discovered that certain character traits are dominant in persons whose instinctual life is *anally* oriented. These traits are partly reaction-formations against anal-erotic activities and partly sublimations of them. The main traits are orderliness, frugality, and obstinacy. Anal character traits express concomitant resistance to the environment's demands, obdience to them, and compromises between these two trends. Frugality is a continuation of retention, orderliness implies obedience, and obstinacy is the expression of rebellion (Fenichel, 1945).

As with all character disorders, the client with a *hysterical* character does not suffer consciously from anxiety, guilt, or any other ego-alien symptoms. Glover (1949) has pointed out that a true hysterical character often goes undetected because his behavior is seen as an exaggeration of normal behavior.

Hysterical characters are usually passionate in their social likes and dislikes, and in their sexual and social relations are quite aggrandizing. Frequently they are babyish in their emotional contacts and are subject on occasion to illusions. The character trait expresses the conflict between an intense fear of sexuality and strong but repressed sexual strivings. The hysterical character tends to sexualize most "nonsexual" relations; he or she is usually inclined toward suggestibility, irrational emotional outbreaks, chaotic behavior, dramatization, and histrionics (Fenichel, 1945).

The *psychopath* or *sociopath* suffers from superego lacunae. Either because he has received no training, limits, or controls, or because his training has been overly abusive and punitive, he has refused to develop inner controls, or a conscience. The psychopath is an impulsive individual, extremely narcissistic, who has not been willing to curb his aggressive and sexual impulses because he does not feel any obligation to cooperate with an uncooperative world. Psychologically, he is still an infant who is fighting restrictions and training, refusing to surrender. His only real fear is that of getting caught; he rarely suffers pangs of conscience if he has performed in a socially unacceptable or illegal manner (Cameron, 1963).

Occasionally we see an isolation of guilt feelings in a nonpsychopathic client. Such neurotics perform illegal or socially unacceptable acts without any guilt feelings, but later experience exaggerated feelings of guilt on some other occasion without being aware of the connection (Fenichel, 1945).

The *paranoid* is always afraid of hidden persecutors. He is a guilt-ridden person who anticipates punishment for acts that may be real but usually are fantasied. Frequently hating himself and experiencing much shame for his sexual and aggressive wishes (like the fragile child who believes his parents know everything), the paranoid is always ready for an assault from his omnipotent and punishing environment.

Summary

Before planning intervention for a client, the social worker must make a psychosocial assessment to ascertain what is troubling the client and what personal and situational variables are contributing to the distress. The diagnostic assessment must meet logical and professional criteria for validity and reliability; that is, it must derive from facts that are clearly apparent and would be similarly imterpreted by other professional observers.

In making an assessment, the social worker is always interested in the client's statement of the problem, although he may wish to reformulate it when he gathers further data. Unless the worker can empathize with the client's view of himself and his situation, intervention planning will be contaminated by the worker's biases.

Over the years, social workers have stressed either "the situation" or "the personality" of the client in assessing the client's difficulties. Both components must be taken into consideration for a sound and comprehensive assessment. The worker should ascertain which ego-functions of the client are working well and which are not, and should also determine how the client's social milieu is aiding or hindering adaptation.

For communication with colleagues and supervisors as well as for ease in relating to the professional literature, it is often helpful for the social worker to understand the major clinical categories, such as neuroses, psychoses, and character disorders.

Social-systems theory, role theory, Freudian psychoanalysis, and ego psychology appear to be valuable theoretical perspectives in formulating a diagnostic assessment.

Chapter 4

Planning Intervention

Of what use is it, educationally speaking, to be able to see the end in the beginning? Asking such a question suggests its own answer. To see the outcome is to know in what direction the present experience is moving, provided it moves normally and soundly. The far away point, which is of no significance to us simply as far away, becomes of huge importance the moment we take it as defining a present direction of movement. Taken in this way, it is no remote and distant result to be achieved, but a guiding method in dealing with the present.

John Dewey
Interest and Effort in Education (1928)

Having made a careful psychosocial assessment of the client and his situation, the social worker's next step is to plan intervention; that is, to specify with and for the client specific and individualized goals for improved psychosocial functioning. Whereas Chapter 5, "Implementing the Intervention Plan," deals with procedures for helping the client-system, this chapter focuses on making intervention plans.

Just as the term "diagnosis," because of its medical connotations, has been largely replaced by "assessment" in social-work practice, so we use the term "intervention" in this and subsequent chapters instead of "therapy" or "treatment," because social-work practice must be viewed broadly and our clients need much more than the relief of symptoms which "therapy" or "treatment" has tended to imply (Meyer, 1976).

What Is Planned Intervention?

In contrast to the efforts of a good neighbor or friend, the social worker's plan for help does not rely on good will, faith, and intuition alone. Planning is a deliberate, rational process involving designs for action calculated to achieve specific objectives at some future time (Hamilton, 1951; Perlman and Gurin, 1972). It is concerned with moving from problem-definition to problem-solution, from knowing what is wrong to knowing what is to be done, how, by whom, and in what sequence. The interventive plan usually has goals for immediate, intermediate, and long-term change. It may shift during the course of interviews or even during a single interview as the social worker and client become aware of new developments in person-situation transactions.

Frequently an interventive plan involves others in addition to the client and the worker. Work with an individual might require intervention in his family system, family treatment or group work may necessitate interviews with an individual, and work with a neighborhood council might require intervention with and for individuals and groups. The interventive plan, based always on a thorough assessment, is always individualized. It depends not just on what the social worker offers but on what the client is willing to accept and participate in. The client's motivation, his capacities, his opportunities (Ripple, Alexander and Polemis, 1964), and his degree of discomfort with things as they are will influence the complexity and scope of the interventive plan. "How willing is he to be a client?" is a question that must be answered in shaping the interventive plan.

In order to appreciate some of the issues in planning intervention with a client, let us look at the case of Annabelle:

Annabelle, a black ten-year-old, was referred to the school social worker by her elementary-school principal because of her disruptive behavior in the classroom, inability to get along with peers, poor academic work, frequent absences, and poor motivation. As the social worker assessed Annabelle's problems with her, many conflicts emerged. First, Annabelle felt that she had been very "unfairly" treated by the teacher, who she said made constant negative remarks about Annabelle's race. Secondly, she said the other youngsters in the classroom, with some encouragement from the teacher, teased her about her poor work. Thirdly, Annabelle frequently found her mind wandering away from what was going on in class.

In assessing the client's home situation, the worker found that Annabelle's parents were separated and that her father did not contribute financially to the home, rarely appearing there. Annabelle's mother, although quite depressed and harried, managed to work several afternoons and evenings as a clerk and was often unavailable to her. When the two were together, there was frequent bickering, and each felt very deprived by the other. Annabelle spent most of her time after school alone, or else in some mild delinquent activity with other youngsters.

On the basis of her assessment, which included recognition of Annabelle's distrust of and hostility toward most adults, strong defenses of either withdrawal or attack, moderate depression which interfered with study and concentration, a mutually provocative relationship with her mother in an un-stimulating and unsupportive home and neighborhood, the social worker made several short-term, intermediate, and long-term plans.

In order to have any influence at all on Annabelle and her environment, it was necessary for the worker to make herself available to Annabelle for "on call" interviews as well as scheduled weekly meetings. To establish the girl's trust in her, the social worker had to include in her plan actions that Annabelle would experience as giving and gratifying. She also agreed to meet with the teacher, the principal, and Annabelle's mother to discuss the girl's needs and problems. Both client and worker concurred that these people were "not the easiest to deal with"; consequently, they realized that they would have to jointly devise measures that would make these "significant others" more receptive to Annabelle and to the social worker.

Further plans discussed by social worker and client included recreational opportunities for Annabelle and work with both of her parents, individually and jointly. Later, when the social worker, through her contacts on behalf of Annabelle, learned about certain problems in the school atmosphere, she organized a seminar for teachers in order to deal with some of the interpersonal difficulties that emerged in their classrooms.

In her plans with Annabelle, the social worker not only was interested in improving the girl's self-image and functioning in and out of school but considered the parents' needs as well. Further, it became clear that the interventive plan had to involve the school system, particularly where Annabelle and the school "interfaced." Annabelle, a reasonably bright but emotionally starved and angry child, was helped to accept and contribute to the interventive plans, although suspicious of the social worker at first.

There were, of course, other aspects to the interventive plan that do not need to be detailed here—e.g., "feeding" Annabelle in the interviews (candy, cookies) and arranging for tutoring.

The interventions planned for Annabelle were based on the social worker's individualized assessment of the client's person-situation–constellation. Not only did the plan involve different units of attention, but the social worker had to call on many of her social-work skills—skills in helping individuals, dyads, families, small groups, and parts of the community.

Changing Orientations to Planning Intervention

As was noted in Chapter 1, social work is an evolving profession, and its practice principles are usually in a state of flux; planning intervention is a very different process today than it was in the 1940s or 1950s. In order to sensitize the student and practitioner to the changes that have occurred in intervention planning, we shall briefly review some of the different orientations that have developed since the beginning of social-work practice.

For many decades social-work practice was rigidly constituted around three basic methods, each believed to comprise a cluster of distinctive skills and change-strategies: casework, group work, and community organization. While many of the processes in these three methods were considered similar—e.g., interviewing procedures, making contact with the client, arriving at a contract, arriving at assessments, etc.—the adherents of each method comprised in many respects a cultural island, with their own professional literature, professional organizations, and, to some extent, language. Frequently there was (and still is) a fair amount of competition for status among the adherents of the three methods. Such questions as: "Does changing the nature of transactions and interactions of people and their situations mean modifying the person or the environment?" "Which is more important, institutional or individual change?" and "Is environmental or individual change more difficult to achieve?" were debated at length, both formally and informally at professional conferences, inter-agency seminars, and in schools of social work.

Perhaps the fragmentation of methods in social-work practice was inevitable. The domain of social work, the person-in-his-situation, involves so much knowledge, so many skills, and such varied expertise that it is extremely difficult to train all social workers to be masters of the many dimensions of practice that are required.

However, the realities of practice—clients' needs, workers' experiences, and the accumulation of research—slowly stimulated the profession to question its parochialism. A caseworker in a child-guidance clinic could not confine his work exclusively to the child. He eventually had to plan interventions with the parents individually, together, and with the whole family, or else the child could not be helped. As the parents and family became units for assessment and intervention, it also became apparent that the extended family often had to be seen in dyads and groups as well. By the late 1950s caseworkers in child-guidance clinics were planning interventions for individuals, dyads, families, and mothers', fathers', and childrens' groups; by the 1960s they had become administrators and community organizers in community mental health, working with schools, churches, and neighborhoods.

The experience of caseworkers in the child-guidance movement is also the history of caseworkers, group workers, and community organizers in many other fields of practice. The group worker in a community center soon learned that he had to plan interventions for individuals in and out of the group. He became sensitive to the fact that at intake he had to make specific interventive plans with and for individual group-members. And, as the group process progressed, revised plans for intervening with and for individuals also evolved. Group workers also learned that because the environment is often crucial in the problems of individuals and groups, the group itself had to assume a social-change focus seeking to modify the clients' environment. Furthermore, most group workers and caseworkers by the 1960s found it necessary to move out into the community in order to educate, train, and consult with a variety of significant others—physicians, lawyers, policemen, and paraprofessionals—who were in a position of aiding, stimulating, and enriching helping-services (L. Brown, 1970).

The War on Poverty and the community mental health movement of the Kennedy and Johnson eras sponsored programs in which social workers were forced to make interventive plans for the complete client-system. To organize part of a community, the organizer learned that it was necessary to relate to and help individuals, families, and groups.

In the 1960s a grant to the Bing Neighborhood Center provided funds to help residents of a housing project, virtually all of whom were on welfare. Careful psychosocial assessment revealed that working with these individuals and their situations involved interventive plans on several levels. Landlords, superintendents, doctors and other hospital staff, school officials, the Legal Aid Society, and personnel at the Department of Welfare all had to be enlisted in the interventive plan. Because the tenants in the housing project wanted to participate in influencing "significant others," the social worker not only interviewed these people herself but had several group meetings with the tenants before convening the key people in their environment. Most of the time, when the help of doctors, lawyers, and other professionals was enlisted, tenants were present at interviews, with the social worker acting as catalyst.

The interventive plan included group meetings with the tenants not only in order to consider how situational variables could be modified; group meetings were a necessary ingredient of the interventive plan for other reasons as well. The social worker had to gain the confidence of an essentially distrustful client group, and the tenants needed the group meetings to resolve problems of morale among themselves.

In working on community problems with the residents, it became evident to the social worker and clients that there were many individual and family matters that needed attention—

addiction, alcoholism, economic problems, etc. These problems required individual and family crisis-intervention, family
therapy, advocacy, and social brokerage.

In contrast to the prevailing approach to social work until the
early 1960s, we now conceive of individualized direct services
and social action as complementary activities; there appears to be
no real inconsistency in holding *both* clinical and social-change
orientations (Siporin, 1975). In a study conducted by Taber and
Vattano (1970), no sharp distinction was found between clinical
and social orientations among social workers engaged in practice,
and most workers were able to integrate the two functions quite
well. It would appear that more and more social workers are
recognizing that there is a common base of method, and are using
a combination of "people-helping" and "social-system–change
strategies" (Bartlett, 1970).

Many social-work scholars today have come to believe that the
traditional separation of casework, group work, and community
organization is no longer tenable and that new configurations of
method, constituting a generalist kind of practice, can more effectively translate systemic social-work functions into helping-
procedures (Meyer, 1976; Siporin, 1975).

THE SOCIAL-PROBLEM APPROACH

While the recognition that individuals and their social situations are in constant transaction has required social workers to
merge and integrate traditional methods, it is still evident that no
social worker can be all things to all people. A way of organizing
and planning intervention that has become popular in practice,
theory, and in schools of social work is based on the fields in
which social workers perform their functions (Ferguson, 1975;
Skidmore and Thackeray, 1976). As social workers have identified socially problematic areas—e.g., poverty, delinquency, alcoholism, addiction—they have more and more determined what

the unique contribution of social work can be. Consequently, the social-work student of the 1970s is less likely to be trained exclusively in casework, community organization, or group work, but in many instances selects a particular social problem in which he wishes to work. For example, if the student wants to study and work in mental health, or poverty, or child welfare, he can take courses that relate to this specialization; his field-work placement may be a mental-health center, a facility for economically deprived people, or a setting in child welfare, depending on the student's area of interest and concentration. If, for example, the student's choice of social-problem area is in child welfare, he can take courses on the assessment of children and direct services with them, on marriage and the family, the sociology of child development, social-policy implications of child welfare, law and the child, etc. His research courses would relate to some aspect of childhood or child welfare, and his field-work placement would be one in which he worked with children and their significant others, as, for example, a school, institution, or child-guidance center (Strean, 1974a).

As the student or practitioner plans interventions in his chosen field of practice, he works with people and their problems on many levels. If, for example, his work is in juvenile delinquency, his planned interventions will probably include direct service to an individual client who has been adjudged a delinquent; this will inevitably lead to work with the delinquent's parents and family. The same practitioner or student may conduct groups with juveniles, parents, or others, and concomitantly participate in community efforts that study the etiology of delinquency and seek to eradicate it. The social worker may also involve himself in social-policy formulation and research focused on the etiology of delinquency and its social, economic, and psychological dynamics, as well as on the interventive processes involved in diminishing it.

With a social-problem focus and with expertise in working with the person-situation–constellations on several levels, the social worker's interventive plans may begin at any point of the individual-family-group-community spectrum. The worker might start with an interventive plan for an individual and then move to larger units. Or he might plan interventions in the reverse order: from the whole community to smaller groups, families, and then individuals.

Sometimes the student or practitioner finds himself engaged in social-policy formulation that is specifically designed to stimulate interventive plans for individuals, groups, and communities. As we have indicated, these activities can take place simultaneously.

> At a county welfare-board a student participated in the formation of a social policy that would permit clients on income maintenance to reject personal or family counselling if they so desired and still retain the right to receive monetary allotments. The formulation of this policy involved interventive plans with agency executives, freeholders, city councilmen, and others. Once the policy gained acceptance by the agency and the community, the next interventive plan involved the formation of a voluntary counselling service for those clients who wished to participate in it. Group sessions were planned and executed to interpret the policy change to clients, and it was later decided to continue these same groups as media for counselling. In the group discussions, interventive plans were formed for individuals and families.

The social-problem focus is not without its difficulties and limitations. Just as social workers can become so wedded to a method that they fail to see that people are multidimensional and that intervention must frequently be a multi-pronged effort, so they can become too rigidly focused on a single field of practice. It is still too common in social work that a client seeking help tends to define his problems, or finds them defined for him, in accordance with the function of the particular agency. Thus, child-welfare personnel may not always relate to marital or other familial problems in their interventive plans, and social workers in health care can become oblivious to dimensions of psychosocial functioning that do not at first appear to be related to health.

As Carol Meyer has observed, the social-problem focus may not always follow the natural life-style of people in trouble; Meyer contends that the field-of-practice orientation has forced upon its clientele "a mold that was originally best suited to a practice that was attempting to professionalize itself" (Meyer, 1976).

While some of these limitations of the social-problem focus cannot be dismissed lightly, it is nevertheless possible for the social worker to know the boundaries of his own field of practice and to respect and utilize the contributions of other specialists. Concentration on one social problem in social work does not have to mean that other problems are ignored.

In sum, planning intervention has moved from utilizing one method to combining several; from viewing individuals, groups, and organizations as separate entities to seeing them as units of attention that dovetail, interact, and transact; from recognizing that social workers cannot be all things to all people to a social-problem focus.

Individualizing the Interventive Plan

Regardless of the field of practice or methods used, there are a number of factors that the social worker must take into consideration when planning intervention. Some of these factors have been addressed in the chapters on interviewing and assessment, but they bear further clarification and reinforcement.

THE CLIENT'S ATTITUDE TOWARD THE SOURCE OF REFFERRAL

Clients sometimes appear in social-work offices at their own behest, but frequently they are referred by others—physicians, ministers, judges, attorneys, school principals, families, friends, employers, and so on. How the client feels toward and relates to the referring source will shape his feelings toward the agency and the practitioner. Therefore, there will inevitably be major differences in short-range (and perhaps in intermediate and long-range) interventive plans for clients who appear to be similar but experience their referral parties differently. An adolescent who is referred to the agency by a teacher or physician toward whom he feels positively will greet the social worker much differently than will a teenager of the same sex, age, and presenting problem who has been referred by a teacher or parent toward whom he is ambivalent.

Not only the prospective client's attitude toward the referring person but how that person has defined the problem will also be pertinent. A minister might tell a teenager that he needs group therapy; a family might be told by a physician that they need family therapy; a group might be told by an attorney that they need an advocate; an organization might be told by a civil-rights leader that they need new social utilities. The referral party may be expressing his own biases in assessing the client's needs, and the client may be positively or negatively influenced by his referral party. Consequently, one of the first priorities in any interventive plan is to encourage the client to express his sentiments about the referral party and the possibilities of social-work help. Even if the client feels positively toward the referral party and agrees with the latter's definition of the problem, there is still work to do, as may be observed in the following case illustration:

> Mr. Carr was referred by his wife for "sexual counseling." In the opening minutes of the very first interview at the family agency, he stated: "I'm impotent and have very serious sexual problems. I need help right away or my marriage will go down the drain!" When the social worker explored the Carrs' sexual relationship, Mr. Carr said, "I frequently have to kiss my wife, fondle her, and be fondled before I can have an erection." He noted that "this usually takes from five to seven minutes and gets my wife angry and frantic." On questioning, Mr. Carr added that when his wife rebuked him for his "slowness," he could not help but be angry with her, and then "my erection gets further delayed."

As the social worker explored Mr. Carr's difficulties she discovered that he was a person who tended to sensitize himself as much as possible to other people's wishes, to like himself if he pleased them, and hate himself if he could not meet their expectations. Consequently, one of the first items in the worker's agenda was to question Mr. Carr about why he saw his behavior as problematic and why he was so acquiescent about his wife's referral of him to the agency. If this was not done first, the social worker would emerge as just another person telling Mr. Carr what to do without taking into account *his* wishes, *his* needs, and *his* strivings.

As the worker focused with Mr. Carr on his readiness to accept his wife's referral and heard him out about it, she could then move on with him to an intermediate interventive plan— i.e., mutual reflection on why Mr. Carr needed to be so masochistic and submissive, and what fears interfered with his assertiveness.

As has been mentioned, the client frequently relates to the intervention plan and the social worker in the same manner as he does to the referral party. Mr. Carr, a man who was inclined to be submissive and obedient, expected to be the same way with the social worker. For the worker to encourage this or even go along with it would, of course, have been unproductive.

What is perhaps more difficult to face and resolve is planning intervention for a client who is hostile toward the referral party—and therefore may be negative toward the social worker and agency as well. This occurs frequently with clients who are referred by judges, courts, school personnel, or other figures of authority. This is a difficult situation for client and worker, particularly when the client has been compelled to see a social worker; the client often wants little or nothing to do with him, while he often wants to involve the client in an assessment and interventive plan.

A group of unmarried mothers in a high school had been referred to the social worker by the superintendent of schools. The latter had not called the social worker first, but instead had sent memoranda to the girls ordering them to report to the social worker on a certain date. "Failure to report will compel me to arrange for suspension proceedings," the notice read.

The girls reported to the social worker at the designated time and immediately presented the superintendent's message to him. When the social worker asked the girls what the memorandum was all about, one of them bellowed, "He thinks we're crazy because we're knocked up!" After a silence, several of the other girls spoke up in angry tones. "Why doesn't he mind his own business?" "Who does he think he is?" "It's a free country!"

The immediate goal formulated by the social worker was to help the students voice their resentments toward the referral party. The social worker felt that this might induce them to experience him as an ally and then be more willing to share further aspects of their lives with him. The worker also realized that the prospective clients would test him about his attitudes toward unmarried motherhood; consequently, another part of the interventive plan was to avoid the suggestion, at least at first, that being an unmarried prospective mother was necessarily a problem or a deviancy. Only if the girls wanted to explore this issue with him would he consider their marital and parental statuses as part of the interventive plan.

The social worker put into effect the first part of his interventive plan—i.e., to permit the students to vent their hostility toward the superintendent and eventually toward the entire school system. Later he could plan a discussion with them on their familial relationships and conflicts regarding sex.

As we have reiterated, even if the prospective client regards the referral party positively, his reactions to the suggestion of seeking help are usually mixed, and these reactions color the client's participation in an interventive plan. This is particularly true of individuals who need to see themselves as always autonomous, like the businessmen in the following illustration:

A group of merchants decided that they wanted to help "pre-delinquent" youngsters in the community by sponsoring recreational events and other group activities. Although the merchants appeared to react positively to the suggestion by the Chief of Police that they seek advice from the community social worker affiliated with the Council of Social Agencies in the community, it was clear that before discussing any interventive plan with them the social worker would have to deal with the merchants' reactions to the idea of being helped by a social worker. The men prized their own independence and creativity, and it was clear that they were not about to take direction easily from the worker.

The immediate interventive plan that the worker devised was to support the merchants' strengths, praise their industriousness, and solicit their thoughts on how the boys could best be helped. She reasoned that if she could demonstrate by her attitude and way of relating that they were "the bosses" and that she wasn't going to control them, the men would become less defensive, and that then plans for the boys could be put into effect.

Reactions to the referral party clearly influence reactions to and perceptions of the social worker and must be dealt with as part of any interventive plan. Furthermore, reactions to the referral party give clues to the clients' wishes, fears, anxieties, and defenses. If the client is submissive or ambivalent or hostile toward the referring party, he is telling us how he tends to handle interpersonal situations. What coping and defense mechanisms, anxieties, strengths, and vulnerabilities are at work will all eventually be a part of the assessment and interventive planning.

DEFINING THE PROBLEM

As has been mentioned several times herein, when social workers relate to each unique client-system they are guided by the awareness that people and their situations are in constant transac-

tion and that it is therefore frequently impossible to totally separate internal and external variables. A husband's "marital problem" cannot be viewed as something totally distinct from his
wife's functioning, and vice versa; a group of students' maturational problems cannot be partialized, but must be considered
within the framework of a whole school system; the wish of a
group of merchants to be involved in community activity must be
seen as a phenomenon affected by and affecting the total community. Because people are involved transactionally with many significant others in relationships where everyone influences and is
influenced by everyone else, it is imperative in interventive planning that client and worker agree on a definition of the problem
(Hamilton, 1951). Without this concurrence, the tasks of social
worker and client become blurred, their expectations become
incongruous, and the dropout of the client may occur.

To achieve some agreement on problem-definition is not an
easy task, precisely because the client is in transaction with so
many people who contribute to the problem, all of whom may
(and usually do) have definitions of it different from his own.
Wives frequently claim that their marital problem is caused by
their husbands' provocativeness or limitations, and vice versa;
children do the same with their parents, and vice versa; hospital
personnel frequently ascribe organizational problems to the patients, with the patients blaming the system. Occasionally, people
take too much responsibility for their interpersonal problems, and
this, too, has to be assessed before interventive plans are made.
However, in any interventive plan, it is not the social worker's
task to assign blame; his job is to help people understand themselves better, cope more efficiently, and relate to others with
more maturity.

   In an interracial, interdenominational housing project there
was a great deal of tension among the various ethnic and
religious groups, manifesting itself in verbal abuse, rock
throwing, and many other signs of interpersonal strife. The
blacks felt that the Puerto Ricans had too many privileges,

and vice versa. They both disliked many of the daily habits of the Jews. The Jews wanted to be left alone, and the blacks and Puerto Ricans experienced this wish to be isolated as smugness and arrogance. No group was willing to define the problem as interpersonal, as a power struggle, or as commonly shared anxiety. When representatives of the three groups met with the social worker, each defined the community problem in terms of the other groups' limitations.

The social worker held many meetings with each representative alone before she could have them all come together with her again. Part of the interventive plan, then, was to meet with each of the representatives alone so that each could develop enough trust in the social worker to eventually consider with her how the others might be feeling. It took months before there was even some agreement that maybe the tenants did not fully understand one another, and that maybe each group had some good reasons for perceiving the interpersonal problems the way it did. It took the better part of a year working on problem-definition before the social worker could consider some constructive socialization opportunities across racial and ethnic lines as part of the interventive plan.

Although problem-definition can take a long time, as it did in the situation described above, this does not mean that nothing much is happening. As the client sees that he is listened to attentively, permitted to verbalize his anger, that his perception of the problem is acknowledged, and his vulnerabilities are respected, his self-esteem usually rises. From this more favorable psychological position he can see reality more clearly. Because he feels more self-respect, he is better able to empathize with others. This is why it is important for the social worker to allow plenty of time for the client to present his problems as he experiences them subjectively, maintaining his defensiveness if he is compelled to do so; he should not rush the client to define the problem as the social worker would like it to be defined.

Social workers respect the client's self-determination in the definition of his problems not only because this is a fundamental tenet of social work; domination, manipulation, or paternalism by the social worker seldom, if ever, bring about good results. It is not the social worker's job to play Providence and take the problem away from people; rather, his major task is to help clients mobilize their own capacities to the extent possible (Young, 1937).

SELF-DETERMINATION AND CLIENT MOTIVATION

The notion of planning intervention and positing goals for clients has raised questions in the minds of social-work practitioners and scholars. If one genuinely believes in the importance of self-determination for a client, can one really *plan* treatment *for* him? In this text we have given several examples of situations in which the client's initial request was not gratified by the social worker but explored instead; sometimes it was even frustrated. In the case of Mr. Carr, he was not given instructions on how to improve his sexual performance; instead his submissiveness to his wife and others was explored. The social worker did not promise the teenage girls he would "chew out" the authority figures, as they wanted him to do; instead, he made a plan to help them verbalize their anger so they would be enabled later to better reflect on their interpersonal relationships. However, interventive plans are always made mutually with the client, who is free to reject the worker's proposals at any time. If an interventive plan does not meet the needs and wishes of the client, he will certainly demonstrate this to the social worker by coming to interviews late or absenting himself altogether, by refusing to talk, and so on. These behaviors and the feelings that propel them must be related to in the interventive plan, if help is to succeed.

The social worker can try to stimulate the client to think about himself and his relationships with others, but only the client can actually do it. The social worker has the responsibility of deciding what form of help will be *offered*, but the client exercises control over what he accepts. No form of intervention can be successful if the client lacks motivation to use it.

The degree of a client's motivation to participate with the social worker depends on many internal and external variables. The client may be quite dissatisfied with his current modus vivendi, and this state of disequilibrium may stimulate him to examine the person-situation–constellation with the social worker to see what can be modified. However, as some of the case illustrations in this and other chapters have revealed, the social worker must often summon much skill and expend a great deal of effort to involve people who are not overtly upset by the status quo but are nonetheless potential clients.

If the potential client does not appear to be highly motivated to participate in an interventive plan because he fears exposure, feels too little or too much distress about the problems, is pessimistic about their solution, or holds certain values which discourage his participation in a helping-relationship, these issues must themselves be aired, explored, and understood by the social worker; they should be considered immediate issues for the interventive plan (Hellenbrand, 1961).

UTILIZING ASSESSMENT IN THE INTERVENTIVE PLAN

In addition to the client's reactions to the referral source, his definition of the problem, and his motivation, the transactions between the individual and his social orbit must be taken into account in the interventive plan. Because, as we have indicated, it is virtually impossible to separate internal from external factors, intervention always takes into consideration plans to modify the interaction between clients and their social milieus. The locus of intervention is frequently the points of intersection between people and their situations.

When the worker assesses the ego-functions of the individuals before him; studies their capacities for reality testing, their judgment, and their defense mechanisms; learns in what areas and to what points they have regressed or are fixated; studies the quality of their superego functioning—in short, assesses their complex personalities—he constantly bears in mind what situational factors are either exacerbating problems or supporting efforts to cope. He uses this knowledge to plan with the client what matters may be altered and how to do so. What, for example, are the parents, the school, and the child himself contributing to a school phobia? What is the nature of the transactions among hospital staff, administration, and patients that have led to constant bickering? What is the nature of the personalities and group formations in a housing project that induce racial strife? Knowing about personalities, situations, and their transactions puts the worker in a position to initiate a sound interventive plan.

Mrs. Frank, a 69-year-old black woman living with four grandchildren and on welfare, was assessed by the social worker as extremely depressed. Her history as well as her present circumstances revealed a consistent theme—she felt deprived by family, friends, neighborhood, church, and community. Her mission in life as she saw it was "to work hard for others, and I shouldn't expect too much." The worker sensed a lot of anger underneath Mrs. Frank's depression, but, because the client had such low self-esteem, she "kept it in" and just continued suffering.

On the basis of his assessment of Mrs. Frank's personality-functioning (which of course was more elaborate than is reported here) the social worker deemed it important to relieve her depression, raise her self-esteem, and help her get more pleasure from her daily life. The worker recognized that Mrs. Frank's interactions and transactions with many distressing social variables were contributing to the client's depression and feelings of low self-worth. Mrs. Frank had four children to take care of and received no help in doing so; she lived in a run-down house in a decrepit neighborhood, and there seemed to be no one in Mrs. Frank's social orbit relating to her in an empathic or helpful manner. The dearth of resources in Mrs. Frank's situation paralleled her picture of herself in the present and in the past. She "deserved no more" and never really sought to make it any better for herself.

The social worker was initially tempted to provide material help for Mrs. Frank by getting her a home-maker, more food stamps, and a part-time baby sitter. However, as the social worker reflected on his interventive plan, he realized that immediate provision of material help was contraindicated by Mrs. Frank's long pattern of feeling undeserving, which would make her question the social worker's giving to her. Therefore, the first priority on the intervention agenda had to be helping Mrs. Frank gain some trust in the social worker. The social worker first had to question Mrs. Frank about how she would feel about being in a position of receiving from the worker. If Mrs. Frank could ventilate her suspiciousness, anger, and distrust, and if she could feel that the social worker accepted these expressions, then Mrs. Frank might feel more comfortable with him and be able to consider some modification of the distressing conditions being imposed on her. Mrs. Frank could not accept such a modification of her situation until she could trust the social worker; this could be achieved only by exploring her conflict about taking and her feelings of anger with regard to deprivation in the present and past.

When the social worker senses the discomfort a client experiences in an oppressive environment, he is frequently tempted to move in and correct the unwholesome situation immediately. Unfortunately, many if not most clients cannot easily tolerate quick alteration of the status quo, no matter how dysfunctional it is, because client and situation have evolved through mutually adaptive transactions over time. A self-hating person can feel enormous anxiety when a nicer home or neighborhood, better meals, or more caring relationships are offered. The social situation of a client, no matter how deleterious it is, in many cases mirrors the client's self-image. Consequently, before goods or services are provided for a client as part of an interventive plan, the social worker needs to consult the client on how he experiences being given to. Such questioning usually reveals many ambivalent, angry, and distrustful feelings which demand expression.

Although most social workers deplore the social situation in which a client on public welfare finds himself, they sometimes overlook the fact that the client who distrusts his environmental caretakers is not going to trust the social worker easily. Behind feelings of distrust and depression there is not only a wish to be given to, which is *defended against* by the client, but often latent resentment as well. Hence, in helping a client who is depressed and mistrustful, whether he is a poverty-stricken person or not, the first item on the interventive agenda is to encourage the client to discuss his distrust and anger toward others (which will often include the social worker and social agency). When these processes are encouraged the client is usually in a much better position to reflect on his reality and permit the social worker to act as an advocate or social broker.

Just as the worker must guard against the temptation to modify a client's environment prematurely, so, too, he must avoid making premature interventive plans involving the client's personality dynamics.

At a high school several boys in the senior class had organized themselves to sexually molest younger girls, steal materials from other students, provoke teachers, irritate administrative officials, and harass virtually everybody. The boys called themselves "The Dirty Dozen" and made no secret of membership in this group. They even had T-shirts made with "The Dirty Dozen" written on them; and most of them wore the shirt to school just about every day.

The school authorities, who were "laissez-faire" in their attitudes towards the students and provided limited structure and few limits for them, were aware of the boys' activities. However, it was not until their sadistic behavior reached serious proportions that the officials decided to intervene. For a long time, the guidance officials and the principal labeled the behavior of the boys "typical teenage rebelliousness" and denied that it was serious. However, when the social worker interviewed the boys individually and collectively, he was able to make thorough diagnostic assessments on them. He learned that many of them came from homes where the parents were either divorced, separated, or involved in tempestuous marital relationships. The boys, in virtually every case, were deprived of warm parent-child interaction and were not receiving the limits and structure in their homes that they also desperately needed. Their rebellious behavior not only was an expression of their anger and emotional hunger, but because it was so exhibitionistic, it also could be interpreted as a disguised cry for help.

As the social worker reflected on the problem, his first impulse was to see the boys and give them the warmth they craved and the firm limits that they very much needed. However, he soon realized that unless he had the cooperation of the school authorities and the parents, his efforts might be undermined at worst and only casually supported at best. Therefore, the interventive plan had to be carefully reconsidered. First, the boys' infantile behavior had to be explained to the principal and other school officials, so that they would be able to appreciate the need for firm structure and limits at the school. If the school officials' cooperation could be secured and they could understand the boys' need for warmth and firm limits, they could then help the social worker involve the parents in conferences.

When the school officials were helped (over many interviews) to become more sensitive to the boys' conflicts as well as to the lack of structure and limits in the high school, they could then later help the social worker involve the parents in similar discussions.

Once the parents and school officials were cooperating, the worker could then involve the boys in individual and group sessions where they could verbally discharge their anger, share their mutual feelings of deprivation, and discuss some of their sexual concerns.

Even after the social worker had assessed the boys and their situations, concluding that they were functioning on an infantile level and required warmth, structure, limits, and organization, he was tempted to involve the boys in a premature therapeutic relationship—probably because he, too, was provoked by their behavior. Had he done this, his efforts would have been doomed, because the cooperation and involvement of school officials and parents was vital to the intervention plan. By meeting the problem where the boys and school interfaced and securing the help of the school and family systems first, the worker could then meaningfully involve the boys in a helping relationship.

It is imperative in making any interventive plan to constantly go back and forth between assessment of the clients' ego functioning, maturational level, defenses etc., on the one hand, and their interaction with important situational influences, on the other. As he does so, the social worker begins to see where the locus of entry should be—with an individual client, or with a family, group, or organization. He also determines from whom in the client's environment he will get the best forms of cooperation to further the interventive goals.

All too often social workers seem to feel that they must make a choice between being situation workers, social activists, reformers, or else completely "the clinician." If social work is to be genuinely psychosocial, each social worker must synthesize these elements and be a "situationalist" *and* a clinician—working with the person and his situation, moving back and forth from the individual through the family and larger groups to the community and back to the individual again.

PLANNING THE SOCIAL WORKER'S ROLE IN INTERVENTION

As we have been discussing assessment and intervention in social-work practice, it has become clear that the social worker has many roles to enact as part of his interventive repertoire. In a single case-situation he maybe at times an advocate, a social broker, persuader, therapist, parent figure, group leader, community organizer, and much more. We will examine the social worker's interventive role-repertoire in more detail in Chapter 5, "Implementing the Intervention Plan." In interventive planning it is important for the practitioner to decide not only where, when, and with whom he will intervene, but also how active or passive a part he will play, how firm or indulgent, verbal or unverbal, gratifying or frustrating.

In Chapter 3, referring to Erikson and ego psychology, we pointed out that most individuals who visit social workers are having difficulty with one or more life-tasks. They either have regressed to or are fixated at a certain developmental stage—e.g., trust vs. mistrust, autonomy vs. self-doubt, initiative vs. guilt, and so on—and/or they are having difficulty coping with a current, adult life-task—e.g., generativity vs. stagnation, ego integrity vs. despair. The eight developmental tasks which Erikson (1950) claims that all people must resolve have been used successfully by social workers in making interventive plans.

Erikson (1950) postulates a "radius of significant others" in the person's environment—e.g., parents, teachers, friends, extended family—who can help him resolve a specific life-task. The social worker can conceive of his own role in the interventive plan as that of the key significant other who, through his attitudes and efforts, helps the client move up the psychosocial ladder and resolve his life-tasks. He is also the catalyst helping the specified significant others in the environment enact their roles with more maturity so that the client's functioning can be enhanced.*

Mrs. Frank, referred to earlier in this chapter, is an example of a client functioning at the *trust-mistrust* level. Although, like all people, she showed signs of conflict at all the other life stages (particularly ego integrity vs. despair) and some resolution of

---

*Much of the following section is adapted from "Applying Erik Erikson to Social Work Intervention," in *Personality Theory and Social Work Practice,* ed. H. Strean (Metuchen, N.J.: Scarecrow Press, 1975).

conflict as well, in order to feel and function better she needed first to be helped to trust. Clients showing a high ratio of mistrust to trust usually are or have been psychologically, socially, or physically neglected, battered, or improperly nourished. Angry and frustrated, they have low self-esteem. They usually feel very depressed and the victims of a hostile and oppressive environment. They may be parents who find the role of parenting burdensome because they themselves yearn to be children; they can be so envious of their children they often resort to abusive behavior. In this category, too, are many of the economically impoverished, whose environments are extremely deficient and malnourishing. Here, also, are many of the clients who have suffered such environmental crises as tornadoes, or other depriving situational events such as job layoffs or death.

The client with a trust-mistrust conflict is reminiscent of a child who has been abandoned or unloved and needs the protection of a maternal person who will listen to his angry outbursts (some of which may even be directed at her or him) without rejecting him. The social worker offers a relationship in loco parentis which includes help in verbalizing anger and distrust, later providing necessary tangible and intangible goods and services such as food, housing, safety, an "on call" relationship, and other physical and emotional nutrients that will fill voids in the client's life-situation. When this occurs the client can accept the social worker to some extent as a trustworthy person. As a by-product of the social-worker–client relationship, the client learns to trust himself a little more.

There are two subgroups of clients whose life-tasks and conflicts center around *autonomy* vs. *shame and doubt:* (1) those who have little confidence in their own capacities and limited faith in the social resources of their environments because they have been expected to do too much too soon on their own; and (2) those who have been insufficiently encouraged to perform with some independence, autonomy, and concern for others. While these sub-categories are polar extremes and no client perfectly matches the descriptions, clients having conflicts with autonomy tend towards one or the other; either they were prematurely stimulated toward independence, or else too little was expected from them in their maturing years.

In considering the social worker's role in helping clients who are reacting to imposed high standards (first subgroup), the "significant other in the client's radius" should be an individual or group that will permit and encourage him to relax controls and lessen perfectionistic standards.

People in the second subgroup might be the over-demanding spouse, parent, or child; the recalcitrant student or employee; or the manipulative person with a behavior disorder who throws temper tantrums when called upon to assume responsibility. In making an interventive plan for clients who have been treated over-permissively and indulgently, the social worker should conceive of his role as that of a "trainer." He sets limits when the client acts impulsively and praises him when he appropriately controls himself, reinforcing when he assumes autonomy and independence. The worker should also attempt to influence "significant others" in the client's environment so that they too will provide the kinds of attitudes and relationships the worker is attempting to provide.

Clients who have difficulty accepting and enjoying their sexual roles, but have several concomitant strengths as well, are having conflicts with *initiative vs. guilt*. The client might be someone with anxiety about his or her sexual assertiveness and spontaneity, or may be a parent finding it difficult to cope with his sexually maturing child's amorous advances and competition with the parents. The client may be one who fears success, because being successful stimulates fantasies that he is destroying someone and he must punish himself for these fantasied deeds. The resulting failures at work, school, and elsewhere appear in this category. Sometimes the client appears seductive, charming, and sexually aggressive at a first meeting, but, sooner or later, problems with initiative and anxiety about sexual role become exposed.

With clients who are having difficulty coping with initiative, the social worker encourages the verbal expression of sexual wishes and indicates the universality of the wish to gratify them. He helps the client's significant others also to encourage and accept this expression and universality. Often, marital pairs and family members have a *shared* difficulty in assuming initiative in their respective roles. Consequently, in parent-child, marital, or family treatment where more than one member of a family is participating, a statement by the social worker to any one member is a statement to all, and the worker's attitude of encouragement and acceptance of sexuality and initiative toward one member is often experienced as such by all.

The social worker also encourages the expression of initiative in situations in the client's environment such as work or recreation. He asks, for example, "Why can't you ask the boss for a raise?" "Why don't you allow yourself to enjoy dancing?" "What's wrong with winning at bowling, golf, or tennis?"

Clients who suffer from anxiety in interpersonal situations, feel inferior to their peers, lead regimented lives, and are unable to move beyond the narrow confines of their homes are attempting to cope with the life-task of *industry vs. inferiority*. Here we have the school-phobic child whose parents fear releasing him and who himself fears leaving them for too long. In general, clients who have social difficulties in small-group situations such as the job, recreational groups, and friendship groups fall into this category; abetted by significant others in the past and present, these clients tend to repeatedly seek out the protection of parental figures and do not share well with peers. Though often capable of autonomous activity in many areas and having many intact ego-functions, these clients tend to experience transactions with peers as frustrating.

Clients who fall into this category can usually profit from social or therapy groups where the social worker does not permit too much dependency on himself. Rather, he encourages each client to seek solutions from other group members, helping him to see when he is asking for too little or too much from them. He helps the client acquire, often through group interaction, the social and interpersonal skills that he cannot achieve in his over-protective home. As is true with most clients, a school phobia is not only an expression of the client's fear of separation from his parents and parents' wish to keep the child at home; usually the school and others are also helping to maintain the stability of the transaction. Consequently, the interventive plan not only must involve the social worker fostering industry but must include intervention with the school officials and significant others in the child's social orbit.

When individuals have difficulty in knowing who they are—just what their values, roles, strengths, skills, and limitations are—they are experiencing the conflict Erikson has termed *identity vs. role diffusion*. Here we have the ambivalent teenager who is not sure whether he is an adult or child, the mother whose children are off at school or have left home, the employee in a new job or position, the victim of a job layoff, the divorcée or widow, the newcomer to a community; all wonder to some extent who they are and what the new and different expectations of them by significant others are.

Because clients in this category are often confused about social norms and subcultural expectations, the social worker gears his role to addressing these problems. Often the worker can be utilized as a role-model in his work with individuals and groups as he focuses with them on how they are denying their strengths, are too eager to accept other people's values, and are fearful of appearing unique.

Clients with anxieties about and resistance to intimate interactions, particularly with members of the opposite sex, are attempting to cope with *intimacy vs. isolation*. These may be socially gregarious people who manifest many ego strengths but who nonetheless fail repeatedly in marriage or switch from lover to lover. They may eventually isolate themselves entirely from intimate relationships. In the encounter with such a client, the worker addresses himself to the client's anxieties and fears surrounding intimacy. The worker must feel free to offer and receive intimacy in the social-worker–client relationship. He or she expresses warmth, admiration, and considerateness and explores the client's discomfort in receiving these expressions; when the client does not express similar sentiments to the social worker, this resistance is also investigated.

As the client becomes aware of his unrealistic fears of intimacy in the social-worker–client transaction, as he sees how he fears rejection, he is better enabled to resolve this life-task and take on intimate relationships with others in more comfort.

Clients who are bitter, frightened, angry, or anxious when with their own children or other members of the younger generation are in the midst of a struggle between *generativity and stagnation*. In this category are the angry boss, the frightened or angry parent, and the threatened supervisor or teacher. Essentially, clients in this category fear taking on the responsibilities and role of a parental authority figure. As long as the individual remains in a non-parental role, he is reasonably secure; in a parental role, he becomes very anxious.

If he is a parent, the client can usually derive benefit from family treatment that helps him examine his role difficulties in the here and now. He can also profit from a small group—provided, of course, that his resistances to taking leadership in the group are examined. His relationship with the group leader can be a useful one as he observes a role-model who can assume a parental role, give to others, and enjoy it. Often a group for individuals who share an identical life-task—prospective parents, teachers, foremen, supervisors, etc.—can help the members examine and cope with the anxieties and confusions that their role-set engenders.

The retired person who is depressed and desperate is struggling over *ego integrity vs. despair*. Often feeling unproductive, he can harbor a great deal of self-hate. He questions the contributions he has made to the world and verbally berates himself. To add to his despair, family and extended family may shun him because his dependency induces anxiety in them. Sometimes he is placed in a home for the aged and forgotten.

Because the client in this category frequently needs to talk a great deal about himself and be cared for, a one-to-one relationship is often the intervention of choice. Here the client can reflect on the past and recall his strengths while he is with a social worker who truly values him. This work can be supplemented by helping the client find appropriate political or recreational activities in the community or institution. As the aged person is helped to recognize that he has talents, skills, and a self that can be valued by himself and others, he becomes less desperate.

It should be reemphasized that the notion of life-tasks is only one of several pieces of information that guide the social worker in planning his role repertoire with clients. Different clients, as we have already noted, may share the same life-task but differ markedly in ego resources and other internal strengths. It should also be remembered that clients may have several unresolved life-tasks, so that the social worker has to decide which are most likely to be amenable to confrontation and—perhaps more important—which the client and his significant others wish to face first, second, or not at all.

Erikson's transactional picture of the individual facing specific life-tasks not only provides a means for the social worker to conceptualize his role and attitude as he intervenes for and with his clients but also provides a means of "locating services where people are at the time the services are needed" (Meyer, 1976). Table I suggests a way to view individuals as they interact and transact with life crises and service provisions.

The Agency and Interventive Plans

The social agency's tasks and functions, its program, policies, and procedures, will always affect the interventive plan (Siporin, 1975). If an agency consists of experts in, for example, marriage counselling, child guidance, or income maintenance, the case dispositions made and the plans favored for clients will be heavily influenced by the priorities of the agency. As we have noted, social agencies can become preoccupied with their distinctiveness, and some of the unique needs of the client may be over-

CHART I. Normal Individual Transactions

INDIVIDUAL DEVELOPMENTAL AGE-SPECIFIC TASKS AND NEEDS*	EXPECTABLE TRANSITIONAL CRISES AND TYPICAL PROBLEMS	AVAILABLE INSTITUTIONS PROVIDING SOCIAL SERVICES
I. Infancy, 0–3 *Tasks:* Basic trust *vs.* mistrust; autonomy *vs.* shame and doubt *Needs:* Mothering, care, learning, verbal and conceptual skills	Role transition for parents, working mothers, absent fathers *Typical problems:* Inadequate parenting Unwanted children Neglect and abuse Marital conflict Physical handicaps Mental retardation	Income maintenance programs Prenatal care centers for medical care, advice, and parent education Hospitals, clinics Well-baby stations Family services Child welfare services Homemakers Home helps Day care Protection Placement (foster care, adoption)
II. Preschool, 3–6 *Tasks:* Initiative *vs.* guilt *Needs:* Learning, socialization, play	Child's separation from home Changing tasks of child rearing *Typical problems:* Inadequate socialization Lack of supervision Behavioral reactions	Nursery school care Group care services And see above as appropriate

164

*It is evident that the stages are cumulative; there is overlapping and always residue from previous stages. Thus, "And see above" (in the third column) indicates that available services are applicable at all stages, whereas some are more prominent at certain times.

III. Grade school, 6–13 *Tasks:* Industry vs. inferiority *Needs:* Intellectual and social stimulation	Expanding world and increasing stimuli to be coped with *Typical problems:* Social and learning failures	School guidance services Recreational services Developmental group services And see above as appropriate
IV. High school, 13–18 *Tasks:* Identity vs. identity diffusion *Needs:* Achievement, partial separation from parents	The time for decisions about sexual identity, work, and the future *Typical problems:* Identity crises Alienation Addictions Delinquency School maladjustment	Youth services, hot lines, crash pads, etc. Vocational counseling Correctional services Addiction services And see above as appropriate
V. Young adult, 18–21 *Tasks:* Intimacy vs. isolation *Needs:* Opportunities for self-fulfillment in adult roles	Leaving home Marriage Working *Typical problems:* Unwed parenthood School-work maladaptation Marital conflict Addictions Crime	Marital conflict legal aid services Probation services And see above as appropriate

continued

Individual Developmental Age-Specific Tasks and Needs	Expectable Transitional Crises and Typical Problems	Available Institutions Providing Social Services
VI. Mature adult, 21–65 *Tasks:* Generativity vs. stagnation *Needs:* Expanding opportunities for self-development in life roles	Household management and care *Typical Problems:* Family breakdown, divorce Financial needs or mismanagement Parent-child conflict Work, career failure Disability, personality disorganization Death of family and friends	Family court services Medical and mental health services And see above as appropriate
VII. Aged adult, 65 and over *Tasks:* Integrity vs. despair *Needs:* Living arrangements, physical care, continuing opportunities for self-development in roles of aged	Physical and mental depletion Loss of friends and separation from family Retirement Death of spouse and friends *Typical problems:* Sickness Loneliness	Meals on wheels Centers for the aged Income maintenance programs Foster grandparent programs Foster family care Institutional care And above as appropriate Social isolation Economic deprivation

SOURCE: Reprinted from Carol Meyer, *Social Work Practice*, 2nd ed. (New York: Free Press, 1976). Copyright © 1976 by The Free Press, A Division of Macmillan Publishing Co., Inc. Used by permission of the Publisher.

166

looked as a result. The machinery through which social workers do their work sets boundaries to the ways in which they define problems. As Compton and Galaway (1975) have pointed out, a professional subculture evolves that has its own value system and accepted ways of operating.

Social-systems theory has enlightened social workers regarding the impact of agency structure on intervention. The literature now includes pertinent analyses of the effects of agency policy on the selection of clients for help, on role-expectations for the "good client," and on the social worker's perceptions of the outcome for clients with varying diagnostic assessments (Austin, 1963). Frequently, the agency itself has been viewed as an object for change rather than as a given in the situation (Germain, 1968).

Some writers have taken the position that, with the exception of the personality and skill of the social worker, perhaps no factor plays a greater role in the intervention process than the agency itself and the arrangement it provides when working with clients (MacLeod, 1963). If an agency is inflexible about, for example, holding interviews with clients in an office once a week for fifty minutes, many clients will not be helped. For certain individuals it might be necessary to see them in their homes, at a storefront, or in a park if they are to feel free in relating to the social worker (Riesman, Cohen and Pearl, 1964). Some clients may need to be seen several times a week, while others may be able to tolerate only brief interviews every other week. Similarly, if an agency insists on using a particular modality exclusively, such as long-term or short-term treatment, crisis intervention, one-to-one intervention, or groups, some of the needs of certain clients will be neglected. Furthermore, for some clients it may be necessary to see more than one social worker during the helping process.

As social workers begin to conceive of themselves more as generalists attuned to the complex gestalt of people-in-their-situations, it would seem to follow that cooperation among several agencies will be more necessary. In addition, as the agency becomes perceived more as a system which at times can interfere with intervention plans rather than as an immovable bureaucracy to which clients and social workers alike must adapt, social workers will be encouraged to formulate and implement ways to change institutional arrangements that do not enhance client progress (Compton and Galaway, 1975; Germain, 1968). A recent trend in this regard is to encourage staff social workers to participate in modifying agency policies and practices and even to include clients, the consumers of services, as full-fledged members of agency boards of directors. As a result of this innovation, procedures have been modified in many agencies, and communities and organizations have more often been the target of change.

Choosing Among Practice Modalities*

The past decade has witnessed a proliferation of practice modalities. As he plans his interventions the social worker of the 1970s can choose among: the traditional model of one-to-one long-term "treatment," one-to-one short-term treatment, crisis intervention, family treatment (long and short), group counselling, and many more interventive models.

Much effort has been expended to determine what practice models can be most helpful to specific clients at a specific time. How, for example, does a particular family experience meeting as a group, and how would the family members experience being seen separately? What would the clients under study experience as frustrating when a particular modality is used, and what would be gratifying to them? Would the experienced frustration or gratification enhance psychosocial competence or not?

In this section we will briefly review some of the more popular modalities in current social-work practice and examine some of the indications and contraindications for particular clients.

*This section is adapted from a paper by the author, "Choosing Among Practice Modalities," *Clinical Social Work,* Vol. 2, No. 1, 1974.

FAMILY THERAPY

Using the family as the unit of assessment and intervention is not a novel concept in social work. Mary Richmond in 1922 pointed out that "the concern of the social worker is all those who share a common table" (Richmond, 1922) and social workers since then have recognized that modifications in one family-member's modus vivendi will have an impact on other family members, for better or worse. As a result of a growth of knowledge in system theory and role theory, social workers have come to view the family as a dynamic system with interacting partners all of whom contribute to the system's functioning and dysfunctioning.

Those who champion family therapy (treating the family unit with all members present) have alleged that the use of this modality can help locate the family's "most burdensome problem" as all experience it (Pollak, 1956). Family therapists found ways to expose each actor's responsibility for the state of the family's equilibrium, and for all members of the family to note each actor's role, particularly in family conflict. Proponents of family therapy have demonstrated how communication, mutual understanding, and clarification of role discomplementarities can be enhanced when all family members examine their transactions in the "here and now" together rather than individually (Ackerman, 1954; Pollak, 1956).

Further, in family therapy, as Pollak (1956) has suggested, there is "shared blame," and an individual family member is less likely to feel that he must carry the burden of the family's difficulties by himself. He can learn through family therapy that "the family problem" is a product of shared interaction.

Perhaps one of the more important reasons why caseworkers and other social workers for many decades failed to rigorously conceptualize the family system with its intersecting and interacting parts was social work's strong allegiance to the psychoanalytic treatment model. Although Freud wrote quite early in his career that "above all, our interests will be directed toward the family circumstances of our patients,'' (Freud, 1939) and in 1909, in the case of Little Hans, utilized the actions and statements of both parents to understand the development of the boy's phobic illness, most of Freud's followers have been essentially concerned with the diagnosis and treatment of the individual.

As social workers studied the results of their work, particularly with children, they began to observe the interdependency of family members in and out of the treatment situation. Although family therapy implies that the family as an entity is the unit of attention, social workers engaged in family therapy do not ignore the functioning or treatment of the individual but contend that his adaptive or maladaptive behavior cannot be considered apart from the familial context.

Because the social worker engaged in family therapy is diagnosing a system rather than an individual, a new vocabulary (largely derived from system theory) has evolved. The term "family homeostasis" (Jackson, 1957) or "family balance" provides a framework for the study of those forces that help keep the family stable and those that disturb its equilibrium. For example, a couple may be able to interact quite harmoniously until the birth of a child. The family therapist interested in helping them reach a new homeostatic balance would have to study not only how each of the marital partners experiences the baby but also how the parents now experience each other and how the advent of the child has shaken the marital balance (Zilbach, 1968). The maintenance of homeostasis in general requires the accommodation of four family subsystems: parent-parent, husband-wife, sibling-sibling, and parent-child (Pollak, 1956).

One of the major tasks of the family therapist, as already implied, is to study and treat maladaptive communication patterns. By locating how and when family members fail to express what they feel toward each other and how they misunderstand each other, the worker can eventually help their interaction become smoother. In Chapter 3 we discussed the notion of the "double-bind," in which an individual says one thing and means another, contradicting the verbal message by his behavior.

In the Gold family each member was overtly polite to the others. Mother, father and son Jack (aged eleven) frequently complimented each other, often smiled, and appeared to be physically affectionate. However, whenever they were with members of their extended family or with friends, they used the extended family's or friends' support to berate each other. Thus Jack often complained about his parents at his grandparents' home, and the parents would do likewise at various places. The "double-bind" messages were the expressions of overt love concealing feelings of hatred.

"Double-bind" messages induce much confusion in the recipient, create tension in communication, exacerbate distrust, and alienate family members from each other. The family therapist tries to expose "double-bind" messages when he converses with family members, examine their causes, and eliminate their use as much as possible.

"Pseudo-mutuality" is another concept that appears in the family-therapy literature. Introduced by Wynne and his co-workers (1958), the term refers to a seeming accommodation by family members which is at the expense of the enhancement of individuals. Each member of the family is forced to give up much of his own individuality to maintain the family balance, and unfortunately, each member's pleasure is sacrificed.

Lidz (1963) has emphasized the importance of the "continuing influence of the family environment through the years" and has discussed the concept of "parental coalition." Parental coalition, once established, ordinarily changes to meet new family issues, interactions, and relationships. For example, the emergence of adolescent children in the family represents a new focus of power and demand and can be a basis for modifying the parental coalition, for better or worse.

When the Herman family came for family therapy Sally was sixteen years of age. She had begun to date boys the previous year, and Mr. Herman was very upset about her "late hours" and "growing disinterest" in him. Obviously threatened by Sally's alienation and unsuccessful in his attempts to limit her, he turned to Mrs. Herman for support. Mrs. Herman saw "nothing wrong" with Sally's dating and encouraged it because "it gives me a kick." The parents became tempestuous in their dealings with each other, and each refused to compromise. Neither Mr. Herman nor his wife was able to give Sally the support and guidance she needed to handle her burgeoning sexuality, and their frustrating marriage only increased Sally's uncertainty about her identity and role-behavior.

Ackerman (1954) has pointed out that when family members look at each other as a group and the therapist does likewise, the heightened feeling of "groupness" brings the family's concerns, conflicts, strengths, and weaknesses to the foreground. He has stressed that an important dimension of family diagnosis is the family's "defensive maneuvers," whereby family members support each other "to obscure the identity of the person who is the source of destructive reactions."

Family therapists in their diagnostic formulations have an orientation geared to the here and now. As Weiss (1962) has pointed out, "the social worker must consider what is going on in the present," particularly at the point at which the family comes to the agency.

To assess the family's life-style and its unique sense of identity, many family therapists have utilized the home visit. In observing how the family presents itself to the stranger-therapist, some of the family's coping devices and interactions become exposed (Ackerman and Behrens, 1956).

Because family therapy should be aimed at helping the family accomplish family tasks, most family therapists advise that interventions should be directed to family as a whole. As the therapist focuses on patterns of interaction in the family and as all members learn to participate in the exchange with the therapist, they can eventually supplant the therapist's role (Scherz, 1962). Some family therapists (Leader, 1967) claim that greater activity is required of a family therapist than of one who works with individuals. This is necessary in order to alter the family's customarily maladaptive ways of coping with one another. Frequently the family therapist requires family members to substitute different communication lines—such as listening more to one another, observing one another, and trying new modes of coping with conflict. In family therapy, there is less reflective discussion by any one person and more shared reflection about current interaction (Stamm, 1972).

To determine whether family therapy is the treatment of choice one of the important questions is: "Is the family at a level of psychosocial maturation such that its members can recognize or be helped to recognize a common problem to which all contribute?" A positive answer implies some capacity in the family members (or most of them) to identify with each other, expose their own anxieties and imperfections, tolerate some frustration in order to listen to others and their complaints, and identify with the family as a unit.

Many of the families that confront social workers have members who are functioning at a low level of maturation; they may be quite infantile and narcissistic. They usually do not have the ego-functions necessary to participate in shared responsibility; usually they must fix blame on others. Such a client also tends to lack the frustration tolerance necessary to participate in any group, particularly a family group, and finds it too trying to take note of other family members' anxieties, wishes, and, particularly, their complaints about the client. Clinets functioning at this psychosocial level cannot be expected to profit from a group experience in the form of family therapy but need an experience tailored to their maturational level. This would probably be a one-to-one relationship where the client has access to a parental figure who limits and gratifies, protects and encourages, in order to help the client mature.

An assessment of the family members' defensive patterns can also be useful in determining whether family treatment is the modality of choice. For example, after observing the family's patterns of interaction the social worker may conclude that a strong symbiotic network exists, and that an appropriate intervention goal would therefore be increased autonomy and individuality for the family members. The ties that bind the family members may be so strong, albeit maladaptive, that the worker decides to see the family as a unit simply because separating family members would create too much anxiety for them; however, one of the worker's long-range goals would be to explore with the family these fears of separation and autonomy. A cardinal tenet of social-work practice theory is that the client or client-system must be met "where it is"; even if the treatment structure compounds the client's defenses, we would rather protect the client than have no client at all.

In some families that confront social workers, the family members have strong defenses against communicating and interacting with each other. From a theoretical point of view, family therapy might be the modality of choice, but the individuals involved may not be able to bear the anxiety of sharing. Hence a one-to-one relationship with the social worker should probably be considered initially, so that each family member can receive enough protection and understanding while communicating with the social worker to eventually develop the strength to share problems with the others in family treatment.

WORK WITH SMALL GROUPS

There seems to be little question that society, particularly in the past two or three decades, has isolated people from one another. Paradoxically, the increased popularity of such communication devices as television appears to help decrease the intimacy of personal relationships. It may be that the growth of group therapy and group counselling represents a correction against the social isolation engendered by technological improvement. A strong need has developed for people to get closer together, and it is met to some extent by participating in small groups (Corsini, 1964).

Furthermore, growing recognition of the importance of group influences, coupled with increasing demand for therapeutic help, has led to the rapid development and wide acceptance of group methods of interaction, especially since World War II.

Clients of social workers have been seen in small groups for decades and for a myriad of reasons—for recreation, social action, interpersonal and psychological change, political participation, etc. Groups satisfy the basic human need to belong—what Slavson (1943) has termed "social hunger." The "gifts of the group" have been eloquently delineated by Tropp:

> Belonging implies acceptance by others, and that acceptance is a basic kind of affection from one's fellow human beings. To be in a group also means having opportunities for self-expression under circumstances in which others can appreciate it, so that it becomes achievement and brings recognition—and these are great supporters and strengtheners of that precious feeling of self-worth so necessary for mental health. Finally, to be in a group means having the opportunity for that important communal balance of freedom and limitation which is at the root of social responsibility.
>
> The group is not only an alliance through which normal needs can be met; it can also be a natural healer of hurts, a supporter of strengths, and a clarifier of problems. It may serve as a sounding board for expressions of anxiety, hostility, or guilt. It often turns out that group members learn that others in the group have similar feelings weighing them down in their aloneness, that they are not so different or so alone—and learning this in live confrontation with one's peers is a most powerful change-inducing experience (Tropp, 1968, p. 267).

Group treatment, like family therapy, is a "here and now" experience with the group usually experienced by its members as a symbolic family. In the group the individual member repeats patterns of interaction that he learned in his original family. As he interacts with "siblings" in the "here and now" he learns what he typically does to alienate and isolate others and also what he does and can do to bring others closer to him. Rosenthal (1971) provides an example of these group processes:

In a counseling group session, Mrs. Sanders stresses the stimulating intellectual exchanges that she has with her husband and animatedly describes the books they have read and discussed and the opinions on world affairs they have shared. In her description she uses such words as "superscilious," "extraneous," "repercussions," and "empathic." The other members are silent and an atmosphere of gloom pervades the group. The leader elicits the reactions of the group. Mrs. Weiss responds sadly that for her the session just strengthened her feelings of disappointment in her own underachieving and non-intellectual husband. Mrs. Marks indicates, "I just feel so inadequate next to Mrs. Sanders—I don't even read the newspapers any more." Mrs. Gorden nods agreement with this. A silence of several moments ensues. Mrs. Sanders then thoughtfully comments, "Boy, I certainly did a job here today, didn't I?"

Mrs. Marks says supportively, "You didn't do it; we react with our own feelings to what you say." Mrs. Sanders responds, "Yes, but there is something I'm doing here. Maybe this shows me what effect I have on others." Mrs. Sanders goes on to explain that when she enters a group of people whom she considers intellectually superior, she freezes up. She adds that here, however, she can talk.

Mrs. Marks comments wryly, "Thank you again—so we're a bunch of dummies!" Mrs. Sanders flushes deeply and laughs uncomfortably. She then, for the first time, shares with the group her feelings about her mother's death when she was a young adolescent and her subsequent bitterly competitive relationship with her stepmother (Rosenthal, 1971, p. 313).

The primary function of the social worker as group leader is to create an emotional climate in the group that will enhance the attainment of the group's goals. Therefore, he will exercise care in the selection of members for the group in order to achieve a workable balance among the personalities; he will address himself to helping group members resolve obstacles to communication; he will regulate the discharge of emotion in the group; and, in the interest of enhancing communication, he will be alert to the meaning of non-verbal cues such as lateness, restlessness, and silence. The leader's ongoing demonstration of mature and appropriate behavior in the face of a wide variety of emotional expressions is also an important part of his role. His capacities to deal constructively with aggression, his repeated demonstrations of respect for the group as an entity and for its members as individuals, and his constant attempt to understand the latent meaning of their communications all help to create an emotional atmosphere that will stimulate maturation of the group members (Rosenthal, 1971).

James Mann (1955) has discussed the significance of the leader's behavior in the attainment of group goals:

> The group therapist is forever in a position of showing the way toward more mature relationships so long as he remains aware of this and makes proper use of it. It is through the therapist and the example set by him that each member can move to more mature relations with other group members. It is his impartiality and his understanding of intergroup reactions; his ability to prevent the appearance of a group scapegoat; his subtle protection of the weak and, yet, his refusal to condemn the strong; his display of strength in opposing, if necessary, the whole group at the appropriate time and for the appropriate reason; his capacity for activity as well as passivity; and, most of all, his persistent search for the nature and meaning of the emotional conflicts before him—all these are necessary demands on the leader in his role as leader if the group is to move toward more gratifying relationships (Mann, 1955, p. 239).

In choosing a group for a client, the decision would appear to have some, but not all, of the indications and contraindications that were suggested for family treatment. A group may be very enriching and may serve as a stimulant to maturer psychosocial functioning for children and adults who are too dependent on parental figures but who possess some impulse control and some capacity to relate to others empathically. Group therapy with children, for example, has best been utilized by the child who fears being autonomous in a social or educational setting but who can emerge as less socially anxious with peers with the social worker's direction and interaction (Slavson, 1943). For an adult whose capacity for interpersonal relationships is very weak and who has never experienced intimacy and warm empathy from at least one parental figure, the group may be overwhelming.

Groups have been quite effective for clients who have the capacity to see themselves in a person-situation–constellation similar to that with which others are coping. Mothers, for example, who can experience themselves emotionally as mothers, and fathers who can do likewise as fathers, have profited from parents' guidance and other educational and therapeutic groups (Strean, 1970a). However, ego-fragmented parents with strong unfulfilled childlike wishes and fixations who need to have their own infantile needs attended to often experience a discussion of parental roles as threatening and respond with rage and anxiety—all of which suggests that a parents' group is contraindicated.

Although the social worker might recognize that a particular client's difficulties evolved in an early mother-child relationship (i.e., the trust-mistrust period) and that the conflicts he expresses reveal his need for a corrective emotional experience in a one-to-one relationship, the client may resist such a relationship because his primitive wants have asserted themselves and he is threatened by them. A group can be used by such a client to "hide" so that he does not feel impelled to expose his vulnerabilities. As one client in a group stated, "When I was alone with the social worker I was very scared and felt I had to talk, but in a group if I want to be silent, I can be silent." The group can help such a client to feel strong enough to cope eventually with a one-to-one relationship, where he can be helped to deal with his trust-mistrust conflicts.

Many clients can better use the social worker's help in the initial phase of the process if they meet him in a group with which they are already affiliated. Thus, welfare mothers, war veterans, and members of certain ethnic and minority groups may find that the social worker's entrance is more tolerable if they are in a neighborhood club or interest group in which they already feel some degree of comfort (Meyer, 1976). Just as a home visit is less anxiety-producing for some clients than an interview at the social agency, so the social worker may be more easily taken into the client's life-space when he meets the client on his home ground.

In sum, the use of groups seems to be best indicated for clients whose major difficulties lie in their social and interpersonal relationships. In a group they can examine their interactions with peers, and locate which forms of interaction lead to conflictful and estranged relationships. To be really helpful this modality, like family treatment, seems to require in the client some ability to identify with others, empathy, impulse control, and frustration tolerance; for clients who have not developed these capacities to any appreciable degree, one-to-one help would seem indicated. For those who have these capacities the group modality may serve either as a preparatory medium for other forms of help or as the exclusive modality of intervention.

CRISIS INTERVENTION AND SHORT-TERM TREATMENT

With greater understanding of ego psychology, particularly notions of psychosocial tasks and the maturational timetable (Erikson, 1950), social workers have been better able to understand the inevitable stress that accompanies living in our society. One manifestation of this understanding has been the increased use of crisis theory and crisis intervention (Parad, 1965).

We now recognize that school entry, the death of a loved one, physical illness, pregnancy, and other important life events may induce a period of regression and overwhelming anxiety, but that frequently the client suffering from the effects of these events responds to help and returns to his previous state of equilibrium in a short period of time.

The definition of "crisis" implies that the hazardous event (Rapoport, 1962) and the tension, anxiety, and regressive behavior it induces are quite different from "life as usual." "Life as usual'' implies a relative absence of maladaptive behavior. When maladaptive behavior is not usually present in the client's life, the social worker can reasonably infer that the client has the ego and the environmental resources to cope with the ''disruption of a state'' (Rapoport, 1962) and can pull himself up by the bootstraps rather quickly; consequently crisis intervention and short-term treatment would appear to be the modality of choice. However, some clients have no bootstraps to pull—i.e., they have limited personal and environmental resources—and for these clients it is unreasonable to assume that after many years of malfunctioning they can respond effectively to short-term work.

Crisis-intervention theory created greater cognizance of the fact that many clients come to agencies at times of crisis with the intention of receiving only immediate help. It led social workers to examine the effect of stress and anxiety on individuals, to assess coping mechanisms and problem-solving abilities, and to learn to help clients mobilize their own resources and find new solutions. Crisis theory recognizes that during emergencies people are more receptive to help and adaptable to change; hence, quick and effective responses on the part of the social worker can have a great deal of influence when the client is thus suggestible and vulnerable.

The principal goals toward which short-term treatment and crisis intervention are directed are: (1) modification or removal of symptoms and relief of suffering, (2) revival of the level of adaptive functioning that the client possessed prior to the crisis, (3) promotion of the client's understanding of the most obvious problems that sponsor symptoms, sabotage functioning, and interfere with a more complete enjoyment of life, (4) presentation of ideas about how to recognize these problems at their inception, and (5) provision of some way of dealing with such problems and their effects so as to make a more productive adjustment (Wolberg, 1968).

An examination of effective procedures in crisis intervention and short-term treatment (Parad, 1965; Wolberg, 1968; Rapoport, 1962) reveals the following principles:

1. At the first session the worker attempts to establish a working relationship with the client while getting as complete information from him as is possible. At the end of the first session, the client is given some explanation for his symptoms, in language he understands. He is told that the treatment period will be limited and that results will depend on how he applies himself to the guidance given him.

2. During succeeding visits, the worker tries to identify patterns that have been operating in the client's life, of which the current crisis is one immediate manifestation. He conducts an exploration to see if these patterns have roots in the client's past, particularly in his relationships with parents and siblings. By pointed questioning, he encourages the client to put the pieces together for himself, in particular to figure out why he was no longer able to make an adjustment prior to coming to treatment. Together, worker and client explore why he is unable to work out his present difficulty, bringing him to an awareness of how and why he is resisting or is otherwise unable to resolve his trouble.

3. The client is helped to find appropriate resources in his environment to reduce his stress—an attorney, physician, detective, etc. He is encouraged in self-observation and is taught how to relate his symptoms to precipitating happenings in his present environment.

4. Therapy is terminated with the recognition that the immediate accomplishments may be modest, but that the continued application of self-understanding will help bring about more substantial changes.

Before deciding on crisis intervention or short-term treatment, just as with other modalities, the social worker must assess the client's defensive patterns. There are some clients who find sustained help burdensome, overwhelming, or threatening. These clients may find it quite comforting to know in advance that their defenses will be not attacked but supported and that contact with the social worker and agency can terminate in a short period of time. They may use the social worker as they wish during the short period, returning at a later point for a more prolonged relationship or for intermittent short dosages of help.

Short-term help would appear to be the treatment of choice when the client, with or without the social worker's help, can identify the tasks that have to be accomplished, can see his stressful state as temporary, and has sufficient personal and situational resources to cope with the tasks and their attendant conflicts (Reid and Epstein, 1972). It may also be utilized when the notion of long-term intervention is too anxiety-provoking or threatening to the client's equilibrium.

It should be borne in mind that the modalities we have reviewed are not necessarily mutually exclusive. A client's maturational needs and state of resistance may indicate that some combination of modalities is needed. However, whatever modality or combination of modalities the social worker uses, intervention should be planned in terms of the client's psychosocial level of maturation, his ego resources and limitations, and the resources and limitations of his environment.

Summary

Planning intervention is a deliberate, rational process that involves the choice of actions designed to achieve specific objectives. It is concerned with moving from problem-definition to problem-solution; from knowing what is wrong to knowing what is to be done, for what ends, how, when, and with whom. Goals for clients are arrived at through discussion with them. The interventive plan, based always on a thorough psychosocial assessment, is always specific and unique to the client-system. It depends not just on what the social worker offers but on what the client is willing to accept.

Interventive planning has been moving from a rigidly constituted organization of three distinct methods—casework, group work, and community organization—to a more generalist method with a social-problem focus.

In individualizing and specifying the interventive plan, the social worker must recognize the client's feelings toward the source of referral, toward his definition of the problem, and toward significant others. The client's motivation with regard to accepting help will also influence the interventive plan. It is of crucial importance in planning intervention to understand the strengths and limitations of the client and his social orbit, and the functional and dysfunctional transactions that exist where people and situations intersect. Intervention will take place in that part of the person-situation–constellation that is most amenable to change; that is, directly with the person, the environment, or both.

The social worker plans his interventions in accordance with the client's level of psychosocial maturation, considering himself a crucial member of the client's radius of social relations. The worker's role, attitude, and choice of modalities are based on his appraisal of the life-tasks the client is facing. In his work with the client and environment the social worker is a responsible caretaker manifesting attitudes and behavior that the client needs in order to cope better with his life, and that will help him mature with more comfort.

Chapter 5

Implementing the Intervention Plan

Technique smothers the ideas that put its rule in question and filter out for public discussion only those ideas that are in substantial accord with the values created by a technical civilization.

Robert K. Merton
The Technological Society (1967)

No issue in social-work practice commands or deserves more attention than the matter of implementing the intervention plan. Social-work students, practitioners, teachers, scholars, and researchers devote a considerable portion of their time and energy to exploring and evaluating procedures by which they can help clients to enhance their day-to-day lives. One indication of social workers' concern with interventive procedures is that there are now over twenty typologies in the social-work literature that attempt to classify procedures and roles in the intervention process.

That social workers in every field of practice are preoccupied with these procedures is understandable. For in the end, all social workers want to help their clients; they want to see change for the better. Yet philosophers of science have noted that when there are a number of orientations or theories on a particular subject, there is usually some confusion about the dimensions of the subject (Deutsch and Krauss, 1965).

In this chapter we shall first review the work of other writers in social work who have attempted to clarify existing practice theory, helping procedures, and helping professional relationships. In addition, we will attempt to fill some of the gaps that exist in the conceptualizations of social-work intervention by elaborating on a few dimensions of the social-worker–client encounter that have been relatively neglected in the literature. Specifically, we wish to explicate some of the ways in which clients *experience* interventive procedures—why they resist help at times, how and why they experience the social worker as they do—and finally, we wish to consider some of the subjective, non-rational factors inherent in giving and receiving help that are important determinants of intervention's effectiveness.

A Review of the Literature on Interventive Procedures

Existing typologies on intervention appear to have certain limitations in helping the social worker feel confident as he acts for and with a client. This section will review these typologies, note their contributions and limitations, and offer a few notions designed to remedy some of the deficiencies apparent in existing conceptualizations.

Mary Richmond (1922) discussed four procedures utilized by

social workers to help clients cope with internal and external problems:

1. Providing the client with "insight into his individual personal characteristics."
2. Providing the client with "insight into the resources, changes, and influences of the social environment."
3. "Direct action of mind upon mind"—to "influence and reorganize the client's thinking."
4. Indirect action—enlisting the client's significant others to help him in his social functioning.

Richmond's procedures have often reappeared in the writings of later scholars and practitioners, although different terms have been used to describe them. Thus Porter Lee in 1923 described intervention as comprising two roles:

1. Executive—involving the social worker's discovering a particular resource and arranging for its use by the client.
2. Leadership—the exercise of personal influence by the social worker, as in modifying the client's attitudes in a marital, parent-child, or employer-employee relationship.

Gordon Hamilton devised three categories:

1. Administration of a Practical Service—The social worker helps the client to choose and to use a social resource afforded by the community.
2. Environmental Manipulations—The worker attempts to correct or improve the client's social situation to reduce strain and pressure.
3. Direct Treatment—"a series of interviews for the purpose of inducing or reinforcing attitudes favorable to the maintenance of emotional equilibrium." In this category are included such techniques as "clarification of the client's feelings and thoughts, mobilizing of affect, and interpretation of preconscious thoughts or behavior" (Hamilton, 1951, p. 203).

Lucille Austin, in 1948, referred to social treatment, ego-supportive therapy, experiential therapy, and insight therapy (Austin, 1948). In its meticulousness and thoroughness Austin's typology clearly surpasses its predecessors. She not only listed procedures but specified several criteria for utilizing each of the four types of treatment. Because Austin's typology is a comprehensive one, we will present it in some detail.

1. Social Treatment
    Goal: Modification of the social environment without modification of client's attitudes and behavior.
    Techniques: Helping clients to obtain and use social services; opening opportunities for better social contacts; changing negative environmental factors. Use of encouragement, reassurance, and clarification of reality-issues.
    Relationships: The social worker in his approach to the client should reflect attitudes of courtesy, respect and sympathy.
    Clients Served: Individuals whose reality and social problems lie largely in their social circumstances.

2. Ego-supportive Psychotherapy
    Goal: Maintenance of existing ego-adaptive strengths.
    Techniques: Reassurance, permissive attitudes to relieve guilt, use of social services when indicated.
    Relationship: Helping the client discuss feelings toward the social worker, particularly irrational ones—i.e., use of transference. Protecting client from undue pressure.
    Clients Served: Clients whose ego functioning is weak.

3. Experiential Therapy
    Goal: Modification of the client's attitudes and behavior.
    Techniques: Use of positive transference to provide a corrective emotional experience; fostering favorable life experiences; use of selected dynamic interpretations that are preceded by clarification of the client's reality.
    Relationship: Exploration and clarification of the transfer-

ence as a dynamic for a corrective emotional experience. Promoting attachment to and identification with the social worker.

Clients Served: Adolescents, young people with oedipal problems, those with some ego-functions intact.

4. Insight Therapy

Goal: Partial reorganization of the personality structure. Change in ego-functioning through insight.

Techniques: Interpretations of unconscious feelings and defenses.

Relationship: Use of transference reactions to help client understand himself better.

Clients Served: Clients with mild neuroses and character problems.

Although Austin's typology fails to take into account (among other omissions) how the client's unique ego strengths and limitations are related to his transactions with his environment, it does attempt to weave together assessment of the client and interventive goals and procedures. It considers, albeit in rudimentary form, some of the dynamics of the social worker-client relationship as an instigator of client growth, and it recognizes that clients differ in what they can give to and derive from social-work intervention.

Throughout the 1940s and 1950s typologies either listed procedures separately, as did Bibrings's—suggestion, emotional relief, immediate influence, clarification, and interpretation (Bibring, 1950)—or else placed clients into psychiatric groupings, such as those with "normal," "psychotic," "neurotic," and "character" problems. Specified techniques, such as "advice," were suggested for the most emotionally disturbed clients, and "interpretation" and "clarification" for the less disturbed (Cockerill, 1951).

A typology that evolved in the 1960s and is still popular is the work of Professor Florence Hollis (Hollis, 1972). Her "psycho-social treatment" recognizes both internal psychological and external social causes of dysfunction; her procedures are designed to enable the individual "to meet his needs more fully and function more adequately in his social relationships." Hollis's procedures, as we noted in Chapter 1, are as follows:

1. Sustaining—demonstrations of interest and desire to help, expressions of confidence in the client's competence, reassurance about guilt and anxiety.
2. Direct Influence—suggestions and advice.
3. Catharsis or Ventilation—encouraging the client to discharge pent-up feelings and emotionally charged memories.
4. Reflective Consideration of Current Person-Situation–Configuration—The social worker encourages the client to think about economic, social, or educational problems and about people with whom he is associated.
5. Encouragement of Client To Reflect on Dynamics of His Response Patterns—i.e., why he behaves the way he does.
6. Encouragement of Client To Reflect on Development of his Response Patterns or Tendencies—i.e., etiological factors which affect current functioning.

Hollis has pointed out that intervention is an ever-changing blend of some or all of these procedures. Furthermore, with the possible exception of the sixth item in her classification, these procedures can be used with "significant others" in the client's social orbit and applied in work with dyads and families as well as individuals.

Hollis classified environmental work in terms of the roles a social worker may assume when working with a "significant other" or with another agency. The roles are: *provider* of a resource, *locator* of a resource, *interpreter* of the client's needs, and *aggressive intervenor* (Hollis, 1972).

As situational factors became more prominent in social workers' thinking and activity during the late 1960s and early 1970s, two important shifts took place in the conceptualization and classification of interventive procedures: (1) Further direction was provided in working with the client's environment, and

(2) more social workers became "generalists," working simultaneously with individuals, families, groups, and communities in complex social situations. Intervention procedures were therefore classified around specific roles, such as that of social broker, advocate, enabler, counselor, etc. Elizabeth Meier (1965), stressing that the person-situation–configuration should always be in the forefront in assessment and intervention, has suggested a classification in which intervention attempts to modify either the situation or the person, or both. According to Meier, the situations that clients bring to the social worker may be classified into six groupings. The situation may—

1. be deficient in opportunities for the client to find satisfactions in his "essential strivings"—i.e., fundamental psychological, social, and physical needs;
2. prevent the client from expressing his strivings;
3. make unrealistic demands;
4. reactivate unresolved conflicts;
5. stimulate unacceptable impulses; or
6. make demands contrary to the client's values.

Intervention in the above classification consists of—

1. providing opportunities to increase the client's satisfactions; or
2. modifying the manner in which he expresses his wishes.

In current conceptualizations of intervention the role concept appears to be the most popular. Compton and Galaway (1975) conceive of social-work intervention as involving one or a combination of three roles:

1. The Social Broker Role—The social worker serves as a linkage between the client and other community resources. The primary objective is to steer people toward the existing services that can be of benefit to them. Its focus is on enabling or helping people to use the system and negotiate its pathways. A further objective is to link elements of the service system with one another. The essential benefit of this objective is the phys-

ical hookup of the person with the source of help and of elements of the service system with one another (McPheeters & Ryan, 1971).

2. The Enabler Role—The social worker's activities are directed toward assisting the client to find coping strengths and resources within himself. The major distinguishing element of the enabler role is that change occurs because of client efforts; "the responsibility of the social worker is to facilitate or enable the client's accomplishment of a defined change" (Compton & Galaway, 1975).

3. The Advocate Role—The social worker becomes a spokesman for the client, presenting and arguing his cause when necessary in order to accomplish the objectives of the intervention plan.

Siporin (1975) has expanded the use of the role concept in intervention by linking various roles (e.g., social parent, guide, model, teacher, reinforcer, and social planner) to various outcomes (viability, maturation, and competence) and task functions (adaptation, integration, and pattern maintenance). Goldstein (1973) has also elaborated on various interventive roles: the role of authority, the socializing role, and the teaching role; Pincus and Minahan (1973) have mentioned similar roles. Atherton, Mitchell, and Schien (1971), in an attempt to locate a focus for intervention, developed three diagnostic categories: (1) problems related to performance of legitimate and acceptable roles, (2) problematic roles, and (3) problems in the structure of social systems that affect the behavior of individuals. These authors, like Siporin, prescribe various social-worker roles to deal with the various role problems of clients: social broker, mediator, educator, and crisis intervenor.

Other interventive processes reviewed in the social-work literature have been borrowed from behavior-modification therapy. These include operant conditioning, reward and punishment, and positive and negative reinforcement. Growing in popularity among social-work practitioners, researchers, and scholars, these procedures are based on the premise that all behavior is learned and that maladaptive behavior can and should be unlearned (Thomas, 1971).

If the reader has tried to utilize some of the notions discussed above in his work with individuals, families, or groups, he will have many unanswered questions. Although a few of the authors do attempt to demonstrate how interventive planning is related to the diagnosis of the client, in most cases this important linkage is neglected. Secondly, the client categories that are described are so broad ("adolescents," "neurotics," "role incapacity"), and the procedures and role-models so general, that they provide very little information which the social worker can use to *individualize* intervention for a particular client at a particular time in a particular situation. In addition, with the possible exception of Austin's (1948), these classifications ignore the dynamics of the social-worker–client relationship.

The Dynamics of Intervention

The most important dimension in any change effort is how the recipient *experiences* the activity. The social worker may "sustain," "advise," "reinforce," or be a "social broker," but the client may and often does experience the social worker's activity in a way very different from that in which it was intended. As we have seen from some of the case illustrations in previous chapters, a supportive remark from the social worker may be experienced by the client as demeaning; the firm imposition of a limit by the social worker may be received by the client as an act either of love or of hostility; and the role-enactment of advocate or social broker, a beneficent act in the social worker's mind, can induce negative or at least ambivalent reactions in the client.

Just as any two clients may experience the same situational press—e.g., unemployment, bereavement—very differently, so will they react idiosyncratically to the same intervention, whether it be "support," "advocacy," or "interpretation." For intervention to move progressively, the social worker must understand how the client and significant others experience themselves and the problems addressed, and why. Further, he must take into consideration the fact that every client will resist the social worker's interventions from time to time, may distort the social worker's activities intentions (particularly when they arouse anxiety), and will respond with progress or lack of progress depending on how he experiences himself and the social worker in their mutual relationship.

It is a virtual axiom in social work that one of the most crucial factors that produces change in the client is the helper-helpee relationship (Austin, 1948; Hamilton, 1951; Hollis, 1972; Pincus and Minahan, 1973). This relationship has many facets: subtle and overt, conscious and unconscious, progressive and regressive, positive and negative. Both client and worker experience themselves and each other not only in terms of objective reality, but in terms of how each wishes the other to be and fears he might be. The phenomena of "transference" and "countertransference" exist in every relationship between two or more people, professional or nonprofessional, and must be taken into account in every social-worker–client encounter. By "transference" is meant the feelings, wishes, fears, and defenses of the client deriving from reactions to significant persons in the past (parents, siblings, extended family, teachers), that influence his current perceptions of the social worker. "Countertransference," similarly refers to aspects of the social worker's history of feelings, wishes, fears, and so on, all of which influence his perceptions of the client (Freud, 1953).

Whether an individual is getting advice about a job, a couple is reflecting about their marital conflict, a family is discussing their budgetary problems, a group is planning recreational activities, or neighborhood representatives are convening to discuss a community problem, all the actors have objective and subjective, rational and non-rational feelings and ideas about each other which influence the content and outcome of their discussions. If understanding of these phenomena is lacking, intervention can only be hit-or-miss.

Anyone who has been engaged in helping others make changes in their lives, whether the changes are internal and attitudinal or external and adaptive, has recognized that in the face of all logic and reason the client can often behave in a most obstinate and uncomprehending manner. To try to convince a suspicious client that his spouse is well meaning, or a self-hating client that he is competent in certain areas, usually intensifies his doubts. No client is so consistently rational and no worker so consistently wise that the worker's clarification and interpretation of the client's problems will lead automatically to the client's embarking on a new course of action based on the new insights he has acquired. If this were the case, most clients could be helped easily and quickly, and lasting results would accrue.

Intervention, to be well conceptualized, must always include a full examination of the social-worker–client relationship with its many dimensions and nuances. Although the worker's activity and the client's response to it can never be separated in understanding the dynamics of the intervention process, for purposes of examining each actor's role, activity, and experience more closely, we shall arbitrarily separate them in the following discussion.

The Client's Experience and Activity

TRANSFERENCE

Probably no concept has been more misunderstood by helping professionals than transference. As indicated above, transference exists in all relationships: in the classroom, in marriage, at meetings, and on the baseball field. Because of our unique histories, ego functioning, values, and social circumstances, each of us brings to every new relationship wishes, fears, anxieties, hopes, pressures, defenses, and many other subjective factors evolved from previous relationships that may or may not be appropriate in

the new situation. Because these phenomena are largely unconscious, we cannot will them away or consciously modify them
easily. They influence our perceptions of the people we meet;
however, very often our "explanations" for responding to people
with love, hatred, or ambivalence are rationalizations—i.e., ex-
cuses to justify our reactions.

Every human being has had emotionally charged experiences,
positive, negative, and ambivalent, with parents, siblings, the
extended family, and others, which have left indelible marks on
him; everyone's attitudes toward intimate relationships in the
present are continually colored by these past transactions. We
continue to seek in new relationships what was pleasant in the
past and to resist that which was unpleasant.

The intimate relationship of client and social worker is one in
which the client depends on the worker. This invariably reacti-
vates mixed feelings and ideas about the social worker that the
client experienced with those on whom he depended in the past.
These ambivalent feelings cannot be obliterated, ignored, or neglected, as some social workers have advised (Garrett, 1958;
Hamilton, 1951); they are normal in any interaction and become
intensified in helping situations. If the client has experienced
those who nurtured, advised, and educated him as essentially
positive and well meaning, he will in all likelihood experience the
social worker in the same way. However, in most individuals
there are residual mixtures of love, hate, and ambivalence toward
parents and others, and the social worker will be the recipient of
all these feelings. Typically, the clients of social agencies have
not experienced solid, positive relationships in the past. Hence
they are apt to exhibit strong reactions to the social worker,
ranging all the way from enormous gratitude, hope, and euphoria
to rejection, pessimism, and despair. Sometimes all of these reactions can be observed in one client in a single interview.

It is imperative for the practitioner to recognize that the client
will respond to his words and actions not only with his rational
faculties but also on the basis of transference. The practitioner
is loved, hated, demeaned, or adored by his clients not only

because of what he says and does but because of how they experience him.

> When Mr. Zeller was referred to the family agency for job counselling he broke three screening interviews. Each time the social worker telephoned him, Mr. Zeller said that he had "forgotten" about the interview or "something had come up" and he could not make it. Sensing his reluctance to receive help, the social worker in the fourth phone conversation said, "I get the impression you'd rather do without me." Mr. Zeller protested and said he'd come in. He arrived twenty minutes late for his first interview, apologized profusely for his tardiness, and went on to report that he was going to get a job by himself and didn't really need the social worker's help. "I'm a self-made man and I'll do things by myself."

Mr. Zeller was clearly transferring to the social worker his negative feelings toward people in his past who were in a helping position. To depend on someone aroused feelings of anxiety, humiliation, and anger. The social worker, merely by being a social worker, was the recipient of negative transference feelings, and these feelings were exacerbated by Mr. Zeller's joblessness and need for help.

Transference reactions occur, of course, not only in one-to-one relationships but in dyads, families, and other groups as well. In these situations, not only are there individualized transference reactions to the social worker but the group members' relationships with one another are also colored by their past experiences, values, hopes, wishes, fears, etc. When a particular theme is introduced in a group discussion, the theme will be experienced in part transferentially. The following excerpt is from the thirteenth session of a group of adults in a mental-health center. All of the members had previously dropped out of one-to-one treatment. The discussion centered on bringing in a new member to the group.

> When the social worker said, "There is the possibility of bringing in a new member. How do you feel about it?" Mike

quickly replied, "OK by me." After a two-minute silence, Roberta stated, "I would like to know more about him or her. Is it someone who couldn't get along with his social worker? Is he like one of us?" Another silence. Zelda remarked, "Look, we're one big happy family having a good time!" Several members nodded assent and then Mike said, "That's why it's all right with me to have another member in the group. We'll have one more person to knock all those social workers we didn't like." Jerry turned to the social worker and said, "How do you feel about it? Do you want another member?" The social worker asked, "How do you think I feel about it? Do I want to increase the membership of the group?"

The group members then attacked the social worker, Mike said, "You pompous ass! You never answer questions. You are not only ungiving but you just want more talk from us!" Grace, Sally, and Mike took turns saying, "Right on!" "Bravo!" and "Hurrah!"

After attacking the social worker the group members slowly began to examine themselves. Zelda recalled how she felt when her youngest brother was born—"I was out in the cold"—and began to weep. Other members recalled how they had felt displaced by their siblings and how their parents didn't understand their anger and feelings of impotent rage.

In this session and in the next two, the social worker was badgered further with angry statements from the members. Further memories of having been displaced in their own original families were recalled by them. Slowly, the members began to offer each other some compassion and identified with each other as they reexperienced past deprivations.

What is particularly noteworthy in this vignette is that when the social worker did not respond to Jerry's question but instead frustrated him, the whole group attacked the worker for several sessions. It can be hypothesized that the group members were angry not merely because Jerry's question was unanswered but because they were transferring to the social worker their angry feelings toward their parents for depriving and frustrating them in the past. The negative transference reactions were, of course, revived and exacerbated by the proposal to bring in somebody new (a new sibling figure). They all experienced the social worker as they had their parents who had imposed a new brother or sister on them without much preparation.

Many client reactions can be understood in terms of transference. The client who has always yearned for a protective, omnipotent parent may transfer this wish to the social worker, then feeling highly elated and functioning beautifully for weeks only to regress severely when some of his fantasies are punctured by reality. The client who frequently felt subordinate to a sibling might react negatively to a dyadic marital-counselling relationship. The deteriorating family that depended on a grandparent who recently died may experience the social worker as the grandparent reincarnated and feel together again. The black neighborhood council may greet the white social worker with scorn because they have had negative experiences with white people in the past (Compton and Galaway, 1975). These examples and many others attest to the ubiquity of the transference phenomenon.

John Bowlby, a well-known developmental psychologist and a teacher and supervisor of social workers for many years, has pointed out that transference and countertransference reactions "are the stuff of which the social worker's daily life is made" (Bowlby, 1962). His job is not to avoid them but to learn how to deal with them, recognizing always that how he and the client treat each other is neither wholly a mere repetition of their pasts nor wholly a coping with the present but is the result of each one's unconscious appraisal of the present in terms of similar past situations. Bowlby asks, "How could it ever be otherwise?"

The notions of countertransference and counterresistance will be discussed in more detail later in this chapter.

RESISTANCE

In the early days of social work, when a client did not respond favorably to the social worker's activity, the case record read:

"Case closed, client uncooperative." Today, when a client does not cooperate, the record may read: "The client's resistances were powerful, his defenses intractable, and his motivation was poor—case closed." The social worker of the 1920s and the social worker of the 1970s both recognized that every client, no matter how much he seeks change and how much he is suffering in the present, also seeks in many ways to preserve the familiar status quo. The child who is suffering the consequences of a school phobia will nonetheless resist going to school for a long time even when much reassurance and support are offered; the married couple who deplore their lack of compatibility and their frequent squabbles may find that the tension in some ways is protective; the family that scapegoats one member may be aware of the deleterious consequences but still covertly demonstrate that the scapegoating preserves some kind of family cohesion; the group that is bitterly divided on virtually every issue may recognize that the divisiveness is counterproductive but still go on fighting; and many a neighborhood and community has recognized the futility of racial and religious bigotry but continues to act out its prejudices.

When the individual enters into a relationship with the social worker, part of him unconsciously works against progress. The child with the school phobia may not wish to feel, face, or discuss the hateful feelings he has toward his parents. Leaving them to go to school may mean to him that he is killing his parents; therefore, just as he stays home to avoid the painful conflict, he will stay away from the social worker by being either absent or very reluctant to talk. The reistance here stems from a fear of his aggressive wishes, which he wants no one, particularly himself, to know about.

Very frequently the idea of a change threatens certain values or superego admonitions. The client may not be receiving much pleasure in life, but each time he considers something pleasurable he feels an unexplainable anxiety.

Mr. and Mrs. Young, a couple in their late twenties, came to the family agency because there was acute tension in their relationship. Although they shared similar values, and many aspects of their marriage were conflict-free, neither could experience sexual enjoyment, and each of the partners blamed the other. As they reviewed their individual histories with the social worker, both Mr. and Mrs. Young reported many instances in their original homes when anything pertaining to sex was hushed up. Sex was seen as a dimension of life that had to be suppressed and repressed, almost as if sexual wishes should not exist in any human being. Mr. and Mrs. Young had therefore made an unconscious pact with each other that sex was to be virtually avoided in their marriage.

When the social worker and the Youngs began to recognize that they were in many ways repeating their childhoods, the Youngs did not quickly jump into the marital bed and enjoy sexual bliss ever after. On the contrary, they experienced the social worker as "a dirty old man" (which was a projection of their own id wishes) and felt he was forcing them to "betray" their parents, their church, and their current and past values. The resistance the Youngs shared was a fear of sexual pleasure. To enjoy sex was experienced as a rebellion against parents, family, extended family, and church. Though parts of each of them wished to rebel, they were afraid of the punishment to follow.

To many people the idea of change, with its connotations of "success" and "achievement," can activate much anxiety, so that they subtly or actively fight the social worker's help. To arrange for one's life to be better often conjures up the thought that one is surpassing parents, family, friends, and colleagues, and may therefore anticipate abandonment. Even clients whose parents are deceased or far away may experience conflict about making lives for themselves better than those of their parents.

The Wayne family was plagued with all kinds of financial difficulties. Each time the social worker attempted to make up a budget with the family members, they all resisted him by not listening or changing the subject. Finally, when the worker explored their resistance with them, after many rationalizations Mr. Wayne said, "Look, I was always poor and I'm used to it. Our life-style is probably much better than the way we had it at home, and I don't want it any different." Mrs. Wayne supported her husband and said, "If my parents knew we had a car and a TV and took vacations, they'd roll over in their graves."

The Waynes were engaged in self-destructive resistance. They wanted to surpass their parents, yet they feared psychological alienation and abandonment. Therefore, they unconsciously arranged to punish themselves for wanting a better life and for a long time resisted the social worker's efforts to help them with their finances.

Resistance to help is always present to some degree in every client. It manifests itself in a variety of ways, and the reasons for its unique expression must eventually be understood by both client and social worker. The client may persistently come late for interviews or absent himself altogether; he may refuse to accept a tangible service, a referral, or a series of interviews; he may refuse to talk or be very reluctant to discuss certain specific issues; he may focus excessively on certain parts of his reality because he is afraid of facing feelings or motives, or he may obsess about certain feelings to avoid facing current realities; he may dwell on the past to avoid the present, or vice versa (Fine, 1971).

An expression of resistance that is sometimes overlooked by social workers is the client's tendency to overvalue the help he gets from the social worker, thus resisting becoming autonomous. Experiencing the social worker as the parent he always wanted, he checks with him every time he has to make a decision. Frequently, the client's helplessness and passivity induce the social worker to take over, thus gratifying and reinforcing the client's excessive dependency so that it appears over and over again in other situations.

Whenever the representatives of a housing project decided to meet with the freeholders, the school principal, or any "significant other," they inevitably checked in with the social worker. Even though the social worker did not modify any of the plans they had agreed upon, the representatives needed to know that "he knows what we're doing." The social worker, enjoying his position, did not realize for some time that he was encouraging the clients' dependency and was also subtly demeaning them. When he finally became aware that he was compounding the clients' resistance to becoming more independent and autonomous, he decided to discuss it with them and learned a great deal about the reasons for their resistive behavior. The members talked about the social worker as being a "powerful white" and experienced themselves as "weak blacks." They idealized the social worker's intelligence, knowledge, and modes of relating.

The resistance was an expression of the self-hate and negative self-images which the clients were maintaining by being too dependent on the social worker. To act on their own meant that they were "as good as the social worker," something they wanted but feared.

Certain, if not all, transference reactions may be considered a form of resistance. The social worker is idealized, scorned, praised, or condemned, and these perceptions of him preserve defenses, diminish anxieties, or keep unrealistic wishes alive. Resistance is anything that works against progress, and most transference reactions serve this function (Fine, 1973).

Sometimes the client appears to accept the social worker's suggestions, clarifications, or interpretations but does not truly believe them. For many clients the relationship with the social worker is reminiscent of a child-parent transaction. Feeling so intimidated by the social worker, they agree with the worker because they anticipate that dissent will lead to some form of condemnation. Therefore, overt compliance of clients often covers up distrust, hostility, and rebelliousness.

In a group of parents meeting with a social worker because they all were participants in child abuse, discussions were held on how children did in fact induce much anger in adults and that this was inevitable. The social worker frequently

pointed out that though parental anger was a universal phenomenon, this did not mean that feelings had to be acted
out. The parents agreed and even gave further reasons to
substantiate the social worker's message. However, after
some weeks of meeting with the social worker, it became
clear that many of the parents were continuing to beat their
children. On the surface, the clients were showing much
compliance, but underneath their cooperative defense
lurked much rebelliousness. It was only when the social
worker dealt with the clients' transference reactions to
him—their anger, their wish to defeat him—with these feelings being verbalized by the clients, that any headway could
be made.

Just as overt acceptance of the social worker's remarks does
not mean internal conviction, so too, overt rejection does not
necessarily mean complete refusal. Many clients feel humiliated
in a dependent relationship and react by being competitive with
the social worker. They try very hard to show themselves and the
social worker that he is not having any effect on them; they try, in
effect, to make and keep the social worker impotent.

A social worker met weekly with a group of Army sergeants
to discuss the emotional and social needs of the men under
them. In the discussions, the sergeants constantly argued
with the social worker; even when the worker agreed with
some of the men's remarks, they had to oppose him. It became quite clear that the notion of helping soldiers threatened
the sergeants, and they very much resented being helped by
the social worker.

Although the social worker began to feel that his work was
having only limited effect, when he visited the sergeants at
their own companies it was clear that they were all to some
extent implementing points that the social worker had
brought out. Away from the social worker, they could act as if
the ideas were their own, not his, and they did not have to
lose face among their peers for being in the demeaning position of cooperating with him.

OTHER RESPONSES TO INTERVENTION

As already mentioned, when the social worker advises, interprets, enacts the role of social broker, or locates a service, the client will respond in his own idiosyncratic way. Because of his ever-present transference and his resistances, he may believe something that is false, reject something that is true, avoid a resource that may help him, or accept a service that may not. Even the most carefully worded and least ambiguous statement is frequently received by the client in some sense other than that intended. The client may react to a clarification, interpretation, or question as though it were criticism, threat, praise, reward, exhortation, or any number of other unintended things. For example, many social workers have noted that clients frequently interpret the shortcut question "Why not?" not as an inquiry about their motives but as a command: "Why don't you go ahead and do it?" (Herma, 1968).

Frequently the client refrains from verbalizing his reactions to seemingly innocuous remarks of the social worker for some time. The writer recalls a client who was making excellent progress until, for no apparent reason, he suddenly stopped coming to the agency. It turned out that the client experienced the social worker's casual statement at the end of the interview, "We have to stop now," as a rejection meaning that the worker did not want to see him ever again.

Silences of the social worker in the interview have been experienced by the client as everything from reassurance that he will not be pressured into discussions for which he is not ready to lack of interest, contemptuous rejection, or outright condemnation (Aull & Strean, 1976).

Thus the social worker is never in the situation of a surgeon operating with sterilized tools; contamination always occurs. The client is frequently, and usually unconsciously, contributing a dimension of meaning beyond the one intended, either to the act of communication or to its content. He perceives the social worker's remarks and activities partially through the lens of his transference and resistances, and this always contains a subjective, non-rational component.

In order to conduct a progressive and productive helping relationship, the social worker must observe, understand, and relate to the client's responses to his interventive acts. The decisive question with regard to the social worker's remarks (clarifications, suggestions, interpretations) or his activities (social brokerage, advocacy, locator of resources) is not whether or not the statement or activity is correct but *how the client reacts to it,* and in turn what the social worker does with the client's reactions (Fine, 1968). Perhaps in the majority of occasions the social worker offers the "correct" interpretation or provides the "correct" resource; yet his words and actions may not bring about the results he strives for if he has not attended sufficiently to how they were received and elaborated on by the client.

During the course of social-work intervention, the client is faced with the possibility of new actions and new ways of looking at things. Before he can choose which solutions to take, he has to have some inner conviction about what is being offered to him. Such a conviction is most firmly held when it is based on thoughts, feelings, and ideas that the client himself has produced. If, for example, he himself has brought out many instances of hating figures of authority, he will be more able to accept the social worker's interpretation that part of his modus vivendi is provoking rejection for his anger. If the client goes on to produce more material from his past and present corroborating both the social worker's ideas and his own prior to the worker's interventions, we can be reasonably confident that he is moving in the right direction. If the client begins to be less provocative on his job and sustains this behavior for a while, we can be surer that progress is taking place.

Of course, the worker must always be alert to the differences between manipulative emotion or action and expressive, assertive emotion or action (Fine, 1968). Manipulation involves an unconscious effort to influence the social worker's responses. Assertion is direct release to enhance the client himself. Anger, for example, can be used defensively to cope with anxiety, and in this case its expression will do nothing for the client. However, when a client has feared the expression of anger, his ability to release it usually connotes that he is becoming less fearful of inner and outer authorities and that true progress is being made.

SELECTIVE LISTENING

There is ample evidence in the literature of social and experimental psychology that people do not listen impartially and objectively; we all perceive selectively (Proshansky, 1970). The issue is by no means trivial when it concerns the client's receptivity to the social worker's remarks. Some clients simply do not listen to what the social worker says; others listen partially; and many gather from the statement whatever they please. The same phenomenon can, of course, be observed among social workers as well. What a social worker records after an interview may reveal glaring discrepancies from what actually occurred in the interview, as a tape recording will later show.

> The Thomas family came to the County Welfare Office several times to discuss with the social worker many familial and environmental problems. As the discussions went on, it became clear to the social worker that unless the Legal Aid Society could petition the landlord to make some necessary changes in the Thomas's house, many of their difficulties would continue. Although the social worker clearly stated a date and time when she would meet with the Thomases to go to the Legal Aid Society, when the day came the Thomases were not available. Although they had faithfully and cooperatively attended all family sessions, and although they seemed to converse easily with the worker and among themselves, the idea of going to Legal Aid turned out to be an emotionally charged notion for them which they did not want to deal with. It later became clear that they had many fears of lawyers, fantasied them as "persecutors," and were

quite convinced that lawyers did not aid clients but punished them.

THE CORRECTIVE EXPERIENCE

Whether the social worker conducts one-to-one interviews exclusively with a client, does family or group interviewing, or spends most of his time locating or providing resources, aggressively intervening in the client's environment, the client will not enjoy the benefits of these activities unless he begins to experience himself differently. Once an individual, a family, or a group becomes a client, acceptance of the worker's services will be influenced by idiosyncratic ego strengths and limitations, values, and subsequent transference reactions and resistances.

Correction of negative self-images takes place when the client is convinced that who he is, what he wants, what he fears, and what gives him pleasure are acceptable to the social worker. The black client begins to feel more self-worth when his hostility, rejection, and distrust of the white social worker are responded to with genuine empathy. The husband and wife who fear sex cannot truly enjoy it until they are convinced that their sexual fantasies and practices are not rejected by the social worker. The family that needs legal assistance will not feel free to seek it until they vent their fears and angers to the social worker. The group cannot cease being divisive until the wishes and fears that propel the divisiveness are ventilated and accepted. The social worker offers a corrective experience to his clients when he demonstrates that such things as anger, sexual drives, wishes to provoke, feelings of inferiority, and power struggles between groups will be understood, not condemned or rejected.

These same guidelines pertain to work in the client's social orbit. Unless the client experiences the worker's advocacy, social brokerage, mediation, or location of resources as something he truly deserves and wants, he will somehow sabotage the intervention plan. He can accept the tangible service and use it to enhance himself only if it emanates from a social-worker–client relationship in which he feels understood, valued, and respected. Only if the client feels genuinely accepted as he is can growth take place and the client usually senses how the worker truly feels toward him.

The Social Worker's Experience and Activity

COUNTERTRANSFERENCE AND COUNTERRESISTANCE

The social worker, like the client, is a human being who is not infallible or omnipotent; therefore his activity too will be unconsciously influenced by feelings, attitudes, biases, and anxieties that reflect the story of his life. This is what is meant by "countertransference" (Freud, 1953). No social worker is exempt from reacting on occasion to his client's productions in a subjective manner. For instance, in the course of his work, the social worker may find himself so sympathetically disposed toward a client that it becomes difficult, if not impossible, to deny inappropriate requests; the worker who overidentifies with the client's plight may offer help that the client does not really need. Occasionally, a client reminds the social worker of an angry parent, a rejecting teacher, or an old girlfriend or boyfriend; interventions may then be colored by fear of the client's hostility, wish for his love, or sexual fantasies toward the client.

The social worker usually finds that he can achieve greater rapport with some clients than with others. The neglected child may appeal to him more than the rejecting spouse, or he may find more kinship with the provocative adolescent than with the law-abiding adult. Frequently a client stirs up in the social worker feelings of identification with him, and the worker may then reject those parts of the client that he dislikes in himself and champion those aspects that he likes in himself.

A social worker in a child-guidance clinic was working with a seven-year-old girl who was quite depressed in reaction to the recent birth of a baby brother. This stirred up in the social worker memories of a similar event in her own life. Overidentifying with the client's situation and feeling enormous hostility toward the girl's parents and brother, the social worker found herself withdrawing in the interviews and feeling depressed herself on occasion. She was unable for some time to help the client ventilate her own anger and fear of retribution.

This vignette is quite representative of many social workers' countertransference reactions. As is true of a client's transference reactions, countertransference is not something to be ignored. The social-work practitioner learns rather early in his career that no one can be strictly impartial, fully aware, and in control of personal biases at all times. However, just as we want to help clients eventually face some of their transference distortions, so too the social worker must confront his feelings toward his clients.

How can a social worker recognize when countertransference reactions might be interfering with client's progress? There are many ways. First, if the client is not making much progress or if his situation is worsening, the social worker should review his activities to ascertain whether there are blind spots or overinvolvement on his part. Second, periodic review of his cases with peers, a supervisor, or a consultant often can reveal resistances that prevent the social worker from relating to certain dimensions of the client's person-situation–constellation. Third, the social worker should always observe his own behavior and feelings as he engages the client-system. Is he himself late for the interviews? Is he too talkative? Does he ask too many questions? Does he prolong interviews? Is he too quiet? Does he shut off anger, love, sex, aggression? Is he bored, tense, or excited?

Countertransference reactions are even more likely to develop in dealing with a client-system involving more than one person. Workers frequently identify with a child against a parent, with one spouse against the other, or with one member of a family against the rest. Nor is it difficult to overidentify with certain subgroups of a neighborhood against others, or with certain individuals against others.

It is sometimes thought that a social worker's preoccupation with the feelings encountered in his relationships with clients amounts to an unhealthy indulgence in introspection and can bring too much self-consciousness into his work, thereby interfering with naturalness and spontaneity. While concern with one's feelings can reach obsessive proportions and be used defensively, if the introspection leads to self-awareness its value in contributing toward being a disciplined professional cannot be denied. It is the capacity to meet the difficulties of others calmly and without undue involvement that frees the worker to respond with empathy, communicate understanding, and extend tangible help (Ferard and Hunnybun, 1962).

ENACTING HELPING ROLES

As was indicated in our previous discussion on adapting Erikson's theoretical orientation to intervention, when the social worker and client have defined the nature and purpose of their relationship, agreeing upon a contract, and when the client's person-situation–configuration has been assessed as well as possible, with the formulation of an intervention plan, then the social worker chooses the role or roles that he will enact. On the basis of the client's maturational needs, the unique nature of his personality and situation, and his transference reactions and resistances, the social worker decides how he will use himself to best enhance the client's functioning. The procedures the worker utilizes— e.g., advice, clarification, locating a resource—are determined by the various roles that he has elected. For example, if the client is struggling with trust-mistrust problems, which will be manifest in his transference reactions and resistances, the social worker will make comments (questions, confrontations, and possibly interpretations) that will encourage the client to verbalize his distrust and anger. When he perceives that these feelings are accepted by the social worker non-defensively and calmly, the client may then be able to take suggestions, direction, and advice from the worker.

The roles that have been chosen by the social worker evolve from an assessment of where the client's personality-situation places him on the maturational psychosocial scale. If the client needs, for example, to develop further autonomy and to learn how to exercise more self-direction, the social worker will frustrate requests for advice and support. Hence, when the overdependent client asks what to do about his marriage, his parent-child relationship, and so on, his question should be returned with a question: "What is your thinking about this?" "You seem to feel so helpless in describing what to do about your marriage, how come?" Frequently the client who is overdependent will react with anger when frustrated, resenting the worker who is trying to help him become more autonomous. As the client verbalizes hostility without censure from the social worker, he begins to feel more like an equal rather than a patronized child. The weaning, the frustration, and the struggle help him gain confidence in himself and in his ability to make his own decisions.

As we have noted, countertransference reactions may interfere with the social worker's ability to take on the role of frustrator and limit a client's demands. Like the parent who has fears about weaning his child, the social worker who overidentifies with the client's plight may enjoy the client's dependence on him. The worker's unconscious objective may be to obtain love rather than to help the client work through his problems. Nagelberg (1959) has suggested that if requests for help are granted directly, the social worker may encourage primitive modes of adaptation to the world and may, by fostering the client's dependence, set himself up as an invaluable figure with powers for ordering and manipulating another's life.

The following case-vignette* describes the enactment of an interventive role-set in some detail. Here we wish to demonstrate the social worker's use of himself and certain procedures in work with an adolescent boy who was in constant power-struggles with virtually all figures of authority. Fearing his own dependency and feeling humiliated by those to whom he ascribed power, the boy adopted as his major defense the attempt to defeat all adults around him—a very common maneuver of teenagers. The vignette also demonstrates the timely location and provision of a social resource.

Joe M., a fourteen-year-old, was referred to a child-guidance clinic by school officials. He had failed several subjects, could not read, was very withdrawn, and participated in virtually no extracurricular activities. His persistent negativism and social isolation were apparent in all of his relationships. He wanted "nothin' from nobody."

Prior to referral to the clinic, Joe had been involved with several social workers, psychologists, and psychiatrists, but was able to defeat all of their efforts. In each instance he withdrew from the helping situation and could not be persuaded to return.

In his first interview with the social worker, Joe said that he hated coming to a clinic or an agency, that nobody had helped in the past, and that "it's useless." The social worker responded with "Then I guess I won't be able to help you either, huh?" Joe said, "You're probably right!"

Asked by the social worker, "What should I do?" Joe answered, "I can tell you're the same as the other guys and I'm not coming." He then was silent for about fifteen minutes. The social worker told Joe that he reminded him of Gandhi, the Indian leader who won many battles by passive resistance, and asked, "Maybe you can teach me some of those techniques." Joe responded that the social worker talked too

*This case illustration is from "The Use of the Patient as Consultant," *New Approaches in Child Guidance,* ed. H. Strean, (Metuchen, N.J.: Scarecrow Press, 1970).

much and that he might consider "for a short time" teaching the worker how to be silent. If the social worker were silent, Joe said, he might consider another visit to the clinic. However, he insisted, "You have to promise to say nothing; I'll be the boss around here."

Several interviews passed uneventfully. Joe, instead of talking or teaching, remained silent. The social worker and client merely looked at each other with no exchange except "Hello" and "Goodbye." In the middle of the sixth session, Joe broke the silence, exclaiming, "I'm quitting; I don't like it. Nothing is happening. You're no better than the other guys." The social worker replied that he must be doing something wrong. He asked Joe where he was erring and what he could do to make coming to the clinic more worthwhile for him.

Joe told the social worker that he no longer wished to demonstrate his techniques of passive resistance. "I'm not getting anything out of it," he remarked. Though the social worker felt that he, the worker, *was* getting something out of it and then wondered aloud what he should do now, Joe merely returned to his silence and doodled with a pen. He devised electrical circuits and fantasied out loud how he would burn down the clinic. He cursed the social worker and the building, yet made it clear that he had some skill in electricity. When the social worker wondered if Joe could teach him something about electricity, Joe got up, walked out of the interview, and stated dryly, "You've got a lot to learn. I'll think about coming back to show you."

Joe did return for two silent sessions, and then, without encouragement, undertook to show the social worker several electrical plans. Electricity became the sole subject of communication for several weeks, with Joe as teacher and the social worker as pupil. However, again Joe's ever-present negativism asserted itself. He told the social worker he was "tired of being the big shot" and that it was about time something was done for him by someone else. The social worker asked Joe what he thought could be done. Joe renewed his hostile barrage and stated that the clinic was the same as school, "plain awful." The only difference was that at the clinic he could dabble in electricity. The social worker then asked

Joe how he would feel if the worker tried to find an electrical
school for him to go to. To this Joe replied, "There is no such
thing; you couldn't do anything about it." Again the worker
asked, "What should I do?" He was advised not to get "so
excited," to do less talking, and to "give with more action."
At this point the social worker began trying actively to locate
an electrical school for Joe.

Although it took weeks to find the appropriate school, Joe
was extremely tolerant of the social worker's slowness. "Take
your time, it's not that important," he frequently remarked.
Eventually Joe entered a vocational school and specialized in
electricity. As he spoke with enthusiasm of his studies and an
occasional relationship he developed at the school, he finally
"confessed" that he was learning how to read quite well.

When Joe had learned how to read and had attained other
academic and social successes, he suggested that his case
be closed. He himself wrote a closing summary in which he
both criticized and praised the social worker, giving a colorful
picture of the client–social-worker encounter.

In examining the interventive process in this case, it should be
recognized that the worker could have used other means in helping the boy resolve some of his resistances to help and his fears of
dependency, and with equal success. Joe needed a certain kind of
attitude from the social worker: He needed to feel that he would
not be controlled or directed, that his resistances and defenses
would be respected, and that he could not easily involve the
social worker in a power struggle. The procedures utilized by the
social worker were designed to communicate the feeling, "I can
tolerate and accept your wish to boss me. I know how painful it is
for you to be bossed. I'll try to show you that one doesn't have to
crumble when confronted with someone in an authoritarian
role." The attitude the social worker reflected helped Joe to be
less afraid of himself and to eventually permit the social worker
to intervene aggressively in his environment in the role of social
broker and advocate.

In the intervention process the social worker may frequently be called upon to serve as a role-model, demonstrating behaviors with which the client can identify and which he can emulate. This is usually necessary in the social worker's responses to conflicted parents, who often need to be shown how a mature parent deals with the demands and angers of a child. The worker's attitude toward the parent who behaves childishly in encounters with him can be later recapitulated by the parent in his relationship with his own child.

The following session of a father's group is presented in full to illuminate this principle:

Mr. King started off the fifth session by asking me in a rather quiet, but semi-hostile and challenging tone if I thought they were "getting anywhere in these group sessions." I wondered aloud what *he* thought and asked him to address this question to the group, as I felt it was a very good question. Mr. King then turned to the group and said he had been coming to every meeting and was "sort of wondering if we were getting anywhere." He had some concern about whether they were or not, and, as he thought it over, felt he hadn't gotten enough solutions for himself to make it worthwhile. After a silence, I asked the other members how they felt about this, and Mr. Wolfe commented, "At least it's a night off from the wife," at which the other members laughed.

Mr. Lewis then commented that he was getting a great deal out of the group and couldn't quite understand how the other members could feel otherwise. After a period of silence, I asked him to elaborate. He said he felt much more confidence in disciplining his daughters and being "more of a father." Mr. Wolfe then commented that perhaps one of the problems in the group was the wide disparity in age among the children of the members. For example, his son, Harvey, was twelve years old and Mr. King's daughter was only eight. At this point I asked Mr. Berg what he felt, and he said his feelings paralleled Mr. King's. He had been coming to many of the meetings and working very hard, but he didn't feel that there were enough solutions to the problems. While regular attendance has helped him some, he said he thought it should have helped him more. He said it was a little too early to evaluate it, but he saw himself struggling and not getting enough results.

Mr. King agreed that it might be too early to evaluate the group and added that he might be expecting more than could be gotten from four sessions. I said to the group that perhaps I was not giving them some things they wanted or was doing some things they didn't want. Mr. Berg said that he was bothered by our tendency to "jump around" too much and felt that I should "control the discussion more." When I asked him to explain, he mentioned that we had discussed allowances, rivalries between their children, conflicts between the generations, and a number of other things. While he got something out of each discussion, he felt that it would be a much better idea to stick to one topic throughout a session.

Mr. Wolfe and then Mr. King agreed that this would be a good idea. Mr. King said, "Maybe it wouldn't be so rough on us if we stuck to one thing." Mr. Lewis suggested that since we were in a position to experiment, "Let's try it." The other members assented. Mr. Lewis added that sticking to one subject might be a little easier than jumping around in view of the fact that group members arrived after a hard day's work. He further commented that if there were more members in the group perhaps they wouldn't have to work so hard.

Mr. King said he liked the idea of a "small informal group," to which Mr. Berg and Mr. Wolfe agreed. Mr. Berg then said, addressing me, that it would be helpful if in addition to sticking to one topic each session I could give them some material first. The other members all voiced approval of this sentiment. When I asked the group what sorts of material they would like me to give them, Mr. Lewis answered that I should provide "some theoretical material as a sort of springboard." The other members agreed, noting that "sometimes it is hard to get started."

It was interesting to me that all the members at this point were affirming and reaffirming each other, and were really saying that they wanted to be given to more by me and to do less work. I repeated to the group at this point what they were asking for (realizing that they wanted more from me)

and asked them if there was anything else they were dissatisfied with. Mr. Berg then said he felt for the most part
that "everything has been going pretty well," but that we
might experiment with these few additions and see where
it got us. Mr. Lewis, Mr. King, and Mr. Wolfe nodded their
heads.

I asked the group to pick a topic and Mr. Lewis then commented, "Children all have peculiarities, such as nail-biting
and thumb-sucking, and perhaps we could discuss these."
Mr. King and Mr. Berg liked this idea. Mr. Berg then asked
me if I could give them some theoretical material about
thumb-sucking and Mr. Lewis and Mr. King seconded this
idea. I asked them what they meant by theoretical material.
Mr. Berg said the causes of thumb-sucking might be a good
subject, and the others nodded assent.

Since I felt that this request was related to the men's own
unconscious needs, I started off by telling them that very
often when we see a child sucking his thumb, in fact he is
communicating that he is not being gratified on some other
level. For example, a child who has had insufficient breast or
bottle might very well suck his thumb; later on the same child
might suck his thumb when disappointed or disgusted. I
amplified this by noting that during times of tension, many
adults turn to smoking cigarettes. Mr. Berg said this made
him think. Mr. King laughed and said, "That really hits
home." Mr. Wolfe said his daughter sucked her thumb a lot
and "It really irritates me quite a bit." Mr. Berg then went on
to say that both his son and daughter sucked their thumbs,
and he realized now that they must be annoyed by something that was happening; his son's thumb-sucking might be
related to the feeling that he was losing his father's approval,
so he sucked his thumb to "gratify himself." He said that if he
had better conversations with his son, perhaps the boy
would not need to suck his thumb so much.

Mr. King then noted that something had happened between
him and his daughter regarding thumb-sucking that he would
like to tell the group about. The child had asked for a dog;
when Mr. King said no, first she pouted and then sucked her
thumb. Mr. King, while puffing on his cigar, expressed a

great deal of annoyance at this, and said at her age his daughter should not be sucking her thumb. Mr. Wolfe commented that she was "probably very angry at you, and if you discussed it further with her she might not have sucked her thumb." Mr. Lewis joined the other members of the group in attacking Mr. King and said, "You're too rough on your daughter, you're expecting too much from her." Mr. King said perhaps he was, but thumb-sucking bothered him when he saw it in his daughter. Mr. Berg said, "Up until tonight it bothered me, too." He said that maybe what bothers parents so much is that somehow thumb-sucking is not "very socially acceptable. . . . I guess it's a question of worrying about keeping up with the Joneses."

Mr. Wolfe commented that it was interesting to note that a child sucking his thumb is like an adult smoking a cigarette. He said his daughter sucked her thumb mainly when he and his wife were out of the house, and that was pretty easy to figure out: "She misses us, so she takes her thumb instead." Mr. King pointed out that this was really a problem of thumb-sucking but that the thumb-sucking showed something else wasn't going right. Mr. Lewis felt that was a good way to look at it, and Mr. Berg and Mr. Wolfe agreed.

I asked for some elaboration on this, and Mr. Lewis said that when he admonishes his younger daughter for something, she often says, "So what?" Mr. Berg reminded us that Mr. Stein (who was absent tonight) had said in the last session that his son, when upset, hid in the bathroom; then Mr. Stein laughed with the other group members at how the struggle came to be over the bathroom. Similarly, Mr. Berg said, the problem is not thumb-sucking, but what the child is basically upset about.

Mr. Lewis and Mr. Wolfe both nodded their heads, but this did not seem to sit too well with Mr. King. He said that at his daughter's age, she should learn to accept limitations. He went on to say how he himself would like to go to Florida, own a Cadillac, and have many other things, but he doesn't feel envious of his neighbors and he can postpone these things to maybe another time or forget about them altogether. Mr. Berg commented that Mr. King failed to realize the difference between a child and an adult. "When a child wants something, he really wants it, and hasn't learned to postpone his wish, but yells right then and there." He went on further to say that it is our job as parents to meet the need if we can, but if we can't, we have a real job to help them to understand why we say no. This is where we fall down and "this is what we need to work on further."

Mr. Wolfe commented that he was just thinking about something similar to thumb-sucking, and that is that very often Harvey, when he goes to bed, takes a piece of cotton and wipes behind his ear, and that is the way he falls asleep. Mr. Lewis said that is like masturbation, to which Mr. King said "that's probably right." Mr. Wolfe then went on to say that he now knows that just as you don't tell a child to take his thumb out of his mouth, because that doesn't do any good (to which Mr. King said he's a real witness to that; it never works), he's got to find out what is going on in Harvey's mind.

Mr. Lewis then commented that his parking meter was up, and the other members of the group realized that we had gone beyond the time limit. Mr. Berg said this was a real good session today, to which Mr. King said it was much better than any before, and Mr. Wolfe said, "I liked it a lot." Mr. Lewis said, "Maybe next time we can talk about helping our children to accept limits." Mr. Berg said if we can get the answer to that, we'll really be well off. Mr. King said that he would like to continue along the same lines as tonight, and discuss this further.

It was interesting that at the end of the session, all four members came over to me individually to shake my hand and tell me it was a good session.

In the group session presented above, the social worker's role is quite clear. Sensing that the group members were feeling angry about being "worked so hard," he first helped them express their anger and dissatisfactions. Enacting his role "in loco parentis," in a quiet, encouraging, and accepting manner he helped his symbolic children discuss their irritations with him and what they wanted from him. Interestingly, the men chose thumb-sucking as the area to be discussed, demonstrating their own hunger and inevitable inability to satisfy their children's dependency needs. After the social worker had "fed" the fathers information, they were able to have a constructive discussion with one another and eventually began to appear more sensitive to their children's needs, thus identifying with the social worker, who was sensitive to the fathers' angers and emotional hunger.

Role Theory and the Intervention Process

ROLE INDUCTION

Social worker and client like any two people in an interpersonal situation, will engage in efforts, frequently subtle, to induce each other to enact the role or roles that each deems necessary to maintain the interpersonal situation (Meerloo and Nelson, 1965).

It would appear that the concepts of transference, countertransference, and resistance can be fused into the single construct: "role induction." Transference can be seen as the client's efforts to induce the social worker to abandon his chosen role of helper, enabler, social broker, and so on, and instead project a role such as parent or sibling; resistance can be viewed as noncompliance with the role the worker prescribes for him. Because the client's efforts at role induction are paralleled by those of the social worker, we may regard as countertransference those efforts of the social worker to persuade the client to enact prescribed roles when he resists them.

ROLE EQUILIBRIUM AND DISEQUILIBRIUM

The interventive decisions the social worker has to make always involve the choice of promoting either equilibrium or disequilibrium in the interaction. During the initial phase of the encounter, when the social worker is attempting to induce the client to move from the applicant role to the client role, some role equilibrium is necessary; otherwise there is the danger that the client may leave the situation prematurely. Consequently, for the action-oriented client, some form of social-worker action would probably be indicated; for the verbal client, some form of verbal interaction would appear to be the procedure of choice.

As we pointed out in Chapter 2, the social worker in the early interviews should first state how he views his own role and how he feels he and the client can work together (Varley, 1968). Then, he should discuss with the client what is expected of him, so that early discomfort and confusion can be avoided.

Certain role prescriptions that the client offers must be frustrated; otherwise he will not learn new and more adaptive roles. For example, to gratify the wishes and obey the role prescriptions of a demanding, self-destructive client is, in effect, to join him in his self-destructiveness. Although this client may enact an explicit role that at first seems logical to the social worker, such as one of consistently asking for advice and guidance, if the social worker acquiesces to this induced role he may further weaken the client's sense of self and autonomy. If the role of the social worker is that of frequent giver, the frustration tolerance of the client will not develop. Instead, he will find it difficult to express disagreement or deal effectively with external reality because his role status as dependent, helpless child is consistently reinforced.

There are certain situations in which the social worker can comply with the client's prescriptions to the client's eventual benefit. Perhaps the client's prescribed roles have never been acknowledged by previous social workers or other significant people in authority, and no amount of persuasion or appeals to logic on their part seems to have dissuaded him from his pleas. Such clients are usually individuals who have suffered a great deal of deprivation—psychological, social, or economic. In many ways they are trying to prove that "no one cares," and the worker's refusal to consider their prescriptions, which frequently appear absurd on the surface, convinces them of this.

Regardless of the method utilized, the social worker seeks to offer clients new experiences designed to enhance their psychosocial functioning. One of his major tools is his own role repertoire as a professional. He gives to those who need giving; he frustrates those who need frustration; he is broker, advocate, leader, follower, expert, or neophyte depending on the dynamic unfolding of the case situation. The social worker attempts to offer a corrective experience by being a new and different role partner who did not exist in the client's previous socialization experiences. The social worker, in sum, enacts those roles that will help his client assume and strengthen those social roles of his own that have to do with his individual growth and development.

Summary

No issue commands more attention in social-work practice than the implementation of the intervention plan. Intervention is action by the practitioner intended to induce change in some parts of the client's person-situation–constellation.

A review of the social-work literature on the intervention process reveals important gaps. Although many procedures and roles have been suggested, few writers have linked their typologies to the assessment and interventive plan, and most have failed to consider sufficiently the dynamics of the social-worker–client relationship, in particular how the client experiences himself and the social worker in the encounter.

Whether interventions are in the client's social orbit or with the client directly, they are always experienced idiosyncratically, on the basis of the client's previous life experiences, personality characteristics, aspirations, and the like. Consequently, a crucial aspect of helping a client-system is always being aware of the client's responses to intervention, adapting one's role or roles accordingly.

The intimate relationship of client and social worker is one in which the client depends on the worker. This invariably activates feelings and ideas about the social worker that the client experienced with those on whom he depended in the past. These transference reactions constantly influence the client's responses to the worker's interventions.

In any therapeutic relationship, part of the client unconsciously works against progress. To many people, change means hurting or displeasing others or violating important values. Resistance to help is always present to some degree in every client. It manifests itself in a variety of ways, and the reasons for its unique expression must eventually be understood by both client and social worker.

The social worker, like the client, is a human being who is fallible; therefore his activity will be unconsciously influenced by feelings, attitudes, and biases that reflect the story of his life. While the worker's concern with his own feelings can reach obsessive proportions and can be used defensively, if the introspection leads to self-awareness its contribution toward his development as a disciplined professional cannot be denied.

Chapter 6

Termination

People who belong together do not have to be glued together.
Theodor Reik
Listening with the Third Ear (1948)

The complex dynamics of termination and separation are generally neglected in the social work literature. Yet they constitute a dimension of the social work encounter that all clients and social workers must inevitably confront.

While ending a relationship can be a joyful and positive experience, more often it is a painful, frightening, sad, and ambivalent affair. Separation can be an anxiety-ridden situation particularly for clients of social workers. Usually one becomes a client because one is having difficulty coping with oneself and one's environment and is under some kind of stress. The need for social-work help in itself, as well as the problems and the processes that produce the need, frequently induces a state of vulnerability and powerful emotions. If the client has found the social worker an empathic ally, separation will not be a matter-of-fact phenomenon but, like any other human loss of importance, can generate a sense of helplessness and grief (Briar and Miller, 1971).

Separation from the client can be discomforting for the social worker as well. He too has had an emotional investment in the process and in the client's life and is not immune to feelings of loss and grief.

It may very well be that the superficial attention paid to this important event stems from the fact that termination conjures up painful associations for both social worker and client—memories of rejection, abandonment, and loss. As Fox, Nelson, and Bolman (1969) have suggested, the gap in the literature is "a reflection of the social worker's defensive processes against the affects involved in termination—a sort of institutionalized repression."

Another possible reason for the professional neglect of the subject of termination and separation, is the fact that unsuccessful intervention is often the reason a case is closed. For example, in a study of family agencies it was reported that one-third of clients seen in a first interview did not return for a second interview, and that fifty percent of all applicants had only one interview or less (Beck, 1962). When a client terminates the social-work encounter prematurely, he often feels some antagonism toward the worker and agency; many social workers might wish to overlook the reasons why the client does not want to have anything further to do with them or their agencies.

Social work is a mobile profession, and social workers frequently leave a job in the midst of an intense social-work process with clients. Facing the end of a relationship with a client while planning bigger and better things may contaminate the social worker's objectivity; he may defend against his guilt and regret by not giving full attention to the client's feelings of hurt and abandonment.

As much as social workers and clients wish to avoid confronting the end of their relationship, the feelings and ideas associated with separation, as with every other issue of importance in the client's life situation, must be expressed, understood, and mastered. If not, some of the gains of intervention may be lost, and the client will not receive the help he needs in confronting future separations in his life.

In this chapter we wish to discuss the dynamics of the separation process from two vantage points: the client's perspective and the social worker's. We will also review the evaluation process that precedes formal termination of the social-worker–client relationship.

The Client's Perspective on Separation

LENGTH OF SERVICE

One of the factors that will influence the client's reactions to separation is the duration of his relationship with the social worker. If the contact between client and social worker is of short duration, involving such specific services as the provision of a home-maker, referral to another agency, summer-camp plans, and the like, the involvement will be relatively superficial and termination will probably not be fraught with too many difficulties. According to some of the proponents of short-term service, clients react well to termination in response to time-limits that are agreed on early in the encounter. Furthermore, it has been observed that when a termination date is set well in advance, clients seem to accelerate their progress (Reid & Epstein, 1972; Reid & Shyne, 1969).

What has not been sufficiently considered by practitioners involved in short-term work is that in these circumstances the client may believe that he does not have the right to express his feelings and thoughts about termination. The conditions of help have been structured by the social worker, very often in the first interview, and the client may feel very uncomfortable about questioning the contract he initially agreed to. In addition, the social worker in short-term work is often task-oriented and may be oblivious to the client's latent feelings of remorse, dejection, and anger.

When the Perry family was seen at intake, Mr. Perry's first question was, "How long will this last?" The social worker replied, "I'd like to know why you ask." Then Mr. Perry, with the other members of the family joining him, reported, "At the last agency they told us in advance that we would need only five interviews, and they gave us some homework to do during each week. We did the homework, they praised us for it, and soon after they told us we should be on our way. We were sore as hell at them, but that was their policy and they did try to help us. None of us thought it would be right to be angry at them and tell them that we had a lot of unsettled problems. We tried to believe at first that things would be OK, but they just weren't. A couple of months ago, they asked to see us to find out how things were. We politely gave them the answer they were looking for. But now we're here!"

If the contract with a client does not take sufficient account of the client's situational presses, psychological needs, wishes, expectations, anxieties, resistances, and so on, the client is likely to muffle his feelings toward the social worker throughout his contact with him and the agency. Consequently, his feelings about separation will be suppressed and repressed as well, and the client, like a frightened, angry, intimidated, but obedient child, will probably tell the social worker only what he wants to hear, refraining from saying anything critical or hostile. Furthermore, if he has not been understood too well, his longing for the encounter will probably not be strong.

Whether a social-worker–client relationship consists of five interviews or a hundred, if the worker has truly related to the client's expectations, perceptions of himself, and transactions with his social orbit, the client will experience the encounter as meaningful and the worker as someone significant; therefore, separation from this "significant other" will inevitably arouse complex and ambivalent feelings. Still, a long-term relationship with a social worker will probably induce more intense emotions at termination than a short-term one. A prolonged relationship has usually stimulated dependency needs and wishes, transference reactions, revelation of secrets, embarrassing moments, exhilaration, sadness, and gladness. The encounter has become part of the client's weekly life, so that ending it can seem like saying goodbye to a valued family member or friend.

Fifteen-year-old Olive had seen the social worker weekly for close to a year, and much progress had been made. Initially a socially isolated and depressed girl who was doing poorly in her academic work, she had begun to date, to feel more pleasure in her life, and to become more successful in her school work. She used her relationship with the social worker to talk about hostile and loving feelings toward her parents and other figures of authority, sexual anxieties, unpleasant memories, and traumatic episodes. In the course of these discussions, Olive felt angry with the social worker at certain times and loving at others. Sometimes she felt very well understood and at other times referred to the social worker as a "ninny."

When Olive began demonstrating less conflict and more autonomy in her day-to-day activities and began to hint that she could "go it alone," the social worker suggested that termination might be considered. After an initial expression of exuberance, Olive declared that her "whole world is caving in." It took many interviews to help Olive express her gratitude for being helped, her rage at termination, and her ambivalence about coping alone. In some interviews there was real despair in her voice and some of her initial problems returned. She talked about the social worker as "the mother and father I've always wanted" and "the best friend I've ever had."

After two months of discussing termination, Olive suggested that the interviews be held every two weeks instead of weekly. Again, the longing for the relationship, although lessened, was still present. It took three more months for Olive to feel comfortable with the idea of being "weaned," and even more work was necessary before she could genuinely welcome being independent.

The feelings that Olive experienced at the idea of termination were expressed quite directly. Often clients communicate their separation-anxiety non-verbally, through lateness, new crises in their lives, reluctance to share material with the social worker, somatic complaints, and unaccountable feelings of depression.

ATTAINMENT OF CLIENT GOALS

We have noted that at some point, usually quite early in the contact, client and social worker set the goals they wish to accomplish. A task force may want to establish a day-care center; a group may set as its goal some piece of social or political action; a family may want to learn how to communicate with less hostility; an individual might want a better job. But does the client always want the social-work encounter to end when the goals have been realized?

One of the reasons that termination and separation are sometimes an unsuccessful experience for clients is that the social worker has failed to differentiate between task accomplishment and the termination of the relationship. Many a client has been able to improve his functioning and accomplish what he and the social worker contracted for, but is nonetheless not ready to leave the agency. If the social worker is too task-oriented, he may be insensitive to the client's desire for a continued relationship with him. We are not implying that the social worker in every case should gratify the client's wishes to prolong the contact. Rather, the social worker has to explore the client's reluctance to leave him.

> A group of tenants met with the social worker over a period of six months with the goal of improving housing conditions and gaining certain rights. They accomplished all of their planned tasks and even a few they had not anticipated. However, when the social worker suggested that the group be disbanded, the members protested. They all felt a commonality of interest and a feeling of kinship, and wanted to continue to see one another and the worker on a regular basis. When the social worker pointed out that the group members all lived near one another and could easily meet, the members protested even more strongly, claiming that they needed and liked the social worker and that he was their "ally" and "mediator."
>
> It took several months of discussion among themselves and with the worker, in which group members worked out their fears of autonomy and "feelings of emptiness," before he could appropariately disengage himself from them.

Just as some social workers have incorrectly utilized the client's goals as the sole basis for determining when termination is indicated, others have not been sufficiently attuned to what the client is seeking for himself. Lack of clarity regarding goals may endlessly prolong the social-work effort; with no goals established, the client can maintain a dependent relationship that is not necessary for him. He feels no clear sense of accomplishment because he has never been sure what he was striving for in the first place. Within this nebulous framework motivation to separate from the social worker and become more self-directing may never develop.

As was suggested in Chapter 2, it is important not only to identify the client's goals from the very inception of the social-work process but also to recognize that they may shift during the process. As the client gets a clearer perception of himself and his situation, he may alter his notions about what he wants for himself. The married couple that initially contracted for divorce-counselling may later wish to try to learn to live with each other (or vice versa); the family that wanted to place a child in an institution may alter its plans and goals; a committee may change its agenda, and an individual may lower or raise his aspirations in one or more areas of living. Whether client-goals shift or persist, the social worker must keep a watchful eye, an open mind, and a receptive ear to the client's expectations of help and change; otherwise, successful termination can never be effected. If the client is not sure why he started and continues a process, he is hardly ever in a good position to discuss its ending.

Premature Termination

Many clients wish to leave the social worker long before the social worker thinks they should do so. This is often a serious problem for the clients and an embarrassment to the practitioner. While no social worker can be all things to all people, better understanding of clients can reduce premature terminations.

If the social worker imposes goals of his own which are at variance with the client's, client dropout will occur. Also, the modality of help offered may be more compatible with the agency's needs and the social worker's predilections than with the client's modus vivendi and psychosocial needs. Thus, long-term help may be imposed on a client and tacitly accepted by him when he would feel more comfortable with just a few interviews; family therapy may be overwhelming for certain families; and a group may not be the medium of choice for certain individuals. Many clients, pleased with the idea that help is being offered and fearful of the power they ascribe to the social worker, apparently acquiesce, but later abandon the social worker prematurely because they have felt misunderstood, over- or understimulated, and, of course, very angry. This is why it is extremely important to study the needs of the client and his situation, his resistances, wishes, and expectations of help, before deciding on the means of help.

Perhaps the most frequent cause of abrupt separation by the client is a social worker's insensitivity to the client's latent transference feelings which go unexpressed in the interviews. Lurking behind the client's overt compliance may be resentment toward the social worker; rejecting and negative responses may cover a wish for love from the social worker; aggressive, sexual, and ambivalent feelings toward the social worker may be deflected or unnoticed by the worker, only to be acted out by the client in the form of premature separation (Fine, 1971).

> A social worker conducting a series of discussions for a PTA noticed that the attendance had been declining from meeting to meeting. Although the parents had initially agreed that the format would be a group discussion with the social worker acting as catalyst, it became clear that the parents resented hearing so much from one another and wanted more direction and advice from the worker; with no opportunity to express their resentment toward the social worker's role, they absented themselves from the meetings.

Many clients resist what might be "good" for them, and this resistance will manifest itself in the relationship with the worker. Before progress can be made the client's feelings must be aired; otherwise he may disappear before the process has begun.

Often a social worker is quite able to sense a client's discomfort with him when the issue is latent distrust or anger, but finds it difficult to help the client feel comfortable with feelings of love and sexual desire toward him. Because so many clients have felt unable to love another person, and a helping relationship with a social worker often unleashes these long-suppressed feelings, the social worker must be extremely sensitive to unexpressed feelings of sexual desire or love; otherwise the client feels scorned and may leave the agency prematurely.

> When Mrs. Jones discussed her marital problems with her (male) social worker, frequently making derogatory remarks

about her husband, she would smile intermittently and appear to be awaiting a response. When none was forthcoming, she would go on discussing her marital woes, but would leave each interview in an agitated state.

After a dozen interviews, Mrs. Jones called the social worker to say that she was quitting. She charged the social worker with being inattentive to her, said he was the same as all men in that he was uncomfortable with her love, and vowed she would never again ask for help from a man.

It must be emphasized that the way for the social worker to have kept Mrs. Jones coming to the agency was *not* to assure her of his love or tell her she was an attractive woman. However, if she could have been helped to see what she wanted from the social worker, to verbalize and understand her wish to have a man respond to her, she might have sustained her relationship with the worker.

It should go without saying that when the client wants to separate prematurely from the social worker, his wishes should never be accepted at face value but should be explored. Some clients threaten to leave to test the social worker. If the social worker and the client together examine how the worker is failing him, the client might be able to express his doubts and discomforts and through discussion feel reassured. The client often experiences the social worker's attempt to understand his dissatisfaction as an act of love. Furthermore, a client who threatens to leave is still in communication with the social worker; part of him, it can be hypothesized, wants to stay in the relationship.

Often a social worker can learn about some of his mistakes when he examines the client's wish to terminate the encounter prematurely. Hidden expectations, resentments, and misunderstandings come to the surface and frequently can be resolved.

A group of physicians met weekly with a social worker in a hospital to discuss some of the emotional and psychological factors involved in physical disease. After a few lively initial discussions, the doctors soon appeared to be bored and uninterested, and expressed the wish to dissolve the seminar. When the social worker asked the group what she was doing wrong, after several evasive replies and intermittent silences the doctors revealed their feeling that the worker was too "authoritarian" and did not respect the doctors' knowledge of and expertise in the psychosocial aspects of disease. They felt demeaned by the social worker and hostile toward her.

When the worker thanked the doctors for their frankness and asked for ideas about how the format of the meetings could be changed, they cooperated, and interest in the meetings was revived.

The social worker who welcomes a client's criticism and advice thus appears less authoritarian to the client and helps him feel more like a respected equal. Feeling like a true participant in a reciprocal process, the client is less apt to sever the relationship prematurely.

INDIVIDUALIZING SEPARATION

In order for it to be a positive experience, separation, like any other human event, must be individualized for each client-system. The few writers who have dealt with the separation process have not linked it to psychosocial assessments and intervention plans but instead have offered statements of a global nature which pertain to only some clients some of the time. Thus Siporin (1975, p. 338) writes:

> In certain termination situations clients, and sometimes social workers, may develop severe emotional reactions of resentment about what is perceived as violated trust; anger about implied abandonment or rejection; hurt or grief over loss and separation. Such feelings may be mutually traumatic for client and worker where there has been much investment of self in the helping relationship and in group relationships, as well as a development of strong, personalized affectional bonds and dependency gratifica-

tions. Mutual ambivalences or resistances may arise, manifested in defensive behavior of denial, repression, and withdrawal. The client may show some degree of regression to justify remaining in the relationship, as a return of low self-esteem or of disabling symptoms. In a group there may be an outbreak of explosive or delinquent behavior. Unrealistic transference or countertransference feelings may recur and add to the difficulties. The social worker may feel guilty about ''deserting'' the client, particularly if he or she is leaving the agency.... On the other hand, the termination experience often is a positive and painless one for both client and social worker.

If the social worker understands the individual client and his situation well, he will be better able to anticipate the probable reactions to termination and govern his own behavior accordingly. It may very well be that the majority of clients terminate on their own without mutual agreement because their feelings and ideas about separation have not been sufficiently linked to their maturational needs and social situations.

Garland, Jones, and Kolodny (1965) have noted a number of reactions which take place in groups in the process of termination:

1. Denial—The members forget that eventual termination is a reality.
2. Regression—The groups return to less mature forms of functioning.
3. Expression of need—The members, through their behavior in the group, demonstrate that the leader's presence is still needed.
4. Flight—May be a destructive reaction to separation in which there is a denial of the positive meaning of the group experience, or it may be a positive experience in which constructive moves are made toward disengaging from the group.

Many of these reactions are found in one-to-one relationships as well (Pincus & Minahan, 1973). Specific reactions of individuals, families, or groups to the termination process will depend on who they are, their situations, and their transferences to the social worker.

Just as the Eriksonian framework (1959) offers clues to the appropriate choice of role for the social worker, so it can also serve as a guide for the worker in the termination and separation process. For example, if clients are coping with crises and conflicts involving "trust vs. mistrust," it is inevitable that the gains derived from the helping process will be both trusted and mistrusted. If the client was manifesting difficulties that made him doubt his ability to manage his own life, separation will probably rekindle the "autonomy vs. self-doubt" conflict.

A group of men in a halfway house for alcoholics demonstrated enormous anxiety about taking initiative. From their histories, ego-functions, and social situations, it appeared that all were individuals who experienced success and assertiveness as highly aggressive and destructive; hence, they felt guilty when they accomplished anything and regressed to self-destructive behavior, expressed and symbolized by their alcoholism.

Although there were, of course, individual differences among the men and their situations, as they discussed their life situations and interacted in the group they all demonstrated the fear that they would hurt others if they let go and succeeded. As the social worker became sensitive to the members' conflicts, she was able to determine that the men feared aggression because they had huge quantities of it that they kept repressed and suppressed.

As the expression of aggressive fantasies and wishes was encouraged by the social worker, the men slowly became surer of themselves and began to take more initiative in their jobs and family lives. However, after much progress had been made and the social worker introduced the idea of termination to the group members, they joined forces in trying to make her feel guilty. "You are doing something cruel!" "How dare you be such a big shot!" and "That's a nasty idea!" were some of the remarks directed at her.

Termination induced in the group members a regression to their problem of "initiative vs. guilt," and their feelings were projected onto the social worker. Recognizing the projection, the social worker subjected her own behavior to the group's examination. As the men discussed *her* "aggression" and *her* "meanness" for a few meetings, they recalled previous discussions of their own anxieties about taking initiative. Slowly, they realized that they were experiencing the prospect of leaving the group and being on their own in the same way that they perceived other independent acts in the past. As one member put it, "If we act on our own and are successful, we are not murdering a soul. We used to think so."

In this situation the members shared a similar conflict and tended to experience discussions around separation in a similar way. It is perhaps more common in a group for different members to experience separation in different ways, because their psychosocial situations vary. This has been observed, for example, in mental hospitals when patients with different life-styles plan to return to their own communities (Lennard & Bernstein, 1969). Each has experienced hospitalization in his own idiosyncratic way, and each will be returning to a different family and community; hence, each patient's responses to leaving the hospital can best be understood by a thorough reappraisal of the original psychosocial assessment and of what has happened since it was made.

THE MODALITY OF INTERVENTION

Reactions to termination will vary depending on the modality that has been utilized. We have already noted that clients' reactions to separation from short-term work are sometimes less intense and complex than their feelings about leaving a long-term relationship. In family therapy, the members are in most instances going to continue living with each other; consequently, family members' reactions to separation are usually focused around how they feel about functioning in the absence of the social worker. In other small groups, however, members have to cope with separating from each other as well as from the worker, and the separation process may be more complicated. With community projects the social worker sometimes expects to deal with the group members again in the future; therefore, "there may not be any termination of relationships, though there is a termination of the specific planned change effort" (Pincus & Minahan, 1973).

Sometimes the relationship with the worker does not terminate but changes, and the clients may need help in moving to this modified relationship with the worker and each other. For example, a task force established initially to see if a day-care center is needed may become its board of directors when it is established.

CHANGE OF CLIENT STATUS

If social-work intervention has been successful, the client should begin to feel more like the social worker's equal. Since here the client's social and/or psychological condition places him more on a peer basis with the worker, the affects associated with termination may be especially intense.

After years as a camper at a facility for emotionally disturbed youngsters, Bill was invited to become a junior counselor. Instead of reacting with pleasure, as the camp staff had anticipated, Bill became very depressed, regressed from his mature behavior, which had been quite consistent, and became quite destructive in his interactions with his peers and figures of authority as well.

Apparently Bill could feel autonomous and like himself only when he felt the protection of parental figures. He resented the change in his status and did not want to be "on the same level" with his counselors. Through his regressive behavior he was fighting the idea of being considered an adult. Not only did he fear competing with the staff, but he experienced the relinquishing of his peer status with the other campers as a real loss. Like many teenagers, he experienced his newly acquired status as a giving up of many pleasures and privileges and anticipated that all kinds of onerous responsibilities would be imposed in their stead.

It took many sessions with the camp social worker to help Bill ventilate his anger, mourn his losses, and clarify his distortions.

Giving up the client status is often associated in the client's mind with entrance into the adult world. None of us completely enjoys being a full-time adult, and therefore the anticipation of no longer being a client is never fully welcomed. Discovering what it is that the client prizes psychologically about being a child will help to explain his reluctance to enter the non-client world.

The Social Worker's Reactions to Termination

As we have pointed out, the social worker is by no means immune to countertransference reactions at the time of termination. If the worker is not aware of his own feelings about termination, he may over- or underidentify with the client, be too supportive or not supportive enough, become too active or too passive, or feel too pressured and thus not be sufficiently directive.

Helen Northen (1969) has focused on some of the reactions a social worker may have when ending a group activity. Her analysis seems applicable to one-to-one and other social-worker–client relationships as well. Facing terminations, Northen has pointed out, stirs up feelings about both the members' and the social worker's roles in the group. It is natural that the worker will feel pleased about the progress of the group and his part in it, and equally natural will be the sense of loss. The termination will also activate feelings about the quality of the worker's performance; for example, he may feel some guilt for not having had the time or the skill to be more helpful to more members. Finally, the worker may have doubts about the nature and the permanence of the gains made, leading to a desire to hang on to the group.

Separation means different things to different social workers, and sometimes many reactions coalesce—loss, anger, depression, a sense of accomplishment, pleasure, etc. Furthermore, each social worker finds that his various clients affect him differently; some will induce a wish to hold on while others will activate a wish to let go. Some will stimulate a sense of failure and others a joyful feeling of mastery and success. For the social worker to effect a positive termination-experience for the client, he has to be sensitive not only to the client's feelings about it but also to his own feelings toward the client. Perhaps most often the social worker harbors mixed feelings which can include joy, a sense of accomplishment, sadness, and guilt for not having helped the client more.

EVALUATION

The termination process has an important assessment component; it is necessary for the social worker to make a comprehensive evaluation of what has transpired during the whole social-work encounter. This evaluation should not be a cumbersome or overwhelming process if, throughout the life of the case, the social worker has periodically checked with the client and with himself to ascertain that the objectives that were initially formulated (and perhaps later modified) were being accomplished. With periodic evaluations, impasses between social worker and client can be assessed and negotiated, unworkable objectives revised, and procedures reformulated in response to client resistances and situational limitations (Siporin, 1975).

Social workers have learned through evaluating the outcome of their efforts that goals have to be specifically formulated and well defined. "Personal happiness," "improved ego functioning," and "restored mental health" are constructs that are much too global in nature (Briar and Miller, 1971). On the other hand, specifying symptomatic changes such as "improved attendance at school," "less marital friction," "better group morale," or "improved community spirit" does not help very much in evaluating how the client is feeling and functioning in his situation. These terms neither describe how the client is experiencing himself and others nor provide information regarding this ego functioning or modifications in his situation.

In evaluating the outcome of social-work intervention, there should be a careful psychosocial reassessment that includes an examination of the client's ego functioning, his transactions with his significant others, and the availability of resources to meet his needs (e.g., housing, food, school, legal aid, etc.). This psychosocial reassessment is necessary at termination whether the client is an individual, a family, a group, or a community.

In evaluating the progress of an individual client a valuable barometer of real change is, of course, his functioning in the social-worker–client encounter. Has the distrustful client become more trusting of the social worker? Is the very dependent client more autonomous? Is the client who could not take initiative in the interviews now more self-directing? Inasmuch as the client's transference reactions are a composite of his strengths and limitations and offer a readily identifiable index of how he sees himself and others, changes in transference usually indicate alterations in the client's coping capacities; i.e., the client will be liking himself better, relating to others with more maturity, and functioning with better judgment, reality testing, and frustration tolerance.

The same variables used in evaluating the readiness of an individual client for termination are applicable to other units of attention. However, in terminating with dyads, families, and groups the social worker looks for shifts in interpersonal patterns among individuals. What has happened, for example, in the power struggle between parent and child, husband and wife, leader and member? Have the anxieties diminished so that there is more empathy and identification between individuals? Are there

realignments and apparent shifts in role relations and responsibilities? Have new roles of authority emerged which can sustain
the changes that have been achieved?

In the evaluation of organizations and communities, it should
be determined whether an organization's attempts to revise pro-
hibitive policies have been successful and whether new services
have been created to combat particular social problems.

Changes in organizations or communities may require
modifications in existing programs, policies, and services. New
tasks and objectives may evolve from the immediate changes
(Goldstein, 1974).

The evaluation process which precedes formal termination is
based on the objectives that have been agreed upon with clients.
The achievement of both process and outcome objectives is always appraised in terms of clearly stated objectives. The social
worker is extremely sensitive to the client's ongoing reactions to
him as well as to his own role in the transaction (Carter, 1971).

INTERVENTIONS AT TERMINATION

The social worker's specific interventions at termination are
not very different from his activities at any other time during the
social-work process. He will plan his activities on the basis of his
assessment of the client and his situation, the client's level of
maturation, and the meaning of termination to the client. If the
prospect of termination has activated feelings of rejection, remorse, and mourning from the client's prior situations, the social
worker needs to encourage him in verbalizing, discharging, and
understanding the meaning he ascribed to these earlier separations. As the client realizes that his own anger and unrealistic
fantasies might have been at work in past relationships and therefore may have caused him to experience separations very personally and punitively, he may come to appreciate how he is distort-
ing his current experience with the social worker. Thus, the
worker can provide learning experiences for the client on the

meaning of separation and loss and how to cope with them (Siporin, 1975).

It is the social worker's job to sensitize first himself and later the client to the mixed feelings that separation inevitably induces. Feelings of anger, depression, joy, exhilaration, and fear not only reflect how the client experiences the social worker but suggest what termination and separation in general mean to him. When distortions are unravelled and the client begins to understand emotionally that "the end" is also the beginning, that life does not stop because a relationship has ended, and that he is not being personally rejected, new perceptions evolve, self-esteem rises, and he can face himself and the world with added strength.

The social worker's role in the termination process is largely governed by how the client is experiencing both termination and the social worker as they talk about it. For the client who distrusts the gains he has made, the social worker offers opportunities to express his feeling that the experience was worthless. As the client does so and finds that the worker does not censure him, he eventually comes to see himself, the worker, and the world a little more clearly. Similarly, if the client, despite the many gains made during the social-work process, fears being autonomous and insists on relying on the social worker, the worker should help him verbalize his demands once again so that he can reflect on his doubts concerning his autonomous capacities. As he does so, the client will recall past interviews, reconsider old distortions, and eventually move on with more self-confidence.

Many social workers fear that at the termination phase the client may regress back to where he was at the beginning of the contract. This seems to take place in all modalities and with all units of attention. If the social worker recognizes the regression as temporary and does not feel that all his work and the client's has gone down the drain, he can help the client discharge his anxious feelings, empathize with his reluctance to be on his own, and help him to understand the unique meaning separation has for him. With this understanding, the client can usually face independence with more certainty.

Summary

The dynamics of termination and separation has generally been neglected in the social-work literature, perhaps because of the professional's defensiveness against the painful affects involved in termination—"a sort of institutionalized repression" (Fox, Nelson, and Bolman, 1969).

To understand the dynamics of the separation process several factors must be taken into consideration: the length of the social-work process, client and social-worker goals, the social-worker–client relationship, the modality of intervention utilized, the psychosocial assessment of the client, the meaning of separation to client and worker, and the client's maturational level. The social worker's specific interventions at termination are not very different from his activities at any other stage of the social-work process and are determined on the basis of how the client experiences separation and termination.

Chapter 7

Research on Social-Work Practice

In our first contact with a set of propositions, we commence by appreciating their importance. . . . We do not attempt, in the strict sense, to prove or disprove anything, unless its importance makes it worthy of that honor.

Alfred North Whitehead
The Aims of Education (1960)

The 1970s in social work have been referred to as "The Age of Accountability" (Briar & Miller, 1971), and the need for research into practice problems by investigators skilled in research methodology and grounded in both theory and practice has been

245

declared several times. If the practice of social work is indeed effective, it is important that this be demonstrated to the profession and the community at large. Yet the problem of measurement in social work is not an easy one to resolve; and practitioners often resist subjecting their work to scrutiny, researchers and practitioners often operate on dissimilar wavelengths and in different languages, and many research projects on social-work practice utilize questionable methodology.

Resistance to Research

In an article on "The Practitioner's Use and Evaluation of Research" (1968), Aaron Rosenblatt concluded that "social workers need to make a long-range commitment to research [and] pay attention to research findings." Although similar cries have been uttered since then it would appear that this counsel has not been heeded to any appreciable extent.

Many practitioners are not entirely clear about what is meant by "research." From the researcher's point of view, social workers often fail to conceptualize their goals and procedures so that outcomes can be measured accurately (Geismar and Charlesworth, 1976). It is virtually axiomatic in research that if one is trying to examine the effect of a given intervention, the goals and procedures must be explicated in advance. This is frequently not done by many practitioners.

To many social workers it seems unrealistic to divert time and staff from their caseloads to prepare records for research. They are likely to believe, instead, that case records themselves provide the pertinent data for research. Yet, Briar (1971) noted that although case recording accounted for one-third of the operating costs in most agencies, the recording did not provide much information for research. "Much of the time spent [on recording] was devoted to the production of material primarily of use to supervisors for non-administrative purposes."

Garfinkel (1970) has described the task of extracting any consistent and useful information from case records as similar to "trying to make a silk purse out of a sow's ear." It is not that records are poorly kept, for the recorders do have a purpose in mind, but it is a different purpose from that of the researchers who come after them. Trouble is inevitable, according to Garfinkel, when the research investigator tries to answer questions which depart theoretically or practically from the organizationally relevant purposes and routines of the record-keepers.

If research is to be part of the social-work process and social work is to be directly accountable to the users of the service, agencies will have to standardize and reorder their recording processes so that goals, intervention plans, and procedures are clearly and specifically described.

According to Geismar and Charlesworth (1976, p.4), interventive procedures

> ... should be subjected to the same vigorous tests determining degree of reliability and validity that are applied to research instruments. There is no reason why these tools should be freed from the necessity of undergoing critical scrutiny. It would seem that the helping professions, challenged as they often are to justify their existence, are reluctant to demonstrate data validity in the fields of practice for fear that this will open the way to additional attack. Unfortunately, this lack of openness militates against the building of knowledge and the improvement of services. If the helping professions sincerely wish to improve and upgrade [intervention] they must insist upon using the best tools, those that have been carefully evaluated and have proved to be most effective.

The Problem of Measurement

One of the most difficult dimensions of research in social work is the problem of measurement. If one is a behaviorist and looks solely at external behaviors, there is little problem. For example, Briar and Miller, behaviorists in social work, have stated that goals and objectives should be "symptom-oriented" and posed in such a manner that the degree to which they are attained can be measured. Thus, they contend,

> ... a youngster who, for whatever reasons, is judged to be a problem because he will not attend school can be thought of as successfully treated when his school attendance becomes reasonably frequent. A child who suffers from enuresis is "cured" when he no longer wets himself. The case of an impotent man can be closed when he experiences erections. An unemployed father is satisfactorily treated when he obtains and holds gainful employment (Briar and Miller, 1971, pp. 168–169).

But for those social workers who view the human being as a complex biological, psychological, and social organism, measurement poses problems. If the social-worker–researcher believes that hopes, dreams, emotions, fantasies, and other internal states are significant, then his research activities must take these phenomena into account.

In order to appraise social-work activity scientifically, particularly the dynamic nature of human change, one must consider the internal environment as an "intervening variable." Some social workers and other professionals, particularly those of a behavioristic orientation, feel very squeamish about such concepts. MacCorquodale and Meehl (1948) have noted that "tough-minded" practitioners tend to use such terms as "unobservable" and "hypothetical" in an essentially derogatory manner and demonstrate "an almost compulsive fear" of passing beyond the directly observable data.

In a sense, once we start dealing with intervening variables, as psychologist Reuben Fine points out, the whole fabric of behaviorism becomes radically altered.

> If we must rely on inference again, why should we eliminate introspective data? Introspection after all leads to another series of inferences, which can then be collated with behavioral data. But then the original argument of behaviorism, that we should only deal with observables, obviously collapses. ... Thus behaviorism, when pushed to its conclusion, ... leads to an inherent logical contradiction. If we confine ourselves to purely objective data, we

cannot explain them. And if we try to explain them we get away from pure objectivity.... The behavioristic position rests upon certain essential misconceptions of scientific theory and scientific method. The crucial role of inner psychological data cannot be denied (Fine, 1960, p. 93).

The difficulty with much research on human beings, and with social-work research in particular, is that it must take full account of introspective data. If one human being asks others a question, the answer will be a variable one, depending on the question, the relationship between questioner and subject, and many other factors. If a person introspects, the nature and meaning of his findings are variable. These two empirical observations of variability, easily subject to confirmation, form the heart of the measurement problem.

Few theories, with the exception of psychoanalytic theory and ego psychology, take the measurement problem into full consideration. As has been demonstrated in previous chapters, these perspectives allow for internal motives and thereby recognize that what a subject tells the experimenter (whether in response to written questionnaires or interviews) depends on the relationship between the two. Unless the motivation of the subject is taken into account in research experiments the observations will be contaminated. The fact that, unlike certain other types of behavior, motives cannot be enumerated does not mean that research should dispense with this important dimension of the human being.

Because so many examinations of social-work practice have failed to take into account the client's internal evaluation of his own transference to the social worker and agency and the relationship between the subject and the investigator (viz, H. Meyer, 1965; Brown, 1968), the results of the research have to be questioned. This does not necessarily mean that social-work activity that was judged ineffective should be declared effective, or vice versa, but pertinent intervening variables that affect outcome (and the client's perception of it) must be considered.

In a recent review of some of the problems and pitfalls in the methods utilized in social-work research, Florence Hollis (1976) contends that some of the disappointing findings on social-work intervention may be attributable to faulty research methodology. Salient parts of Hollis' analysis will be reviewed below, particularly her discussion of experimental and control groups and the inadequacy of measuring instruments.

Experimental and Control Groups

A failure to establish a significant difference between experimental and control groups does not necessarily mean that intervention was ineffective. Weaknesses in the research design or instruments or sampling technique can obscure a difference between the outcomes. Many studies in social work deal in small samples; when experimental and control groups are used, enormous success is required in the experimental group for the experiment to be considered statistically significant. Consequently, positive results that do exist are often not credited.

Generalizing Findings

There has been a tendency to take the disappointing results from well-publicized studies, such as *Girls at Vocational High* (Meyer, 1965) and *The Multiproblem Dilemma* (Brown, 1968), and assume that they apply to social work as a whole. Although the findings of these researches demonstrated that the involuntary adolescent clients in *Girls at Vocational High* and the multiproblem welfare clients studied in *The Multiproblem Dilemma* were not helped appreciably by casework and group-work services, these results clearly cannot be generalized to all social-work intervention. For example, in an examination of thirteen well-designed studies in social work, only four reported no statistically positive findings in support of the major hypotheses or desired objectives (Mullen and Dumpson, 1972).

Inadequate and Inappropriate Measuring Instruments

Questionnaires and other measuring devices developed for studies in other fields are often used in social work, whether or not they are applicable to social-work populations. For instance, an instrument like the Gordon Marketing Scale, which measures overall family functioning, deprecates the family that shops in small, independent grocery stores and assigns higher value to those who shop in supermarkets. Consequently, the modal family in the slums, inclined to shop at independent grocery stores because supermarkets are virtually nonexistent in its neighborhood, is penalized for its shopping habits by the Gordon Scale. Similarly, certain questions in research on child-rearing tend to regard middle-class practices as generally normative. For example, taking a family for a car ride on a Sunday (which is one criterion used to measure family cohesion in several questionnaires) is not a reliable means of measuring the solidarity of the many families that do not own a car.

Many questionnaires used in social work (as in other disciplines) are culturally biased, favoring the predilections and values of the deviser of the questionnaire rather than the psychosocial needs of the client. For example, the reunion of an estranged married couple is given positive weight on questionnaires testing the effects of marital counseling, but it may in fact be indicative of the social worker's failure to help the partners become more autonomous. Similarly, the placement of a child for adoption is considered a change for the worse in some instruments, even though it may in some circumstances be a positive rather than a negative outcome.

Positive Research Results on Social Work

Although there is some research evidence that social work has failed, there is also some evidence that it has succeeded. While the instruments utilized in most outcome research studies leave a lot to be desired, there are data available attesting to the effectiveness of social-work intervention. For example, of thirteen recent, controlled studies of social work with the poor, nine showed positive results (Mullen and Dumpson, 1972).

Follow-up studies of social-work effectiveness based on client evaluations sometimes demonstrate very positive results. In a 1970 national study of family-agency services, 80% of the clients reportedly found the service helpful, 84% were satisfied with their relationship with the social worker, and 70% reported improvement in their status (Beck and Jones, 1973). In a study of child-welfare services, 85% of the clients reported being satisfied with the service and the social worker (Siporin, 1975). And, finally, in research on the treatment by social-work students of hospitalized patients diagnosed as schizophrenic, over thirty of the forty clients studied demonstrated much improvement in their functioning (Strean, 1976).

Carter (1971) has emphasized that there are important political aspects involved in social-work research, and these have influenced the choice of objectives studied. One example of a questionable objective is reducing the number of clients on public welfare; a better goal might be studying the social services for clients who need to stay on public welfare. As Siporin (1975) has pointed out, the research findings on social-service programs have been used for political purposes—for example, to blame the profession of social work for the "welfare mess" and shunt professional social workers out of administrative and service positions in federal and state welfare agencies. The result is an insidious attack on the poor and other deprived individuals who have been aggressively represented by social work.

As Tropp (1974) has argued:

> All that can be asked for in effectiveness in any human-service profession is that a person perform well enough to meet reasonable expectations, with the best available knowledge and skill, under given circumstances. . . . If a social worker can help a significant

number of people cope more successfully with conditions, then that social worker has been both accountable and effective.

Utilizing Social-Work Skills in Social-Work Research

As we noted in Chapter 2, one of the procedures in social work that has proved to be of enormous value in gathering information from people is the helping interview. In order to appraise what has happened to a client as a result of social-work intervention, it would appear that there is no better way than to interview him, studying with him his reactions to the interviewer as well as to the social worker who helped him and examining with him in detail changes in his circumstances, internal and external. Then the evidence of change, for better or worse, can be trusted with some confidence. Fine (1971) concluded, in a review of the available psychotherapeutic research, that "the only effective method of evaluating the results is a clinical one" and that at the present time "no available statistical technique can provide a substitute for clinical judgment. Even the American Psychoanalytic Association, which organized a gigantic fact-finding undertaking, pursuing a routine statistical course with diagnoses, outcomes, and so on, was faced with the meaninglessness of its results."

It would appear that follow-up interviews with clients by a second social worker, attuned to and knowledgeable about psychosocial functioning, interpersonal and intrapsychic dynamics, and transference and resistance phenomena, can produce valuable research results. This procedure, tried in and out of social work (Hollis, 1976; Pfeffer, 1959; Weissman and Paykel, 1974), appears to elicit the necessary information for adequate evaluation of the results of intervention.

While research can fill in many gaps in our knowledge and point to many unanswered questions, there are already sufficient data available (Hollis, 1972, 1976; Mullen and Dumpson, 1972;

Siporin, 1975) to state with confidence that social-work intervention based on thorough psychosocial assessments and intervention planning that objectively relates to the clients' history, maturational conflicts, and internal and external dynamics in interaction and transaction, and takes into account transference, resistance, and the other salient phenomena presented herein can be
quite effective.

Summary

Research on social-work practice has reported good, bad, and
mediocre results. It has often been based on questionable
methodology, such as inappropriate measuring instruments,
faulty use of experimental and control groups, and generalized
conclusions from limited samples.

In order for social-work research to be effective it is necessary
to take into full consideration introspecitve data and the interaction of the person being investigated with the investigator, because they always affect findings. Follow-up interviews conducted by a second social worker may be a source of valuable
research data.

Epilogue: The Growth of the Social Worker and the Growth of Social Work

> *When organizations are not meeting the challenge of change, it is as a rule not because they can't solve their problems but because they won't see their problems; not because they don't know their faults but because they rationalize them as virtues or necessities.*
>
> John Gardner
> *The Creation of Settings and the Future Societies* (1972)

Throughout this book we have emphasized that while the main actor in the attempt to maximize the client's functioning is the client himself, the social worker is a crucial participant. Just as we assess clients by focusing on their transactions with their environments, in any examination of the maturing professional

255

consideration must be given to his transactions with his working and learning environment.

In this chapter we will consider some of the psychosocial dynamics involved in the growth of the practitioner, relating this process of professional maturation to some of the practices and problems in schools of social work, social agencies, and the profession as a whole.

The Growth of the Social Worker

Perhaps more than any other helping profession, social work requires "thinking, feeling, and doing" (Bartlett, 1970). The social worker must be expert in many of the interacting social, psychological, economic, political, physical, and biological variables that comprise the person-situation–constellation. To intervene effectively in the complex life of diverse clientele also requires a great deal of intellectual competence, social conviction, and personality integration. Social workers deal with the most disturbed of the population—the mentally ill, the criminal, the poor, the "hard to reach," and the unmotivated. The most problematic family situations, the most pressing interpersonal situations, and the most chaotic community and urban problems are part of their professional domain. Consequently, their helping repertoire must be wide and rich, and they themselves must be especially flexible and creative in structuring helping relationships.

As the social worker contributes to the growth of other human beings it is inevitable that he will also experience both personal and professional growth within himself. As Harry Stack Sullivan (1961) noted, both social workers and clients are "more human than otherwise." As the social worker participates in a dynamic helping relationship, he not only assists his client to discover and clarify aspects of self and environment but, because he is more similar to the client than otherwise, he embarks on a human and interpersonal journey that is one of self-discovery for him as well.

Many students and young practitioners become disturbed upon finding parallels between some of their clients' ways of functioning and their own. Rather than recognize their essential similarity to their clients, they attempt to deny it. This can only lead to anxiety in the interviews, lack of spontaneity, smugness and a false professional air at times, and, most important, an inability to feel with, think about, and act professionally in the client's behalf.

Merkle and Little (1967) have reported on a phenomenon they term "the beginning psychiatry training syndrome", a set of reactions that appear in the psychiatrist when he first goes into practice, which has much appliability to social-work training as well. Many signs of anxiety, including neurotic symptoms and psychosomatic complaints, become manifest in the young psychiatrist's day-to-day professional functioning. Sometimes he finds it difficult to continue his professional work and enters into a therapeutic situation of his own.

Merkle and Little report that the majority of psychiatric residents suffer a syndrome of this kind to greater or lesser degree. Similarly, many social-work students feel considerable anxiety as they move into the helping process and have direct involvement with clients for the first time. Furthermore, Merkle and Little report that psychiatrists who do *not* report anxiety reactions turn out to be the worst therapists; similarly, social-work supervisors and educators have noted that students who move into the helping situation without some shaking up of their equilibrium usually do not turn into competent practitioners.

The helping situation in social-work requires a disciplined use of the self that no previous interpersonal situation demanded of the social worker. In past interpersonal encounters, he could stop listening if he was so inclined; now, he must keep a watchful eye and "listen with the third ear" (Reik, 1948). Earlier, if individuals angered, saddened, or stimulated him, he could give spontaneous vent to his feelings; now, he must use his feelings in a professional manner and verbalize only what is helpful for the client. In the past, if an individual asked a favor of him, he could take on the task or reject it; now, he must explore and act in ways which he may find frustrating, inasmuch as he is not expressing his usual and characteristic responses.

Some anxiety seems to be a normal aspect of the attainment of competence as a social worker. When it is taken with the recognition that it not only is due to a shake-up of the worker's usual ways of behaving but also reflects identification with his clients and their problems, he is manifesting the first genuine signs of professional maturity. If the social worker does not take his anxiety seriously, wards it off by projecting it onto others, or uses some other defensive maneuver, he will remain an "over-defensive technician" (Fine, 1971) who will do his clients little good.

When the prospective social worker can accept the fact that he, too, could be on the other side of the desk as a client, he has come a long way. In most cultures the idea of being helped usually provokes hostility, sarcasm, and derision in many people, particularly in those who receive help. When the social worker can truly incorporate the notion that participating as recipient in a helping process not only connotes having human problems but also reflects a mature desire to understand and master self and environment and actively solve problems, cultural defenses against help like laughter and sarcasm are dissolved. The social worker is then freer to listen, empathize, and intervene professionally.

It has repeatedly been demonstrated in case conferences, consultations, and supervision that very few social workers can get their clients beyond the point of their own maturational development (Reik, 1948; Fine, 1971). If the worker has a bias against or in favor of a particular ethnic or socio-economic group, this prejudice will be subtly conveyed to those he is trying to help (Hollis, 1972). If he is anxious about his own sexual or aggressive thoughts or fantasies, this anxiety will block his clients' communications to him, and vice versa. If he is uncomfortable in certain social situations, this discomfort will be transmitted to the client (Hamilton, 1951). It is crucial for one who wishes to help people with unresolved interpersonal difficulties to attempt to resolve his own irrational hatreds, excessive preoccupations, ambivalent feelings toward authority, and blind spots.

As Finch (1976) has pointed out: "Conflict experienced by a worker may be caused in part by personal concerns stemming from the difficulty workers often have addressing client problems they have not solved for themselves." As the social worker feels less anxious and more comfortable about the variety of problems that confront him, he can usually make a substantial contribution to communities, groups, families, and individuals. For example, social worker August Aichorn made an extremely valuable contribution to the treatment of juvenile delinquents after overcoming his fear of their aggression (Aichorn, 1935); similarly, Selma Fraiberg (Pharis, 1976), a pioneer in social work with children, was able to feel much more compassion with her clients when she resolved some of her own childhood conflicts.

While there is probably no better way for a social worker to resolve his personal limitations, enrich his helping repertoire of skills, and truly empathize with clients than by undergoing some form of therapy himself, psychoanalysis or psychotherapy is not the only learning experience that can increase self-awareness and the capacity for empathy. These important attributes may evolve, to some extent, from real-life experiences, ongoing self-scrutiny, peer supervision, and regular seminars, case conferences, and the like (Leader, 1971).

No matter how great the social worker's technical skill, only the consistent understanding of himself provides a secure foundation for satisfactory results with clients (Fine, 1971). There is scarcely any field in which the personality of the helper is impressed on the interventive procedures so strongly as in social-work practice.

Professional growth involves not only the emotional maturation of the social worker; he must continue to deepen his understanding of people and refine the skills required to help the diverse clientele that daily confronts him. This necessitates ongoing supervision in his agency, case conferences, consultation with peers, and staff meetings. A social worker cannot be expected to be completely autonomous when he graduates from a bachelor's or master's program. The development of truly effective helping skills takes a minimum of three years of daily professional activity beyond a professional degree in social work, with constant supervision, consultation, and the like. In addition, most schools of social work have programs of continuing education in pertinent aspects of practice, and social-work practitioners should avail themselves of these. Frequently, local chapters of the National Association of Social Workers sponsor institutes designed to help practitioners master some aspect of practice with more facility and skill.

The Growth of the Profession

Client growth and social-worker growth are dependent to a large extent on the institutional arrangements that exist in social-work agencies and schools. What the profession sets as its priorities, what work-incentives it provides, the kind of staff hierarchical structures that exist, and the relationship between schools of social work and agencies will in many ways affect how both social workers and clients function personally and professionally. We will consider in this section several vexing issues relating to such institutional arrangements that seriously hamper the emergence of social work as a socially conscious helping profession.

THE FLIGHT FROM THE CLIENT

Although it is not their manifest intent, public and private social-work agencies tend to organize their professional personnel in such a way that the psychosocial needs of clients are not their paramount concern. As a practitioner gains skill, he is often rewarded by being removed from practice and promoted to a supervisory or administrative position. Thus the practitioner is frequently motivated to deepen his skills and expand his role repertoire by the paradoxical promise that he will be rewarded by being given responsibilities away from practice. If the practitioner is considered mediocre by his supervisors, he is frequently "relegated" to the position of working exclusively with clients—supposedly the major focus of social work! In this way, social agencies are saying to their staff members almost explicitly: "Learn how to work well with your clients! If you do, we'll reward you by diminishing the importance of practice for you!" Rare is the social agency which declares that expertise in practice is worth more in money and professional status than supervisory and administrative responsibilities.

One of the latent functions of the modal social-work agency's organizational structure is to perpetuate a system that makes the assumption of supervisory responsibilities a goal to be sought. If a social worker wishes to remain within the established system and ascend the hierarchy of status and income he *must* move away from clients. To maintain a strong interest in practice and direct participation with clients yet at the same time achieve monetary gain usually requires leaving the established system and becoming an "entrepreneur"—i.e., a private practitioner. This move, however, often results in his being shunned by many colleagues, frequently forcing him to form his own study groups and join organizations only peripheral to the mainstream of social work's endeavors. It is quite clear that one of the difficulties private practice can pose is "the possible crisis of professional isolation" (*Handbook on the Private Practice of Social Work*, 1974).

In an article, "Private Practice Is Alive and Well," Levin (1976) stated:

> One of the most seriously damaging deficiencies of the social-work profession is its failure to devise a system of career opportunities with an appropriate reward system that would provide incentive to the young and not-so-young social work practitioner to spend a lifetime in practice. Not only has this failure damaged

social work as a profession, but it has further deprived the host of consumers of social work services who, for the most part, are already disadvantaged.

While private practice "allows upward progress on a career ladder without blurring the identity of the social worker as practitioner" (Levin, 1976), it does not really solve the problems we are addressing. There are many clients of social work who cannot afford to pay private practitioners and never will be able to do so. As Kurzman (1976) has recently stressed, social work has

> ... a responsibility to serve not only those who can afford to pay, but those who cannot; to help not only those who seek services, but those who need protective care and are in a relatively poor position either to request or to pay for such services.

Because social workers will continue to operate mainly as institutional employees, they will have to face the problem of developing their professional practice within agency systems that have tended to demean the practitioner and ascribe enormous status to the supervisor and administrator. Most social agencies tacitly affirm that those who serve clients directly are the least important and most expendable of their staff. It is probably one of the reasons turnover is greater among practitioners than among other professional categories within social work.

If social work unreservedly valued enhancement of the psychosocial functioning of individuals, families, groups, and communities, it would serve its clientele with its best manpower available, and accord those on the direct-service firing line the most prestige, status, and income. Social work would do well to emulate baseball and other professional sports where the practitioner is on the vertex of the hierarchical pyramid. Although without much authority, as he deepens his skills and expands his role repertoire as a player, he makes more money, has more status, and is less expendable than a coach or a manager.

Is not the practitioner demeaned, derogated, and confused when he is told, in effect, "If you are doing a good job, we'll remove you to the periphery of the game. If you are not doing a good job, we'll keep you in the game''? How valuable is participation in the game for the practitioner when he is penalized for remaining in it? How valuable is practice to the profession when it maintains this organizational dysfunction? Until the profession recognizes the abdication from social-work values that is implied in the hierarchical arrangements in most agencies, delivery of services will not be at the optimum level and social-work practitioners within an agency setting will not mature professionally.

DEVALUING CLIENTS' NEEDS

The nature of the status hierarchy in social work is such that it can foster an inhumane orientation to the recipients of social service. Where the psychosocial needs are greatest among clients, where caseloads are largest, is where the least trained manpower appears.

Social work, which theoretically aligns itself with human needs and attempts to meet them on an individual, group, and community basis, places its best manpower where the need is least severe and the ratio of clients to worker correspondingly low; concomitantly, where the need is greatest, the ratio of clients to worker is very high, and the modal social worker is an inexperienced practitioner. For example, the client on welfare is typically assigned to a social worker with very little training and experience, and is seen once every three to six weeks, often to work on only superficial problems, while the client in an affluent middle-class community with less severe problems than those of the welfare client might very well receive one-to-one weekly treatment, family therapy, or group treatment for a long period of time.

Although American social work has rediscovered poverty at least three times in the past fifty years (Kahn, 1973), it is still true today that in terms of social-work service most welfare clients are getting charity doles while middle-class clients frequently receive what welfare clients very much need—intensive individualized service. Only two percent of the personnel within the public-welfare system have Master's degrees.

In contrast to medicine, which takes the position that the patient who is most severely ill should have the most expert help available, social-work manpower is so organized that those who need the most extensive and intensive help—such as the poverty-stricken, the victims of racism, the mentally ill, the retarded—are serviced by some of our least trained and experienced personnel. Social workers would be quite critical of their medical counterparts if cancer-ridden and other seriously ill patients were treated by interns.

If a profession's method of distributing its most trained and skilled manpower is a valid index of where its priorities lie, it must be concluded that in social work poverty, racism, crime, mental retardation, and many other crucial social problems are not considered serious priorities to be faced by the profession.

DYSFUNCTIONS WITHIN SCHOOLS OF SOCIAL WORK

The status hierarchy in most schools of social work mirrors that in most agencies, whereby the educator who usually has the best practice skills is at the bottom rung of the status ladder. The field-work instructor, who is closest to practice and therefore to what are, at least theoretically, the student's paramount interests, is rarely a full professor with a high salary. Rather, educators, like practitioners, are rewarded by being moved away from direct service if they perform well in it. The field-work instructor is rewarded by being given a classroom assignment and, of necessity, moves into more theoretical matters. The classroom instructor, if he masters social-work theory well, is often rewarded by being made a sequence chairman or dean. Schools of social work, like agencies, do not as a rule dignify those concerned with practice.

By and large, there are two sizeable groups of faculty members whose qualifications to teach practice skills are extremely dubious; the "old-timers" and the newcomers. The old-timers are people who may have been excellent practitioners in their day but often have not seen a client in five, ten, or even twenty years. Yet these individuals, who are very removed emotionally from the anguish, anxiety, ambivalence, problems, and hopes of real people, have become conceptualizers and theoreticians. These faculty members may be likened to a heart surgeon in a medical school who spins beautiful theories but has not felt or seen a heart in years.

If the older faculty member is not a conceptualizer removed from practice, he often is a teacher using practice models popular when he was a practitioner but much less pertinent for current students. It is very difficult to teach crisis intervention, family treatment, short-term work, task-oriented work, or the generalist approach when one has not used these models in practice. If the faculty member does not practice what he preaches, the student senses the emotional detachment of his mentor in the classroom, and teaching and learning are hindered.

The newcomer to social-work faculties also brings obstacles to the teaching-learning process. He typically has graduated from an M.S.W. program and moved right into doctoral work. Most doctoral programs, however, do not value direct practice but champion theory exclusively, and therefore the D.S.W. who teaches in a school of social work has had very limited opportunity to interact with clients; yet, it is he who teaches students the basic social-work skills.

Florence Hollis has commented,

> ... younger practitioners are undertaking doctoral work after only a few years of experience and then going directly from their studies into teaching posts. It is undeniable that, as content has expanded, doctoral work has become more and more essential in the preparation of faculty members. These new instructors are often better prepared than their predecessors in their knowledge of the literature, ... their sophistication about research, and the breadth of their familiarity with modern social and behavioral

science. This in itself is good; but if the art [of practice] is to be passed on in schools of social work, course content must be the product of seasoned, first-hand practice; if new ideas are to be adequately screened for their usefulness, teachers must find ways to continue to engage in... practice. In other disciplines the teacher does not give up the practice of his profession.... [We have here] an administrative problem, but one that can be solved if faculty members and deans become convinced of its importance (Hollis, 1972, pp. 353–354).

If classroom teachers in schools of social work are not engaged in some form of practice, they provide a poor counterpart to the student's field-work instructor, who is most of the time actively engaged in work with clients. Theory and practice do not become an integrated experience for the student if class and field are not complementary and if, as many students complain, "The classroom content is irrelevant!"

If part of a social-work–method teacher's work-week involved practice, not only would he become a better and more relevant teacher but there would be other gains as well, for the students, for education, for the profession, and for the teacher himself. By entering the social agency and working with clients, the classroom teacher would be confronted with practitioners, and dialogue would inevitably ensue. This dialogue could reduce many of the strains and gaps between the academy and practice (Schacter, 1969; Strean, 1976). The academician would need from the practitioner some input in the area of new practice models, interventive procedures, and practice trends. The practitioner, feeling less threatened by someone to whom he has given, would be able to rely with more comfort on his colleague for theoretical underpinnings, conceptualizations, and research advice. The student would then be in a position of experiencing his two mentors and role-models as working together in his behalf; most important, the content that the student would be exposed to would have elements of both practice and theory. Selma Fraiberg (1962) has gone so far as to say that in order to close the gap between practice and professional education, we must make it possible for all teachers in schools of social work to spend at least a third of their time in practice. In the case of the teachers especially, this should be direct work with the clients in a social agency or clinic.

CURRICULAR PROBLEMS IN SCHOOLS OF SOCIAL WORK

The flight from the client has had several adverse effects on the curricula of schools of social work during the 1970s. As practice has become less and less a preferred activity in many social agencies, more and more M.S.W.'s have moved into supervision and administration right after graduation from school. Schools of social work have made an accommodation to this trend by emphasizing programs and courses in administration and supervision. More and more agencies and schools of social work are, in effect, demeaning practice by propounding the notion that increments of education and experience are a guarantee to the social worker that he will be removed from clients. As time marches on, the modal practitioner seems to be a B.S.W. who is supervised by an M.S.W. with limited practice experience; both have been educated by a D.S.W. who has worked with clients for only a short while or who has not seen a client in years!

Although contemporary social problems and policies are part of today's curriculum in schools of social work, discussions of racism, poverty, social security, income maintenance, and so on have a tendency to remain abstract and insufficiently relevant to the student because they are frequently taught by faculty members who are not grappling with these problems in daily practice. If a student is to become more sensitive and astute in relating to social problems, these problems must be viewed within the context of field-work experience where he can observe their effects on real people. Furthermore, as he discusses and conceptualizes his experiences in the classroom, he needs a professor who is not a theorist and conceptualizer alone, but who has also confronted these problems in practice.

Grinding poverty, discrimination, poor housing, the population explosion, pollution, and other acute social problems have induced professionals, particularly social-work scholars, to widen their conceptualizations of the person-situation–constellation. Findings from sociology, anthropology, and social psychology have helped many students, practitioners, and practice theorists in locating some of the salient social factors which impede sound psychosocial functioning. The knowledge-explosion has certainly entered our schools of social work, and today's student is exposed to role theory, systems theory, organizational theory, learning theory, and communication theory, to name but a few social-science orientations now in the curricula.

One of the pitfalls in applying social-science material is that social work may be surrounding itself with a flock of theoretical orientations of possible interest in themselves but having limited applicability to social-work intervention. Although sufficient empirical proof is lacking, one may at least question whether the new social-science conceptualizations truly enhance practice so that the social-work student is both eager and knowledgeable in intervening in social problems. A reasonable hypothesis to investigate would be whether or not these newer conceptualizations have a suble tendency to dehumanize the client. Are today's students really appreciating that there are unique individuals in "the client-system"? Appreciation of the fact that the client is part of a socio-economic class, a role carrier, a unit in a system, almost always enriches psychosocial understanding of the person-in-his-situation and helps interventive planning; however, he is also an individual who is frequently in stress, suffering, feeling anxiety, defending himself from feeling just what is really happening to and in him, and needing a helping human relationship. The newer social-science conceptualizations must not blur our understanding of and ability to relate to a unique individual in a unique situation. As Professor Hyman Grossbard (1976) has observed: "We in the field of social work, because of our wide multidisciplined base, are particularly vulnerable. In many quarters our traditional commitment to problem solving is whittled down from the person with a problem to the problem. We pigeonhole people into roles and tasks, and lose sight of the unifying genetic and experiential base and the dynamic interaction of its parts."

THE PRACTITIONER AND SOCIAL ACTION

Becoming socialized to the social-work profession is a difficult task for any student or practitioner. Usually the individual who enters the field is one with a strong social conscience and much eagerness to help people, but he soon recognizes that his love, spontaneity, and idealism must be tempered with discipline, skill, and restraint. His lofty ambitions about achieving a more humane society with better-functioning and happier human beings are often frustrated as he recognizes that social, interpersonal, and individual change is a very slow process. As Wilensky and Lebeaux (1965) have stated, in referring to the social-work student,

> ... he comes to school, as cursory examination of applications will show, imbued with a desire to help people; and from the school he wants training in the techniques of help. To his distress, however, he soon finds out that clinical (phenomena are) expressed in ways quite alien from those suggested by the ... impulse to help. The humanitarian in him would bind the client's wound directly; the professional clinician, he is taught, explores the wound.... The humanitarian takes people at face value; the clinician is sure that faces are but masks for deeper drives that must be probed. The humanitarian, feeling that all men are brothers, offers friendship to those he succors; the clinician knows he must maintain social distance from those he would help.... The ambivalence of the professional social worker toward participating in social action on the local scene suggests that those who do go on

into practice seldom resolve the professional versus humanitarian conflict completely (p. 322).

It is not only because the student or practitioner is conflicted between his "humanitarian" and "professional" impulses that he does not participate in social action or social reform; actually, a good professional can and should be a real humanitarian concerned with people and ready to help them. Students and many practitioners become so involved in the taxing process of developing a professional self—utilizing appropriate interventive procedures, drawing up workable interventive plans, making difficult assessments, working with resistance, transference, and countertransference problems—that they can easily become oblivious to where their profession is going, what the restraints and constraints on themselves and their clients are, and whether the social-work profession's priorities are being addressed. Although social work started as a profession very much aligned with social reform and social action, professional development and the size of bureaucracies in and around social-work practice have diminished the importance and prospects of social action and reform in the minds of many practitioners.

If the social worker truly relates to the person-in-his-situation, he cannot fail to recognize "the flight from the client" in social work, the retreat from priorities, the constant demeaning of practice, and other pertinent organizational problems which affect clients and social workers deleteriously. Particularly in the past decade, an extremely serious problem has been developing within the social-work profession: those who work directly with individuals, families, and groups have been in one ideological and political camp, while those who are interested in social policy, social action, and social reform have been in another. However, if those who shape policy are not sensitive to the concerns of people, policies will be unrelated to human concerns. If practitioners overlook societal problems, professional values, and the human problems induced by the contexts of social agencies, they will operate in a vacuum and be nothing more than technicians.

Indeed, as Alfred Kahn (1973) has averred, "Practice enacts policy." He has pointed out that what the practitioner does, how he relates to clients, how he exercises discretion, the priorities he places upon his time, and the details of his role-structuring are all ways of setting the direction and atmosphere of programs. "The practitioner sets, modifies or negates policy in his every action. He often settles what programs mean and do to and for people."

If social work is to be a truly humanistic profession, then all social workers must be experts in the basic social-work skills that have been addressed in this text. Whether one spends most of one's time in policy formulation or in work directly with clients, one must understand and relate to human beings *and* social structures.

> One cannot successfully solve problems of interrelationships without a sound economic and political structure, but it is also true that one cannot solve—and this is less easily granted—economic and social problems without a profound understanding of human behavior. . . . There are those who urge social workers to become community organizers and administrators, but do not yet realize that an adequate concept of personality and behavior is as essential to sound legislation, to programs, to institutions, and to administration as it is to treatment (Hamilton, 1952, pp. 317–21).

Social workers must never lose sight of the social and psychological dynamics of a case and must never be oblivious to the community structure and other social and political variables that have helped create it (Wilensky and Lebeaux, 1965). In the "generalist" orientation to social work, all social-work students should be trained to be enablers in individual, group, and community problems, with skills and knowledge "in institutional and policy intervention, planning-policy input and social provision, as circumstances may warrant" (Kahn, 1973).

If social work is to mature as a profession, social workers in education, practice, policy formation, and elsewhere must resolve to place the client's needs in the forefront. Through interagency teamwork, collaboration between the academy and practice, and active N.A.S.W. organizations, they will be more able to agree on priorities and their means of implementation. Briar, in a recent edition of *Social Work,* (1974) concluded that "current trends are not entirely bright." Another pessimistic note was sounded by Specht (1972), who pointed out that professionalism in social work is being undermined by four ideological currents: activism, anti-individualism, communalism, and environmentalism. Because of these currents, he claimed "the social-work profession is undergoing fundamental change and may even be approaching its denouement." On the other hand, Skidmore and Thackeray (1976) contend that although there are critical problems and pressures, "numerous opportunities are available for the social work profession to move ahead on a sound basis, strengthening current delivery of services and innovating services that have been practically untouched to date." They point to an increase in services, a stronger professional identification among social workers, more flexibility in the curricula of schools of social work, more research, and an increase in the status of the social worker.

What transpires in the years ahead in social work will depend not only on the leaders in social-work education and practice and how they work with their colleagues, related professionals, and political leaders but also on whether social-work practitioners can assume the role of mainstays of the profession, performing the most pertinent and crucial tasks within the profession—trying their best to enhance the psychosocial functioning of individuals, families, groups, and organizations.

Summary

As the social worker contributes to the growth of other human beings it is inevitable that he also will experience both personal and professional growth. Many social-work students and practitioners begin to feel considerable anxiety as they move into their work with clients, just as their clients do. This is normal in social-work practice; in fact, absence of anxiety in the beginner is usually indicative of strong defenses against involvement with clients and of other attitudes not conducive to helping people professionally. Professional growth involves constant attempts by the practitioner to increase self-awareness, continued involvement in seminars, continuing education, and familiarity with the literature.

Although social work's status has risen over the years and many improvements have been made in delivery of services and in the curricula of schools of social work, there is still in many agencies a flight from the client, an insensitivity to the profession's real priorities, a demeaning of practice, and a hierarchical structure destructive to both practitioners and clients.

All social workers must relate to people-in-their-situations and have knowledge of personality theory and system theory; all should be trained to be enablers in individual, group, and community problems, with skills in institutional and policy intervention, policy planning, and social provision, as circumstances may warrant.

The profession of social work will not grow and solve its problems without the strong convictions, skill, and dedication of its practitioners.

References

ACKERMAN, N., 1954. *The Psychodynamics of Family Life*. New York: Basic Books.

———— and M. BEHRENS, 1956. "The Home Visit as an Aid in Family Diagnosis and Therapy," *Social Casework*, Vol. 37, No. 6.

ADLER, A., 1927. *The Practice and Theory of Individual Psychology*. New York: Harcourt.

AICHORN, A., 1935. *Wayward Youth*. New York: Viking Press.

ARONSON, H. and B. OVERALL, 1966. "Treatment Expectations of Patients in Two Social Classes," *Social Work*, Vol. 11, No. 1, pp. 35–42.

ATHERTON, C., S. MITCHELL, and E. BIEHL SCHIEN, 1971a. "Locating Points for Intervention," *Social Casework*, Vol. 52, No. 3.

————, 1971b. "Using Points for Intervention," *Social Casework,* Vol. 52, No. 4.

AUERSWALD, E., 1968. "Interdisciplinary vs. Ecological Approach," *Family Process,* Vol. 7.

AULL, G. and H. STREAN, 1976. "The Analyst's Silence," in *Crucial Issues in Psychotherapy,* ed. H. Strean. Metuchen, N.J.: Scarecrow Press.

AUSTIN, L., 1963. "The Changing Role of the Supervisor," in *Ego-Oriented Casework,* H. Parad and R. Miller, eds. New York: Family Service Association of America.

————, 1958, "Dynamics and Treatment of the Client with Anxiety Hysteria," in *Ego Psychology and Dynamic Casework,* ed. H.J. Parad. New York: Family Service Association of America.

————, 1948. "Trends in Differential Treatment in Social Casework," *Social Casework,* Vol. 29.

BARBARA, D., 1958. *The Art of Listening.* Springfield, Ill.: Charles C. Thomas.

BARTLETT, H., 1971. "Social Work's Fields of Practice," in *Encyclopedia of Social Work.* New York: National Association of Social Workers.

————, 1970. *The Common Base of Social Work Practice.* New York: National Association of Social Workers.

————, 1964. *Building Social Work Knowledge.* New York: National Association of Social Workers.

————, 1961. *Analyzing Social Work Practice by Fields.* New York: National Association of Social Workers.

BECK, D., 1962. *Patterns in Use of Family Agency Service.* New York: Family Service Association of America.

————, and M. JONES, 1973. *Progress on Family Problems.* New York: Family Service Association of America.

BENJAMIN, A., 1974. *The Helping Interview.* 2nd ed. Boston: Houghton Mifflin.

BERNSTEIN, A., 1954. *On the Nature of Psychotherapy.* New York: Random House.

BERTALANFFY, L.V., 1968. *General Systems Theory: Foundations, Development, Application.* New York: George Braziller.

BIBRING, G., 1950. "Psychiatry and Social Work," in *Principles and Techniques in Social Casework,* ed. C. Kasius. New York: Family Service Association of America.

BIDDLE, B., and E. THOMAS, 1966. *Role Theory.* New York: John Wiley and Sons.

BOEHM, W., 1959. *The Social Casework Method in Social Work Education,* Vol. 10. New York: Council on Social Work Education.

———, 1958. "The Nature of Social Work," *Social Work,* Vol. 3, No. 4.

BOOTH, C., 1904. *Life and Labour of the People of London.* London: Macmillan.

BOSANQUET, H., 1914. *Social Work in London, 1869–1912.* London: John Murray.

BOWERS, S., 1949. "The Nature and Definition of Social Casework," *Social Casework,* Vol. 30, Nos. 8,9,10.

BOWLBY, J., 1962. Foreword to *The Caseworker's Use of Relationships,* M. Ferard and N. Hunnybun, eds. London: Tavistock Publications.

BRENNER, C., 1955. *An Elementary Textbook of Psychoanalysis.* Garden City, N.J.: Doubleday.

BREUER, J. and S. FREUD, 1936. *Studies in Hysteria.* New York: Nervous and Mental Disease Publishing Company.

BRIAR, S., 1974. "The Future of Social Work: An Introduction," *Social Work,* Vol. 19, No. 3.

———, 1971. "Family Services and Casework," in *Research in the Social Services: a Five Year Review,* ed. H. Maas. New York: National Association of Social Workers.

BRIAR, S., and H. MILLER, 1971. *Problems and Issues in Social Casework.* New York: Columbia University Press.

BROWN, G., 1968. *The Multiproblem Dilemma.* Metuchen, N.J.: Scarecrow Press.

BROWN, L., 1970. "Social Work with Retardates in Their Social System," in *New Approaches in Child Guidance,* ed. H. Strean. Metuchen, N.J.: Scarecrow Press.

BUCKLEY, W., 1967. *Sociology and Modern Systems Theory.* New York: Prentice-Hall.

CAMERON, N., 1963. *Personality Development and Psychopathology.* New York: Houghton, Mifflin Company.

CARTER, G., 1971. "The Challenge of Accountability," *Public Welfare,* Vol. 29, No. 3.

COCKERILL, E., 1951. *A Conceptual Framework for Social Casework.* Pittsburgh: University of Pittsburgh Press.

COMPTON, B. and B. GALAWAY, 1975. *Social Work Processes.* Homewood, Ill.: The Dorsey Press.

CORSINI, R., 1964. *Methods of Group Psychotherapy.* Chicago: William James Press.

CURRY, A., 1966. "The Family Therapy Situation as a System," *Family Process,* Vol. 5.

DEUTSCH, M. and R. KRAUSS, 1965. *Theories in Social Psychology.* New York: Basic Books.

DEWEY, J., 1928. *Interest and Effort in Education.* New York: Columbia University Press.

DINITZ, S., S. ANGRIST, M. LEFTON, and B. PASAMINICK, 1962. "Instrumental Role Expectations and Posthospital Performance of Female Mental Patients," *Social Forces,* Vol. 40.

DUNHAM, A., 1940. "The Literature of Community Organization," in *Proceedings of the National Conference of Social Welfare.* New York: Columbia University Press.

EDINBURG, C., N. ZINBERG, and W. KELMAN, 1975. *Clinical Interviewing and Counselling.* New York: Appleton-Century-Crofts.

ENGLISH, O.S. and G.H. PEARSON, 1945. *Emotional Problems of Living.* New York: W.W. Norton.

ERIKSON, E., 1959. "Identity and the Life Cycle," in *Psychological Issues.* New York: International Universities Press.

————, 1950. *Childhood and Society.* New York: W.W. Norton.

FANSHEL, D., 1966. "Sources of Strain in Practice Oriented Research," *Social Casework,* Vol. 47, No. 6.

FENICHEL, O., 1945. *The Psychoanalytic Theory of Neuroses.* New York: W.W. Norton.

FERARD, M. and N. HUNNYBUN, 1962. *The Caseworker's Use of Relationships.* London: Tavistock Publications.

FERGUSON, E., 1975. *Social Work,* 3rd ed.. Philadelphia: J.J. Lippin-cott.

FINCH, W., 1976. "Social Workers versus Bureaucracy," *Social Work,* Vol. 21, No. 5.

FINE, R., 1975. "The Bankruptcy of Behaviorism," *Psychoanalytic Review,* Vol. 62, No. 3.

———, 1973. "Psychoanalysis," in *Current Psychotherapies,* ed. R. Corsini. Itasca, Ill.: F.E. Peacock Publishers.

———, 1971. *The Healing of the Mind.* New York: David McKay.

———, 1968. "Interpretation: The Patient's Response," in *Use of Interpretation in Treatment: Technique and Art,* ed. E. Hammer. New York: Grune and Stratton.

———, 1962. *Freud: A Critical Re-evaluation of His Theories.* New York: David McKay Company.

———, 1960. "The Measurement Problem," *The Psychoanalytic Review,* Vol. 47, No. 3, 1960.

FINK, A., 1948. *The Field of Social Work.* New York: Henry Holt.

FISCHER, J., 1976. *The Effectiveness of Social Casework.* Springfield, Ill.: Charles C. Thomas.

FOX, E., M. NELSON, and W. BOLMAN, 1969. "The Termination Process: A Neglected Dimension in Social Work," *Social Work,* Vol. 14, No. 4.

FRAIBERG, S., 1962. Letter to the Editor, *Social Work,* Vol. 7, No. 3.

FREUD, A., 1937. *The Ego and Mechanisms of Defense.* London, Hogarth Press.

FREUD, S., 1953. "Freud's Psychoanalytic Method," in Standard Edition, Vol. 7. London: Hogarth Press.

———, 1949. "Further Recommendations in the Technique of Psychoanalysis," in *Collected Papers,* Vol. II. London: Hogarth Press.

———, 1948. "Instincts and their Vicissitudes," in *Collected Papers,* Vol. 4. London: Hogarth Press.

———, 1939. *An Outline of Psychoanalysis.* Standard Edition, Vol. 23. London: Hogarth Press.

———, 1938. *The Basic Writings of Sigmund Freud.* New York: Random House, The Modern Library.

———, 1933. *New Introductory Lectures in Psychoanalysis*. New York: Norton.

———, 1923. *Beyond the Pleasure Principle*. Standard Edition, Vol. 18. London: Hogarth Press.

GARDNER, J., 1972. "Education for Renewal," quoted by S. Sarason, *The Creation of Settings and the Future Societies*. San Francisco: Jossey-Bass.

GARFINKEL, H., 1970. *Studies in Ethnomethodology*. Englewood Cliffs, N.J.: Prentice-Hall.

GARLAND, J., H. JONES, and R. KOLODNY, 1965. "A Model for Stages of Development in Social Work Groups," in *Explorations in Group Work,* ed. S. Bernstein. Boston: Boston University School of Social Work.

GARRETT, A., 1958. "The Worker-Client Relationship," in *Ego Psychology and Dynamic Casework,* ed. H. Parad. New York: Family Service Association of America.

———, 1951. *Interviewing: Its Principles and Methods*. New York: Family Service Association of America.

GEISMAR, L. and S. CHARLESWORTH, 1976. "Parsimonious Practice Research or Have Your Diagnosis and Research It, Too," *Australian Social Work,* Vol. 29, No. 2.

GERMAIN, C., 1968. "Social Study: Past and Future," *Social Casework,* Vol. 49, No. 7.

GLOVER, E., 1949. *Psychoanalysis*. London: Staples Press.

GOFFMAN, E., 1961. *Asylums*. Garden City, New York: Anchor Books.

GOLDSTEIN, H., 1974. *Social Work Practice: A Unitary Approach*. Columbia, S.C.: University of South Carolina Press.

GORDON, W., 1969. "Basic Constructs for an Integrative and Generative Conception of Social Work," in *The General Systems Approach: Contributions Toward a Holistic Operation,* ed. G. Hearn. New York: Council on Social Work Education.

GRINKER, E., ed., 1967. *Toward a Unified Theory of Behavior,* 2nd ed. New York: Basic Books.

———, 1961. *Psychiatric Social Work: A Transactional Case Book*. New York: Basic Books.

GROSSBARD, H., 1976. Book Review of H. Strean, *Personality Theory and Social Work Practice* (Metuchen, N.J.: Scarecrow Press, 1975), *Social Work,* Vol. 21, No. 4.

GYARFAS, M., 1969. "Social Science, Technology and Social Work," *Social Service Review,* Vol. 43, No. 3.

HAMILTON, G., 1958. "A Theory of Personality: Freud's Contribution to Social Work," in *Ego Psychology and Dynamic Casework,* ed. H. Parad. New York: Family Service Association of America.

————, 1952. "The Role of Social Casework in Social Policy," *Social Casework,* Vol. 33.

————, 1951. *Theory and Practice of Social Casework.* New York: Columbia University Press.

Handbook on the Private Practice of Social Work, 1974. Washington, D.C.: National Association of Social Workers.

HART, J., 1920. *Community Organization.* New York: Macmillan Company.

HARTMANN, H., 1951. "Ego Psychology and the Problem of Adaptation," in *Organization and Pathology of Thought,* ed. D. Rapaport. New York: Columbia University Press.

HEARN, G., ed., 1969. *The General Systems Approach.* New York: Council on Social Work Education.

————, 1958. *Theory Building in Social Work.* Toronto: Toronto University Press.

HELLENBRAND, S., 1972. "Freud's Influence on Social Casework," *Bulletin of the Menninger Clinic,* Vol. 36.

————, 1961. "Client Value Orientations: Implications for Diagnosis and Treatment," *Social Casework,* Vol. 42, No. 8.

HERMA, J., 1968. "The Therapeutic Act," in *Use of Interpretation in Treatment: Technique and Art,* ed. E. Hammer. New York: Grune and Stratton.

HOLLIS, F., 1976. "Evaluation: Clinical Results and Research Methodology," *Clinical Social Work,* Vol. 4, No. 3.

————, 1972. *Casework: A Psychosocial Therapy,* 2nd ed. New York: Random House.

————, 1964. *Casework: A Psychosocial Therapy.* New York: Random House.

INGERSOLL, H., 1948. "Transmission in Authority Patterns in the Family," *Marriage and Family Living,* Vol. 10.

JACKSON, D., 1957, "The Question of Family Homeostasis," *Psychiatric Quarterly,* Vol. 31.

JACOBSON, A., 1952. "Conflict of Attitudes toward the Roles of the Husband and Wife in Marriage," *American Sociological Review,* Vol. 17.

JANCHILL, SISTER MARY PAUL, 1969. "Systems Concepts in Casework Theory and Practice," *Social Casework,* Vol. 50, No. 2.

JOSSELYN, I.M., 1948. *Psychosocial Development of Children.* New York: Family Service Association of America.

KADUSHIN, A., 1972. *The Social Work Interview.* New York: Columbia University Press.

————, 1959. "The Knowledge Base of Social Work Practice," in *Issues in American Social Work,* ed. A.J. Kahn. New York: Columbia University Press.

KAHN, A., 1973. *Shaping the New Social Work.* New York: Columbia University Press.

————, 1965a. "Social Work Fields of Practice," in *Encyclopedia of Social Work.* New York: National Association of Social Workers.

————, 1965b. "New Policies and Service Models," *American Journal of Orthopsychiatry,* Vol. 35, No. 4.

————, 1959. "The Function of Social Work in the Modern World," in *Issues in American Social Work,* ed. A. J. Kahn. New York: Columbia University Press.

KIDNEIGH, J., 1965. "History of American Social Work," in *Encyclopedia of Social Work.* New York: National Association of Social Workers.

KLENK, R. and R. RYAN, 1972. *The Practice of Social Work,* 2nd ed.. Belmont, Calif.: Wadsworth Press.

KURZMAN, P., 1976, "Private Practice as a Social Work Function," *Social Work,* Vol. 21, No. 5.

LEADER, A., 1971. "The Argument against Required Personal Analysis in Training for Psychotherapy," in *New Horizon for Psychotherapy,* ed. R. Holt. New York: International Universities Press.

————, 1967. "Current and Future Issues in Family Therapy," *Social Service Review,* Vol. 39.

LEE, P., 1939. "Social Work: Cause and Function," in *Readings in Social Casework,* ed. F. Lowry. New York: Columbia University Press.

LEIBY, J., 1971. "Social Welfare: History of Basic Ideas," in *Encyclopedia of Social Work.* New York: National Association of Social Workers.

LENNARD, H. and A. BERNSTEIN, 1969. *Patterns in Human Interaction.* San Francisco: Jossey-Bass, Inc.

————, 1960. *The Anatomy of Psychotherapy.* New York: Columbia University Press.

LEVENSTEIN, S., 1964. *Private Practice in Social Casework.* New York: Columbia University Press.

LEVIN, A., 1976. "Private Practice is Alive and Well," *Social Work,* Vol. 21, No. 5.

LIDZ, T., 1963. *The Family and Human Adaptation.* New York: International Universities Press.

LOWRY, F., 1937. "Objectives in Social Casework," *The Family,* Vol. 18, No. 11.

MAAS, H., 1971. *Research in the Social Services, a Five Year Review.* New York: National Association of Social Workers.

MACCORQUODALE, K., and P. MEEHL, 1948. "Hypothetical Constructs and Intervening Variables," *Psychological Review,* Vol. 55.

MACLEOD, J., 1963. "Some Criteria for the Modification of Treatment Arrangements," in *Ego-Oriented Casework,* H. Parad and R. Miller, eds. New York: Family Service Association of America.

MANDELBAUM, A., 1971. "Preprofessional Education for Psychotherapy," in *New Horizon for Psychotherapy,* ed. R. Holt, New York: International Universities Press.

MANN, J., 1955. "Some Theoretical Concepts of the Group Process," *International Journal of Group Psychotherapy,* Vol. 5.

MAYER, J. and N. TIMMS, 1970. *The Client Speaks.* New York: Atherton Press.

MCCORMICK, M., 1975. *Enduring Values in a Changing Society.* New York: Family Service Association of America.

McPheeters, H., and R. Ryan, 1971. *A Core of Competence for Baccalaureate Social Welfare and Curricular Implications*. Atlanta: Southern Regional Educational Board.

Meerloo, J. and M. Nelson, 1965. *Transference and Trial Adaptation*. Springfield, Ill.: Charles Thomas.

Meier, E., 1965. "Interactions between the Person and His Operational Situations: A Basis for Classification in Casework," *Social Casework*, Vol. 46, No. 9.

Merkle, L., and R.B. Little, 1967. "Beginning Psychiatry Training Syndrome," *American Journal of Psychiatry*, Vol. 124.

Merle, S., 1971. "The Application of Organization Theory to Social Casework," in *Social Casework: Theories in Action*, ed. H. Strean. Metuchen, N.J.: Scarecrow Press.

Merton, R., 1967. Introduction to *The Technological Society*, ed. J. Eilus. New York: Vintage Press.

———, and R. Nisbet, 1966. *Contemporary Social Problems*. New York: Harcourt, Brace and World.

———, 1957. *Social Theory and Social Structure*. Glencoe, Ill.: The Free Press.

Meyer, C., 1977. "Social Work Practice vs. Clinical Practice," *Alumni Newsletter*, Spring Issue, Columbia University School of Social Work.

———, 1976. *Social Work Practice: The Changing Landscape*. New York: The Free Press.

———. 1970. *Social Work Practice*. New York: The Free Press.

———, 1959. "Quest for a Broader Base for Family Diagnosis," *Social Casework*, Vol. 40.

Meyer, H., 1965. *Girls at Vocational High*. New York: Russell Sage Foundation.

Mullen, E., and J. Dumpson, 1972. *Evaluation of Social Intervention*. San Francisco: Jossey-Bass.

Nagelberg, L., 1959. "The Meaning of Help in Psychotherapy," *The Psychoanalytic Review*, Vol. 46, No. 4.

National Association of Social Workers, 1976. *Register of Clinical Social Workers*. Washington, D.C.: N.A.S.W.

NELSON, M., B. NELSON, M. SHERMAN and H. STREAN, 1968. *Roles and Paradigms in Psychotherapy*. New York: Grune & Stratton.

NEWSTETTER, W., 1947. "The Social Intergroup Work Process," in *Proceedings of the National Conference of Social Welfare*. New York: Columbia University Press.

NORTHEN, H., 1969. *Social Work With Groups*. New York: Columbia University Press.

ORMONT, L. and H. STREAN, 1978. *Conjoint Therapy: Individual and Group Treatment*. New York: Human Sciences Press.

OVERALL, B. and A. ARONSON, 1963. "Expectations of Psychotherapy in Patients of Lower Socio-Economic Classes," *American Journal of Orthopsychiatry,* Vol. 33.

PARAD, H., 1965. *Crisis Intervention*. New York: Family Service Association of America.

PARSONS, T., 1951. *The Social System*. Glencoe, Ill.: The Free Press.

PERLMAN, H., 1966. "Social Work Methods: A Review of the Past Decade," *Social Work,* Vol. 10.

———, 1961. "The Role Concept and Social Casework: Some Explorations," *Social Service Review,* Vol. 35.

———, 1960. "Intake and Some Role Considerations," *Social Casework,* Vol. 41.

———, 1957. *Social Casework: A Problem Solving Process*. Chicago: University of Chicago Press.

PERLMAN, R., and A. GURIN, 1972. *Community Organization and Social Planning*. New York: John Wiley.

PERRY, S., 1958. "The Conscious Use of Relationship with the Neurotic Client," in *Ego Psychology and Dynamic Casework,* ed. H.J. Parad. New York: Family Service Association of America.

PFEFFER, A., 1959. "A Procedure for Evaluating the Results of Psychoanalysis," *Journal of the American Psychoanalytic Association,* Vol. 7.

PHARIS, M., 1976. "A Conversation with Selma Fraiberg," *Clinical Social Work Journal,* Vol. 4, No. 3.

PINCUS, A., and A. MINAHAN, 1973. *Social Work Practice: Model and Method*. Itasca, Ill.: F.E. Peacock Publishers.

POLLAK, O., 1956. *Integrating Sociological and Psychoanalytic Concepts*. New York: Russell Sage Foundation.

PROSHANSKY, H., W. ITTELSON, J. RIVLIN, 1970. *Environmental Psychology: Man and His Physical Setting*. New York: Holt.

QUEEN, S., 1922. *Social Work in the Light of History*. New York: Russell Sage Foundation.

RAPAPORT, D., 1951. *Organization and Pathology of Thought*. New York: Columbia University Press.

RAPOPORT, L., 1962. "The State of Crissi: Some Theoretical Considerations," *Social Service Review,* Vol. 36, No. 2.

REID, W. and L. EPSTEIN, 1972. *Task Oriented Casework*. New York: Columbia University Press.

REID, W. and A. SHYNE, 1969. *Brief and Extended Casework*. New York: Columbia University Press.

REIK, T., 1948. *Listening With the Third Ear*. New York: Farrar, Straus.

REYNOLDS, B., 1935, "Rethinking Social Casework," *The Family,* Vol. 16.

RICH, M., 1936. *Current Trends in Social Adjustment Through Individualized Treatment*. New York: International Universities Press.

RICHMOND, M., 1930. *The Long View*. New York: Russell Sage Foundation.

———, 1922. *What is Social Casework:* New York: Russell Sage Foundation.

———, 1917. *Social Diagnosis*. New York: Russell Sage Foundation.

RIESMAN, F., J. COHEN, and A. PEARL, 1964. *Mental Health of the Poor*. New York: The Free Press.

RIPPLE, L., E. ALEXANDER, and B. POLEMIS, 1964. *Motivation, Capacity and Opportunity*. Social Service Monographs. Chicago: University of Chicago Press.

ROGERS, C., 1962. "Characteristics of a Helping Relationship," *Canada's Mental Health,* Supplement No. 27.

———, 1951. *Client-Centered Therapy*. Boston: Houghton Mifflin.

ROKEACH, M., 1973. *The Nature of Human Values*. New York: The Free Press.

ROSENBLATT, A., 1968. "The Practitioner's Use and Evaluation of Research," *Social Work,* Vol. 13, No. 1.

———, 1961. "The Application of Role Concepts to the Intake Process," *Social Casework,* Vol. 43.

ROSENTHAL, L., 1971. "Application of Small Groups to Casework Theory and Practice," in *Social Casework: Theories in Action,* ed. H. Strean. Metuchen, N.J.: Scarecrow Press.

———, 1956. "Group Therapy in Child Guidance," in *The Fields of Practice,* ed. S.R. Slavson. New York: International Universities Press.

RUESCH, J., 1961. *Therapeutic Communication.* New York: W.W. Norton.

SARRI, R., 1971. "Administration in Social Work," in *Encyclopedia of Social Work.* New York: National Association of Social Workers.

SCHACTER, B., 1969. "Relevance of Direct Practice for Today's Social Work Educator," *Journal of Education for Social Work,* Vol. 5, No. 1.

SCHERZ, F., 1962. "Multiple-Client Interviewing: An Aid in Diagnosis," *Social Casework,* Vol. 43.

SCHOTTLAND, C., 1953. "Social Welfare Issues in the Political Arena," in *Social Welfare Forum.* New York: Columbia University Press.

SCHWARTZ, M., 1965. "Community Organization," in *Encyclopedia of Social Work.* New York: National Association of Social Workers.

SCHWARTZ, W., 1962. "Toward a Strategy of Group Work Practice," *Social Service Review,* Vol. 36, No. 3.

———, 1961. "The Social Worker in the Group," in *The Social Welfare Forum.* New York: Columbia University Press.

SHYNE, A., 1965. "Social Work Research," in *Encyclopedia of Social Work.* New York: National Association of Social Workers.

———, 1957. "What Research Tells Us about Short-Term Cases in Family Agencies," *Social Casework,* Vol. 38, No. 5.

SIPORIN, M., 1975. *Introduction to Social Work Practice.* New York: Macmillan Publishing Company.

SKIDMORE, R. and M. THACKERAY, 1976. *Introduction to Social Work,* 2nd ed.. Englewood Cliffs, N.J.: Prentice-Hall.

SLAVSON, S.R., 1943. *An Introduction to Group Therapy.* New York: Commonwealth Fund.

SMALLEY, R., 1967. *Theory for Social Work Practice.* New York: Columbia University Press.

SPECHT, H., 1972. "The Deprofessionalization of Social Work," *Social Work,* Vol. 17, No. 3.

SPIEGEL, J., 1972. *Transactions: The Interplay between Individuals, Family and Society.* New York: Science House.

————, 1960. "The Resolution of Role Conflict with the Family," in *The Family,* N. Bell and E. Vogel, eds. Glencoe, Ill.: The Free Press.

STAMM, I., 1972. "Family Therapy," in *Casework: A Psychosocial Therapy,* 2nd edition, ed. F. Hollis. New York: Random House.

————, 1959. "Ego Psychology in the Emerging Theoretical Base of Casework," in *Issues in American Social Work,* ed. A.J. Kahn. New York: Columbia University Press.

STANTON, A. and M. SCHWARTZ, 1954. *The Mental Hospital.* New York: Basic Books.

STARK, F., 1959. "Barriers to Client-Worker Communication at Intake," *Social Casework,* Vol. 40.

STEIN, H., 1965. "Administration," in *Encyclopedia of Social Work.* New York: National Association of Social Workers.

————, and R. CLOWARD, 1958. *Social Perspectives on Behavior.* New York: The Free Press.

STEIN, I., 1971. "The Systems Model and Social Systems Theory: Their Application to Casework," in *Social Casework: Theories in Action,* ed. H. Strean. Metuchen, N.J.: Scarecrow Press.

STREAN, H., 1976. *Crucial Issues in Psychotherapy.* Metuchen, N.J.: Scarecrow Press.

————, 1975. *Personality Theory and Social Work Practice.* Metuchen, N.J.: Scarecrow Press.

————, 1974a. "Intervention sociale en bien-être social," *The Social Worker,* Vol. 42, No. 3.

————, 1974b. *The Social Worker as Psychotherapist.* Metuchen, N.J.: Scarecrow Press.

————, 1974c. "Choosing Among Practice Modalities," *Clinical Social Work,* Vol. 2, No. 1.

————, 1972. *The Experience of Psychotherapy*. Metuchen, N.J.: Scarecrow Press.

————, 1971a. "Relief's Abominable Realities," Voice of the People, *The Bergen County Record*.

————, 1971b. *Social Casework: Theories in Action*. Metuchen, N.J.: Scarecrow Press.

————, 1971c. "Role Expectations of Students and Teachers in a Graduate School of Social Work: Their Relationship to the Students' Performance," *Applied Social Studies,* Vol. 3.

————, 1970a. "A Means of Involving Fathers in Family Treatment: Guidance Groups for Fathers," in *New Approaches in Child Guidance,* ed. H. Strean. Metuchen, N.J.: Scarecrow Press.

————, 1970b. *New Approaches in Child Guidance*. Metuchen, N.J.: Scarecrow Press.

————, 1970c. "Recent Developments in Social Casework Theory and Practice: A Social Work Educator's Evaluation," in *Proceedings of the Conference for the Advancement of Private Practitioners in Social Work*.

————, 1970d. "The Use of the Patient as Consultant," in *New Approaches in Child Guidance*. Metuchen, N.J.: Scarecrow Press.

SULLIVAN, H.S., 1961. *Schizophrenia as a Human Process*. New York: W.W. Norton.

TABER, M. and A. VATTANO, 1970. "Clincial and Social Orientations in Social Work: An Empirical Study," *Social Service Review,* Vol. 44, No. 1.

TAFT, J., 1937. "The Relation of Function to Process in Social Casework," *Journal of Social Work Process,* Vol. 1, No. 1.

THOMAS, E., 1971. "The Behavior Modification Model and Social Casework," in *Social Casework: Theories in Action*. ed. H. Strean, Metuchen, N.J.: Scarecrow Press.

————, 1968. "Selected Socio-Behavioral Techniques and Principles: An Approach to Interpersonal Helping," *Social Work,* Vol. 13, No. 1.

TOFFLER, A., 1971. *Future Shock*. New York: Random House.

TRIPODI, T., P. FELLIN, and H. MEYER, 1969. *The Assessment of*

Social Research: Guidelines for the Use of Research in Social Work and Social Science. Itasca, Ill.: F. E. Peacock.

TROPP, E., 1974. "Expectation, Performance and Accountability," *Social Work,* Vol. 19, No. 2.

———, 1968. "The Group in Life and Social Work," *Social Casework,* Vol. 49.

VARLEY, B., 1968. "The Use of Role Theory in the Treatment of Disturbed Adolescents," *Social Casework,* Vol. 49, No. 6.

VINTER, R., 1967. "The Essential Components of Social Group Work Practice," in *Readings in Group Work Practice,* ed. R. Vinter. Ann Arbor, Mich.: Campus Publishers.

———, 1965. "Social Group Work," in *Encyclopedia of Social Work.* New York: National Association of Social Workers.

WATSON, J., 1922. *The Charity Organization Movement in the United States.* New York: Lippincott Company.

WEBB, B. and S. WEBB, 1904. *The Break-up of the Poor Law.* Vols. I & II. London: Longians, Green & Co.

WEISS, V., 1962. "Multiple-Client Interviewing: An Aid in Diagnosis," *Social Caseworker,* Vol. 43.

WEISSMAN, M. and E. PAYKEL, 1974. *The Depressed Woman.* Chicago: University of Chicago Press.

WHITEHEAD, A., 1960. *The Aims of Education.* New York: Mentor Books.

WILDAVSKY, A., 1971. "Does Planning Work?", *The Public Interest,* Vol. 24.

WILENSKY, H. and C. LEBEAUX, 1965. *Industrial Society and Social Welfare.* New York: The Free Press.

WITMER, H., 1942. *Social Work: An Analysis of a Social Institution.* New York: Rinehart & Co.

WOLBERG, L., 1968. "Short-Term Psychotherapy," in *Modern Psychoanalysis,* ed. J. Marmor. New York: Basic Books.

WOOD, K., 1971, "The Contribution of Psychoanalysis and Ego Psychology to Social Casework," in *Social Casework: Theories in Action,* ed. H. Strean. Metuchen, N.J.: Scarecrow Press.

WYNNE, L.C., I. RYCKOFF, J. DAY, and S. HIRCH, 1958. "Pseudo-mutuality in the Family Relations of Schizophrenics, *Psychiatry,* Vol. 21.

WYSS, D., 1973. *Psycoanalytic Schools.* New York: Jason Aronson Press.

YOUNG, P., 1937. *Social Treatment in Probation and Delinquency.* New York: McGraw-Hill.

ZILBACH, J., 1968. "Family Development," in *Modern Psychoanalysis,* ed. J. Marmor. New York: Basic Books.

Index

Ackerman, N., 169, 172
Addictions, 121
Adler, Alfred, 43
Administration, 2, 24–25
Agencies, intervention process and, 163, 167–168
Aichorn, August, 259
Alexander, E., 135
American Psychiatric Association, 115, 123
American Psychoanalytic Association, 253
Anality, 105, 130
Anorgasmia, 126
Anxiety hysteria, 114, 127–129
Aronson, A., 47, 99
Assessment, 14, 39, 77–132
   changing orientations toward, 84–87
   clinical diagnosis, 114–131
   defining problem, 79–80
   ego psychology and, 87, 88, 109–112, 114
   psychoanalytic theory and, 87, 88, 103–114
   role theory and, 89, 97–103
   situation of client, 82–84
   social-systems theory and, 87–97
   utilization of in planning intervention, 151–156
Atherton, C., 191
Aull, G., 204
Austin, Lucille, 128, 167, 187–188, 192, 193
Autonomy, 105, 106, 157, 158–159, 164, 236

Barbara, D., 51
Bartlett, H., 5, 22, 140, 256
Beck, D., 225, 252
Beginning psychiatry training syndrome, 257
Behavior modification, 14, 16, 28–29, 191–192
Behavioral sciences, 26–29

Behrens, M., 172
Benjamin, A., 52
Bernstein, A., 237
Bertalanffy, L. V., 89, 90
Bibring, G., 188
Biddle, B., 46, 97, 99
Bisexuality, 115, 123
Boehm, W., 5, 12, 101–103
Bolman, W., 225, 244
Booth, C., 6
Borderline clients, 120
Bosanquet, H., 6
Bowers, Swithun, 2
Bowlby, John, 198
Briar, S., 225, 241, 245, 246–248, 272
Brown, G., 249, 250
Brown, L., 139
Buckley, W., 89, 96

Cameron, N., 125, 127, 131
Carter, G., 242, 252
Casework, 2, 4, 13–16, 34, 137–138
Character disorders, 115, 129–131
Charity Organization Society, 7–8
Charlesworth, S., 246, 247
Child-guidance movement, 138
Client motivation, 150–151
Clinical diagnosis, 114–131
Clinical Social Work, 35
Closed system, 96
Cockerill, E., 188
Cohen, J., 167
Comments, in interviews, 56–58
Communication theory, 28, 87, 94–95, 268
Community mental health movement, 12, 139
Community organization, 2, 4, 12, 19–20, 137–138
Community Service Society of New York, 33
Complementarity, 89, 97–98
Compton, B., 84, 87, 88, 89, 96, 167, 168, 190–191, 198

Contract, 58–60, 70, 75
Conversion hysteria, 127, 129
Corsini, R., 174
Countertransference, 66, 193, 198, 208–211, 220, 239
Crisis intervention, 21, 33, 179–182

Defense mechanisms, 110–111
Denial, 110
Despair, 105, 157, 162–163, 166
Deutsch, M., 185
Developmental approach, 17–18
Dewey, John, 133
Diagnosis: see Assessment
Dinitz, S., 103
Distrust: see Mistrust
Double-bind messages, 94, 170–171
Doubt: see Shame and doubt
Dumpson, J., 34, 250, 252, 253

Economic approach to personality theory, 112–113
Edinburg, C., 42
Education, 3, 22–23, 34, 264–268
Ego, 85, 108–112, 127
Ego ideal, 85
Ego integrity, 157, 162–163
Ego psychology, 15, 26–27, 87, 88, 109–112, 114, 157, 249
Electra Complex, 125
Elizabethan Poor Law, 6
English, O. S., 121, 126, 128
Epstein, L., 182, 226
Erikson, Erik, 87, 105, 109, 118, 120, 157, 161, 179, 236
Evaluation, 240–242; see also Research
Experiential therapy, 187–188

Family homeostasis, 170
Family therapy, 12, 21, 169–174, 237–238
Feedback, 93
Fees, 71–76
Fenichel, O., 117–120, 122–125, 128, 130, 131
Ferard, M., 210
Ferguson, E., 140
Fields of practice, concept of, 22, 143

Finch, W., 259
Fine, Reuben, 34, 58, 63, 64, 205, 232, 248–249, 253, 258, 259
Fink, A., 6, 7
Fixations, 107, 118
Focus of interview, 60–61, 70
Fox, E., 225, 244
Fraiberg, Selma, 259, 266
Freud, Anna, 87, 111
Freud, Sigmund, 38, 85–87, 103–110, 112–114, 124, 128–130, 169–170, 193, 208
Frigidity, 126–128
Functional approach, 15–16

Galaway, B., 84, 87, 88, 89, 96, 167, 168, 190–191, 198
Gardner, John, 255
Garfinkel, H., 246–247
Garland, J., 235
Garrett, A., 42, 51, 195
Geismar, L., 246, 247
Generalist approach, 21–22, 40
Generativity, 105, 157, 162, 166
Genetic approach to personality theory, 105–107
Genitality, 105
Germain, C., 167, 168
Glover, E., 119, 120–125, 130
Goals of Public Social Policy (N.A.S.W.), 23
Goffman, E., 115
Goldstein, H., 191, 242
Gordon Marketing Scale, 251
Grinker, E., 2, 90, 92
Grossbard, Hyman, 268–269
Group therapy, 12, 70–71, 174–179, 238
Group work, 2, 4, 12, 16–19, 34, 137–138
Guilt, 105, 127, 131, 157, 159, 164, 236–237
Gurin, A., 134

Hamilton, Gordon, 9, 11, 14, 43, 48, 51, 77, 79, 85, 87, 134, 148, 186, 193, 195, 258, 271
Hart, J., 19

Hartmann, Heinz, 87, 109
Hearn, G., 88
Hellenbrand, S., 85, 151
Helping interview, 38, 41–76, 253
  cancellations, 65
  comments, 56–58
  contract, 58–60, 70, 75
  defined, 42
  fees, 71–76
  focus, 60–61, 70
  group, 70–71
  initial, 43–53
  lateness, 63–64
  listening, 51–54, 75
  questioning of interviewer, 68–69
  questions, 54–56
  recording and note-taking, 74, 76
  resistance, 61–67, 70, 75
  role expectations, 45–48
  silence, 65–67, 204, 212–213
Herma, J., 204
Hierarchical factor in social systems, 95–96
Hollis, Florence, 13, 14, 79, 81, 87, 93, 115, 188–189, 193, 250, 253, 258, 265–266
Homosexuality, 115, 123–125
Hunnybun, N., 210
Hypochondriasis, 122
Hysterical character, 130–131

Id, 85, 108, 111, 127
Identity, 105, 124, 161, 165
Implementing intervention, 184–223
  corrective experience, 207–208
  countertransference, 193, 198, 208–211
  dynamics of, 192–194
  resistance, 198–203
  review of literature on, 185–192
  role of social worker in, 208–220
  role theory and, 220–222
  selective listening, 206
  at termination, 242–243
  transference, 193, 194–198
Impotence, 126–128
Industry, 105, 160–161, 165

Inferiority, 105, 160–161, 165
Initiative, 105, 157, 159–160, 164, 236–237
Insight therapy, 188
Instinct theory, 104–105
Integrity, 105, 166
Interactionist approach, 17, 18
Intervention, 14–15, 39; *see also* Implementing intervention; Planning intervention
Interview: *see* Helping interview
Intimacy, 105, 161–162, 165
Isolation, 105, 110, 161, 165

Jackson, D., 170
Jones, H., 235
Jones, M., 252
Josselyn, I. M., 118

Kadushin, A., 10, 12, 42, 52, 54
Kahn, Alfred, 3, 4, 5, 20, 263, 271
Kelman, W., 42
Kidneigh, J., 5, 8
Kolodny, R., 235
Krauss, R., 185
Kurzman, P., 262

Latency, 105
Lateness, for interviews, 63–64
Leader, A., 172, 259
Learning theory, 15, 28–29, 268
Lebeaux, C., 269–271
Lee, Porter, 10, 186
Leiby, J., 6
Lennard, H., 237
Levin, A., 261–262
Lidz, T., 171
Life-tasks, 105–106, 157–166, 236–237
Listening, 51–54, 75, 206
Little, R. B., 257
Lowry, F., 11

MacCorquodale, K., 248
MacLeod, J., 167
Manic-depressive psychoses, 118–120
Mann, James, 177
Masturbation, 128, 129
McCormick, M., 33

McPheeters, H., 191
Meehl, P., 248
Meerloo, J., 220
Megalomania, 118
Meier, Elizabeth, 190
Merkle, L., 257
Merle, S., 20, 29, 91
Merton, Robert K., 26, 101, 184
Meyer, Carol, 21, 37, 83, 84, 86–88,
    103, 134, 140, 143, 163, 178
Meyer, H., 249, 250
Miller, H., 226, 241, 245, 247–248
Minahan, A., 79, 84, 87, 88, 191, 235,
    238
Mistrust, 105, 106, 164, 157–158, 178,
    210, 236
Mitchell, S., 191
Mullen, E., 34, 250, 252, 253

Nagelberg, L., 211
National Association of Social Workers
    (N.A.S.W.), 4, 22, 23, 35, 260,
    272
National Federation of Societies for Clin-
    ical Social Work, 35
Nelson, M., 220, 225, 244
Neurotic symptom formation, 113–114
Newstetter, W., 20
Nisbet, R., 26
Nixon, Richard, 6–7
Northen, Helen, 239

Obsessive-compulsive neurosis, 115–
    116, 126–127
Oedipal fantasies, 105, 124, 125, 127–
    128
Open system, 96
Operant conditioning, 191
Orality, 105, 130
Organization theory, 29, 87, 268
Overall, B., 47, 99

Parad, H., 21, 179, 180
Paranoid, 131
Parental coalition, 171–172
Parsons, T., 81, 89
Pavlov, Ivan, 16
Paykel, E., 253

Pearl, A., 167
Pearson, G. H., 121, 128
Penis envy, 125, 126
Perlman, Helen, 1–2, 13, 15, 99, 100
Perlman, R., 134
Perry, S., 128
Personality assessment, 80–82
Personality theory, 9–11, 14, 85–86,
    103–114
Pfeffer, A., 253
Pharis, M., 259
Phobia, 113, 128, 160–161
Pincus, A., 79, 84, 87, 88, 191, 193,
    235, 238
Planning intervention, 133–183
    agencies and, 163, 167–168
    assessment and, 151–156
    changing orientations, 137–143
    client's attitude to referral source,
        143–147
    crisis intervention, 179–182
    defining problem, 147–150
    family therapy, 169–174
    role of social worker in, 156–163
    self-determination and client motiva-
        tion, 150–151
    short-term treatment, 179–182
    small groups, 174–179
    social-problem approach, 140–143
Polemis, B., 135
Pollak, O., 169, 170
Premature termination, 231–234
Preventive-rehabilitative approach, 17,
    18–19
Private practice, 261–262
Problem-definition, 79–80, 147–150
Problem-solving approach, 14, 15
Projection, 10, 89
Proshansky, H., 206
Pseudo-mutuality, 171
Pseudo-neurotic schizophrenia, 120
Psychic determinism, 103–104
Psychoanalytic theory, 9, 10, 26–27,
    85–87, 88, 103–114, 249
Psychopath, 115, 131
Psychosis, 116–120

Psychosocial approach, 14–15, 26, 188–189
Psychosomatic disease, 121–123
Psychotherapy, 2, 37
Puberty, 105
Punishment and reward, 29, 191

Queen, S., 6, 9–10
Questionnaires, 251
Questions, in interviews, 54–56

Rank, Otto, 15
Rapaport, D., 104, 112
Rapoport, L., 179–180
Reaction formation, 110–111
Reciprocity, 89
Referral party, client's attitudes toward, 143–147
Register of Clinical Social Workers (N.A.S.W.), 35–36
Regression, 110, 118
Reid, W., 182, 226
Reik, Theodor, 224, 257, 258
Reinforcement, positive and negative, 29, 191
Repression, 89, 110
Research, 2, 25–26, 245–254
  measurement problem, 247–251
  positive results, 251–253
  resistance to, 246–247
  utilizing social-work skills in, 253–254
Resistance, 61–67, 70, 75, 198–203, 220
Reward and punishment, 29, 191
Reynolds, Bertha, 11
Rich, M., 11
Richmond, Mary, 7, 9, 79, 84–87, 169
Riesman, F., 167
Ripple, L., 135
Rogers, Carl, 52
Rokeach, M., 30
Role conflict, 98
Role diffusion, 105, 161
Role equilibrium and disequilibrium, 220–222
Role expectations, 45–48, 103
Role incongruency, 98–99

Role prescription, 99–100
Role-set, 101–103
Role theory, 15, 27, 87, 89, 97–103, 113, 114, 169, 220–222, 268
Rosenblatt, Aaron, 101, 246
Rosenthal, L., 16, 91, 175–177
Ruesch, J., 94
Ryan, R., 191

Schachter, B., 266
Scherz, F., 172
Schien, E. Biehl, 191
Schizoid clients, 120
Schizophrenia, 116–118, 120
Schottland, Charles, 23
Schwartz, M., 20, 95
Schwartz, William, 18
Selective listening, 206
Self-determination, 149–151
Self-doubt: *see* Shame and doubt
Separation: *see* Termination
Settlement movement, 8–9, 19
Sexual disorders, 115, 123–126
Shame and doubt, 105, 106, 157, 158–159, 164, 236
Short-term treatment, 21, 33, 179–182
Shyne, A., 25, 226
Silence, in interviews, 65–67, 204, 212–213
Siporin, M., 3, 5, 12, 22, 34, 79, 87, 140, 191, 234–235, 240, 243, 252, 254
Skidmore, R., 140, 272
Skinner, B. F., 16
Slavson, S. R., 175, 177
Smalley, R., 16
Social action, 33
Social Diagnosis (Richmond), 7, 9, 84–87
Social legislation, 33
Social planning, 22–23, 33
Social policy, 2, 22–23, 141, 142
Social-problem approach, 140–143
Social-systems theory, 27–28, 87–97, 113, 114, 167, 169, 268
Sociopath, 131
Specht, H., 272

Spiegel, J., 94, 98
Stability, principle of, 89–92
Stagnation, 105, 157, 162, 166
Stamm, I., 109, 112, 173
Stanton, A., 95
Stark, F., 99
Stein, H., 24, 92
Strean, H., 10, 67, 83, 87, 90, 94, 101, 116, 141, 178, 204, 252, 266
Structural approach to personality theory, 108–112
Sullivan, Harry Stack, 256
Superego, 85, 108, 109, 112, 127
System theory, 27–28, 87–97, 113, 114, 167, 169, 268

Taber, M., 140
Termination, 39, 224–244
    attainment of goals, 229–231
    evaluation, 240–242
    individualizing, 234–237
    intervention at, 242–243
    length of service, 226–229
    premature, 231–234
Thackeray, M., 140, 272
Therapy: see Intervention
Thomas, E., 16, 46, 97, 99, 192
Topographic approach to personality theory, 107–108

Transactional processes, 92–94
Transference, 66, 193, 194–198, 220, 241
Treatment: see Intervention
Tripodi, T., 25
Tropp, Emanuel, 17, 175, 252
Trust, 105, 106, 157–158, 164, 178, 210, 236

Unconscious, 104, 107–108

Values, 29–33
Varley, B., 221
Vattano, A., 140
Vinter, Robert, 17, 18

Watson, J., 7, 8, 9, 16
Webb, Beatrice, 6
Webb, Sidney, 6
Weiss, V., 172
Weissman, M., 253
Whitehead, Alfred North, 245
Wilensky, H., 269–271
Witmer, H., 3
Wolberg, L., 180
Wolpe, Joseph, 16
Wood, K., 107, 113
Wynne, L. C., 171

Zilbach, J., 170
Zinberg, N., 42